The Bible Speaks Today

Series editors: J. A. Motyer (OT)
John Stott (NT)
Derek Tidball (Bible Themes)

The Message of Daniel

D0901840

THE BIBLE SPEAKS TODAY

The Message of Daniel

His Kingdom Cannot Fail

DALE RALPH DAVIS

IVP Academic

An imprint of InterVarsity Press
Downers Grove, Illinois

InterVarsity Press
P.O. Box 1400, Downers Grove, IL 60515-1426
Internet: www.ivpress.com
Email: email@ivpress.com

InterVarsity Press® is the book-publishing division of InterVarsity Christian Fellowship/USA®, a movement of students and faculty active on campus at hundreds of universities, colleges and schools of nursing in the United States of America, and a member movement of the International Fellowship of Evangelical Students. For information about local and regional activities, write Public Relations Dept., InterVarsity Christian Fellowship/USA, 6400 Schroeder Rd., P.O. Box 7895, Madison, WI 53707-7895, or visit the IVCF website at www.intervarsity.org.

Cover design: Cindy Kiple
Image: Marilee Whitehouse-Holm/Getty Images

ISBN 978-0-8308-2438-0 (print)
ISBN 978-0-8308-9561-8 (digital)

Printed in the United States of America ∞

Library of Congress Cataloging-in-Publication Data

Davis, Dale Ralph.
  The message of Daniel : His kingdom cannot fail / Dale Ralph Davis.
    pages cm. — (The Bible speaks today series)
  Includes bibliographical references.
  ISBN 978-0-8308-2438-0 (pbk. : alk. paper) 1. Bible. Daniel—Commentaries. I. Title.
  BS1555.53.D38 2013
  224'.507—dc23

                                    2013015292

P   22   21   20   19   18   17   16   15   14   13   12   11   10   9

Y   32   31   30   29   28   27   26   25   24   23   22   21   20   19

Contents

BST The Bible Speaks Today

GENERAL PREFACE

THE BIBLE SPEAKS TODAY describes three series of expositions, based on the books of the Old and New Testaments, and on Bible themes that run through the whole of Scripture. Each series is characterized by a threefold ideal:

- to expound the biblical text with accuracy
- to relate it to contemporary life, and
- to be readable.

These books are, therefore, not 'commentaries', for the commentary seeks rather to elucidate the text than to apply it, and tends to be a work rather of reference than of literature. Nor, on the other hand, do they contain the kinds of 'sermons' that attempt to be contemporary and readable without taking Scripture seriously enough. The contributors to *The Bible Speaks Today* series are all united in their convictions that God still speaks through what he has spoken, and that nothing is more necessary for the life, health and growth of Christians than that they should hear what the Spirit is saying to them through his ancient – yet ever modern – Word.

ALEC MOTYER
JOHN STOTT
DEREK TIDBALL
Series editors

Author's preface

There are a number of good reasons *not* to write an exposition of Daniel. For one thing, going into print on the book of Daniel makes it too easy for readers of whatever stripe to assign one's lot among either the kooks or the nincompoops. The book is an interpretive minefield and wherever one comes down on various questions he is sure to disappoint people – one fails to take an 'obvious' view here or finds the data too uncertain to take a 'firm' one there. However, with a kind invitation from Alec Motyer it seemed only right to overcome reluctance and begin. I felt it was like eating my oatmeal – it would be good for me.

I had taught Daniel before in several venues, but two years before I left Woodland Presbyterian Church, Hattiesburg, Mississippi, I decided to preach through all of Daniel. That was unusually helpful – at least to me. There is nothing like having to go through the agony of preaching to help one grab the message of the text. Preaching forces one to digest, simplify (hopefully without distorting), popularize, omit, conceptualize – and a whole host of such torturous tasks that are part of the torment of preaching. (I speak of the 'torment' the preacher goes through – at this point I am not concerned with what he does to his hearers.)

Which brings me to a 'dedication', which is to John Burnam, Allen Hawkins, Norman Rowe and Chuck Young, our elders at Woodland, who were always so encouraging about my writing up biblical expositions. It was not uncommon to hear the question raised at a session meeting: 'Are you getting enough time to work on the commentary?' Some pastors might kill for elders like that; I am simply very grateful for these dear brothers. And . . . deep thanks as well to Liz Frazier, my former secretary, who was most forbearing in putting up with a nearly always preoccupied preacher.

DALE RALPH DAVIS

Abbreviations

ABD	Anchor Bible Dictionary (New York: Doubleday, 1992)
ASV	American Standard Version (1901)
AV	Authorized (King James) Version
BDB	F. Brown, S. Driver and C. Briggs, *A Hebrew and English Lexicon of the Old Testament* (Peabody: Hendrickson Publishers Inc, 1996)
DCH	*Dictionary of Classical Hebrew* (Sheffield: Sheffield Academic Press, 1993–2011)
ESV	English Standard Version
HCSB	Holman Christian Standard Bible
ISBE	International Standard Bible Encyclopedia (Grand Rapids: Eerdmans, 1995)
JB	Jerusalem Bible
NASB	New American Standard Bible
NIDOTTE	New International Dictionary of Old Testament Theology and Exegesis (Carlisle: Paternoster and Grand Rapids: Zondervan, 1996)
NIV	New International Version (1984)
NJB	New Jerusalem Bible
NJPS	*Tanakh: A New Translation of the Holy Scriptures According to the Traditional Hebrew Text* (Jewish Publication Society, 1985)
NKJV	New King James Version
NRSV	New Revised Standard Version
TDOT	Theological Dictionary of the Old Testament (Grand Rapids: Eerdmans, 1974–2006)
TWOT	Theological Wordbook of the Old Testament (Chicago: Moody, 1980)

Select bibliography

Where these books are cited in the notes, it is by author only.

Archer, G. L., Jr, 'Daniel', in *The Expositor's Bible Commentary*, vol. 7 (Grand Rapids: Zondervan, 1985).

Baldwin, J., *Daniel*, Tyndale Old Testament Commentaries (Leicester: IVP, 1978).

Calvin, J., *A Commentary on Daniel* (Edinburgh: Banner of Truth, 1995 reprint).

Collins, J. J., *Daniel*, Hermeneia (Minneapolis: Fortress, 1993).

Duguid, I. M., *Daniel*, Reformed Expository Commentary (Phillipsburg: Presbyterian and Reformed, 2008).

Ferguson, S. B., *Daniel*, Communicator's Commentary (Waco: Word, 1988).

Fyall, R., *Daniel* (Ross-shire: Christian Focus, 1998).

Goldingay, J., *Daniel*, Word Biblical Commentary (Dallas: Word, 1989).

Harman, A. M., *A Study Commentary on Daniel* (Darlington: Evangelical Press, 2007).

Keil, C. F., *Biblical Commentary on the Book of Daniel* (reprint ed., Grand Rapids: Eerdmans, n.d. [1872]).

Leupold, H. C., *Exposition of Daniel* (Grand Rapids: Baker, 1969 [1949]).

Lucas, E. C., *Daniel*, Apollos Old Testament Commentary (Leicester: Apollos, 2002).

Luthi, W., *The Church to Come* (London: Hodder and Stoughton, 1939).

Miller, S. R., *Daniel*, New American Commentary (n.p.: Broadman & Holman, 1994).

Montgomery, J. A., *A Critical and Exegetical Commentary on the Book of Daniel*, International Critical Commentary (New York: Scribner's, 1927).

Olyott, S., *Dare to Stand Alone* (Darlington: Evangelical Press, 1982).

Steinmann, A. E., *Daniel*, Concordia Commentary (St Louis: Concordia, 2008).

Thomas, G., *Daniel: Servant of God Under Four Kings* (Bridgend: Bryntirion, 1998).

Veldkamp, H., *Dreams and Dictators* (St Catharines: Paideia, 1978).

Wallace, R. S., *The Lord Is King: The Message of Daniel* (Downers Grove: IVP, 1979).

Young, E. J., *The Prophecy of Daniel* (Grand Rapids: Eerdmans, 1949).

Introduction

Medical staff, according to the clip in *Reader's Digest*, were baffled. They were transcribing medical audiotapes and one of them came upon a perplexing diagnosis: 'This man has pholenfrometry.' Being unfamiliar with that condition one of them double-checked with the doctor. He listened to the tape, shook his head, and translated: 'This man has fallen from a tree.' Sometimes things are that way – not so sophisticated as we suppose. It may be like that with a biblical book. It's usually wise to begin with what's simpler and ask: Just what seems to be here?

1. What do we meet?

So what do we find if we begin with a naïve view of the book of Daniel? Most everyone notes the book consists of about half stories and half visions; there is a series of stories in chapters 1 – 6, followed by a sequence of visions in chapters 7– 12. So, six stories (told in third-person form about Daniel and his friends) and four visions (cast primarily in the form of first-person reports). Moreover, each 'set' of materials seem to stand in chronological order (1:1; 2:1; cf. 5:1, 31 and 6:1, for the stories, and note the specific dates in 7:1, 8:1, 9:1 and 10:1 for the visions). Visually – with the visions in time-tandem with the stories – it looks as shown overleaf.

However, things get a bit more complicated, for whether we read biblical languages or simply follow the footnotes in our translations we note that the book is bilingual:[1]

Hebrew	1:1 – 2:4a
Aramaic	2:4b – 7:28
Hebrew	8:1 – 12:13

---

[1] The fragments of manuscripts from the Qumran caves attest these transition points from Hebrew to Aramaic and from Aramaic back to Hebrew; cf. Collins, pp. 2–3.

Stories

Drawing a line in Babylon	Telling a world-determining dream	Fidelity in a hot spot	Deranged king, a God who is free	Hand wrote, curtain fell	A brief rendezvous with lions
(1)	(2)	(3)	(4)	(5)	(6)

Visions

The 'whole show' of history	Two kingdoms	Restoring Israel: prayer and answer	'What is to happen to your people'
(7) ca. 553	(8) ca. 550	(9) ca. 538	(10 – 12) ca. 536

This scheme seems to 'mess up' the stories-vision pattern, for the linguistic pattern seems to carve off chapter 7 from the visions (now = chs. 8 – 12), place it with the 'stories' (now = chs. 2 – 7), and leave chapter 1 as a sort of prologue. We can look at this in more detail when we consider matters of structure. For the moment chapter 7 appears to have an overlapping role.

But I think one can infer a thumb-nail sketch of the book based on these broad 'language' divisions:[2]

   I. The place in which faithfulness is lived (ch. 1)
  II. The God to whom the kingdom belongs (2 – 7)
 III. The people to whom the kingdom is given (8 – 12)

2. When was it published?

Shelby Foote tells of an episode during the American Civil War. A force of northern troops had overrun some retreating southern soldiers and had captured a ragged Virginia private. The fellow puzzled the northerners – he obviously didn't own any slaves and probably didn't care much about 'States' Rights'. So they asked him, 'What are you fighting for anyhow?' and received the reply: 'I'm fighting because you're down here.' He had no choice! And that's the answer to any who wonder why we need to spill ink on the date of Daniel: we have to face it because others have made a big deal of it.[3]

If one simply reads the extant book of Daniel one may be tempted to think that the book arose in the Persian period near the end of said Daniel's life (ca. 530 BC). One might guess that the stories about Daniel and friends (chs. 1/2 – 6) were edited together with the visions reported by Daniel (chs. 7 – 12) and that Daniel and/or a near col-laborator were responsible for the editing.

But a dominant stream of scholars would say that is all wrong. They hold that the individual stories (chs. 1/2 – 6) were eventually brought together, but that occurred perhaps in the third century BC (ca. 250) – and many would hold the stories to be legendary. Chapters 7 – 12 were not combined with these stories till ca. 165 BC. How do they know that and why is that date so magical? They point to

---

[2] For the focus on God in Division II, note the repeated 'polemical' notes in 2:10–11 and 27; 4:7, 18 and 5:7–9, underscoring the inadequacy of paganism, and yet note how persistently the pagan kings praise and confess the kingship of the true God (2:47; 3:28–29; 4:34–37; 6:25–27). In Division III, note the focus on God's people in 8:24; 9:24; 10:14; 12:1–2.

[3] In this section I will not deal with historical difficulties in Daniel; those will be touched on at appropriate places in the exposition.

11:29–39, all of which they take as describing the activities of Antiochus IV (Epiphanes), a Syrian/Seleucid king who ruled 175–163 BC, and who, close to the end of his tenure, terrorized and persecuted the Jews and tried to annihilate the last vestiges of Israel's faith (more on him later). This section of Daniel 11 is cast in the form of prophecy predicting the activities of this king, but the prophecy is so precise and accurate that – so the argument goes – it could only have been written *after* the fact (i.e., for Latin buffs, *vaticinium ex eventu*); but when the writer tried his hand at genuine prophecy, about Antiochus' end in 11:40–45 (this view assumes that passage is also about Antiochus), he muffed the ball, for Antiochus met his end in Persia, not in Israel (11:45).[4]

The publication of Daniel, then, must have occurred about 165 BC, from a writer (or group) who had witnessed Antiochus' scourge and wanted to encourage Israelites to remain faithful in the face of this lethal assault on their faith even if it meant martyrdom.[5] This means that Daniel is pseudonymous. Pseudonymity is not a disease but a device used by writers from 200 BC – AD 200 to provide 'cover' for their work. They would attribute it to an earlier, respected figure, but no-one was taken in by this. So the claims about Daniel having visions are simply a polite fiction, but this would cause, we are assured, no reader or recipient undue distress.

I have tried to keep this summary as concise as possible. However, enough has been said to keep you from being shocked when John J. Collins opens up his commentary with: 'According to the consensus of modern critical scholarship, the stories about Daniel and his friends are legendary in character, and the hero himself most probably never existed.'[6] And elsewhere with a touch of disdain he writes, 'All but the most conservative scholars now accept the conclusion that the book of Daniel is not a product of the Babylonian era but reached its present form in the 2d century B.C.E. Daniel is not a historical person but a figure of legend.'[7] There are, however, major problems with this position.

The problem of *language*. Even as early as 1927 a 'critical' scholar like Montgomery seemed loath to date the Aramaic section of Daniel (2:4b – 7:28) in the second century. It had, apparently, to be some time earlier.[8] Nine-tenths of the Aramaic vocabulary of Daniel is

---

[4] See, e.g., Otto Eissfeldt, *The Old Testament: An Introduction* (New York: Harper and Row, 1965), pp. 520–521, for this argument.

[5] So G. Fohrer, *Introduction to the Old Testament* (Nashville: Abingdon, 1968), p. 479.

[6] Collins, p. 1.

[7] In ABD, 2:30.

[8] Montgomery, pp. 15–20.

attested in other texts of the fifth century BC or before.[9] That *proves* nothing but indicates Daniel's Aramaic would fit well in an earlier period. However, the Aramaic of Daniel (as well as Ezra) is, according to Kitchen, simply a part of Imperial Aramaic that could fall anywhere from the 600–330 BC range. The sentence pattern of this biblical Aramaic is strikingly different from later Aramaic found, for example, in the 'Genesis Apocryphon' at Qumran.[10] Nor is the case different for Daniel's Hebrew. Archer also compared the Hebrew of Daniel and that of the Qumran sectarian documents (the latter dating from the second century and following) and concluded: 'In view of the markedly later development exhibited by these second-century documents in the areas of syntax, word order, morphology, vocabulary, spelling, and word-usage, there is absolutely no possibility of regarding Daniel as contemporary.'[11]

Linguistic data can prove slippery; most of us are not professional linguists and so are at the mercy of those who are. However, it seems that both the Aramaic and Hebrew of Daniel come from a time substantially earlier than the second century BC.[12]

The problem of *time*. The Daniel texts found at Qumran have implications for the date of the canonical book. Fragments of eight manuscripts of Daniel have been identified among the Dead Sea Scrolls, the oldest dating from 120–115 BC. All twelve chapters are

[9] K. A. Kitchen, 'The Aramaic of Daniel', in *Notes on Some Problems in the Book of Daniel* (London: Tyndale, 1965), p. 32.

[10] Kitchen, pp. 75–76. See especially, Gleason L. Archer, Jr, 'The Aramaic of the "Genesis Apocryphon" Compared with the Aramaic of Daniel', in J. Barton Payne (ed.), *New Perspectives on the Old Testament* (Waco: Word, 1970), pp. 160–169.

[11] Gleason L. Archer, Jr, 'The Hebrew of Daniel Compared with the Qumran Sectarian Documents', in John H. Skilton (ed.), *The Law and the Prophets* (n.p.: Presbyterian and Reformed, 1974), pp. 470–481. A bit of noise used to be made also over three Greek loan words appearing in Daniel (names of three musical instruments noted, e.g., in Dan. 3:5). The presence of these Greek words demanded, it was said, a date after the conquests of Alexander the Great. Naturally, they don't. In fact, they point in the opposite direction. If Daniel came from the second century after Hellenization had been in high gear one would expect to see Greek words and terms appearing like measles. But there are only three – and those in the 'technical' jargon of music. Greek terms in themselves should not be surprising in earlier material, for Greek contacts with the Near East were legion long before Alexander. As Edwin Yamauchi has not tired to point out, the evidence is crushing; see his 'The Greek Words in Daniel in Light of Greek Influence in the Near East', in Barton Payne (ed.), pp. 170–200.

[12] Cf. the matter-of-fact estimate by John E. McKenna: 'Scholars have long been aware that the language of Daniel is earlier than the second century. The consensus was that the Hebrew resembled that of the Chronicler and was earlier than that of the Mishnah. It is indeed noticeably closer to Chronicles than to Qumran (second-first centuries). Similarly, the Aramaic (2:4b–7:28) is closer to that of Ezra and the fifth century papyri than to that of Qumran' (in W. S. LaSor, D. A. Hubbard and F. W. Bush, *Old Testament Survey* [Grand Rapids: Eerdmans, ²1996], p. 574).

represented among the Qumran materials, and the copies of the biblical text show the shift from Hebrew to Aramaic (at 2:4b) and the shift from Aramaic to Hebrew (at 8:1).[13] From allusions to 'the prophet Daniel' in the Qumran materials (4QFlorilegium) it is clear Daniel was regarded as a prophet on the same level as Isaiah and Ezekiel. This proves a bit of a rub for the late-date view of Daniel. If Daniel was produced about 165 BC and yet shows up in a *copy* at Qumran as early as 115 BC, we are looking at a time differential of only 50 years. That strains probability: a mere fifty years for a work to become extant, be circulated and digested among the Jewish people and be accepted as Scripture. I suppose one could invoke miracle here – and it would almost have to be. Harrison's point is well-taken: 'But since all these [Qumran] manuscripts are copies, and not the original composition, the date of the autograph of Daniel must of necessity be advanced by half a century at the very least, so as to allow the absolute minimum of time for the book to circulate and be accepted as Scripture.'[14] That is, the Qumran discoveries require that the latest possible date for Daniel would be ca. 220 BC.

The problem of *propriety*. Here the focus rests on the stories of chapters 1 – 6. The usual view holds that these stories were either produced in or taken over and used in the second-century situation in order to fortify Israel to stand firm in their ancestral faith in spite of the ravages Antiochus IV was inflicting on them. They should, they might have said, take the side of Mattathias, the priest from the village of Modin, who defied the apostasy-baiting of Antiochus' officers and who sparked a rebellion of the faithful against the king (1 Macc. 2:19–28), a rebellion primarily carried on by Judah Maccabaeus, one of Mattathias' sons.[15] The problem is that the Daniel stories are a poor fit for that life-situation.[16] Why depict Daniel manoeuvring to be faithful within and under 'the system' in chapter 1 when one's objective is to stir absolute repudiation of the pagan system of Antiochus? Why show Daniel enlightening Nebuchadnezzar

[13] For a summary, see Collins, pp. 2–3.

[14] R. K. Harrison, *Introduction to the Old Testament* (Grand Rapids: Eerdmans, 1969), p. 1118.

[15] For background, see 1 Macc. 1 – 9 and 2 Macc. 3 – 15; Emil Schürer, *The History of the Jewish People in the Age of Jesus Christ (175 BC – AD 135)*, rev. and ed. by G. Vermes and F. Millar (Edinburgh: T&T Clark, 1973), 1:137–173.

[16] I am not saying the stories would not have been useful as a general encouragement to faithfulness; Mattathias, according to 1 Macc. 2:49–61, cited Daniel's friends' fidelity in Dan. 3 and Daniel's steadfastness in Dan. 6 (along with seven other Old Testament examples) as incentives for his sons to persevere. But late-date critics hold that the material of Daniel was meant to address *specifically* this Antiochus crisis – and, if so, it is an ill fit. David Gooding ('The Literary Structure of the Book of Daniel and its Implications', *Tyndale Bulletin* 32 [1981], pp. 47–49) notes that even a number of late-date advocates have recognized the problem.

in Daniel 2 and simultaneously saving the heads of the pagan dark-arts practitioners? Why pass on the record of Daniel 4 in which Daniel so obviously has a genuine concern and even compassion (4:19, 27) for the pagan king he serves? There seems to be a generally positive attitude toward Nebuchadnezzar and Darius (chs. 2, 4, 6), which is not what a second-century writer/editor would want to depict when he was trying to preach intransigence toward *his* current antichrist from Syria. Even Daniel 3 and 6, which seem most amenable to the 'Maccabean' setting, have something of a square-peg-round-hole character, for neither episode portrays a *general* life or death crisis. The threat to Daniel's friends (ch. 3) only involved 'civil service' employees, not a whole exilic people; and Daniel met the lions (ch. 6) because of the jealousy of some government lackeys – there was no government decree to squash Israelite faith as such.[17] Ronald Wallace put it well:

[I]f the book is intended as a tract with parallels being drawn between the days of the Babylonian captivity and the Maccabean persecution, why did the writer not try to make the Babylonian story fit better into the times he is supposed to be writing for? Why did he not choose more relevant stories; and if he was going to change them, why did he not make a decent job of the whole thing?[18]

So if the stories of Daniel 1 – 6 were specially selected and directed to Israel's second-century emergency, it was ill done. One expects more finesse from an editor than that. He/they would have done better to take the stories of Esther and Mordecai and juice them up with a bit more religion. As it is, the second-century position implies that Daniel's editor was at least singularly inept and perhaps abysmally stupid.

The problem of *psychology*. Here we enter this labyrinth of pseudonymity. Some make the claim that the rationale for writing under a false name from the past was to give status and credibility to one's message – it would pack more clout if folks thought it came

[17] These incongruities have often been noted, by, e.g., Zockler in *Lange's Commentary on the Holy Scriptures*, vol. 13; Keil; Gooding (see previous note); and Raymond B. Dillard and Temper Longman III, *An Introduction to the Old Testament* (Grand Rapids: Zondervan, 1994).

[18] Wallace, p. 20. Note Wallace's further comment: 'Throughout the whole book it becomes obvious that the work is written as a message not primarily for those who are suffering in the midst of deadly persecution but rather for those who are living in a settled condition yet within an alien culture – in other words, not in a Maccabean-type situation, but in a Babylonian-type situation' (p. 21).

from Ezra or Enoch or Daniel.[19] Of course, to be effective the ruse would have to work and the deception really deceive. This raises some minor conundrums such as what authority does a fraudulent 'revelation' have. More recently, we have been assured that the readers were aware of this literary convention (pseudonymity) and would have known how to hear such 'prophecies'.[20] But that's where the 'psychological' problem comes in. As Alec Motyer puts it: How can a recognized fiction help? 'If "everyone" knows what it really is, it can only receive the amused rejoinder, "So what?"'[21] I find it hard to get around that. Why would suffering saints find particular help in a batch of recently promulgated legendary court tales? Why should they give solemn credence to 'prophecies' they knew had been produced by a bunch of visionaries who were their own contemporaries? What divine authority could these pack? We must remember, after all, that the situation the book addresses (according to second-century daters) is the dire suffering of Israel under the rampages of Antiochus Epiphanes. They do not need advice on coping with life's normal challenges but a true word that enables them to go on holding on by their fingernails. I think that what some call the 'quasi-prophecy' of Daniel would give such sufferers nothing more than quasi-encouragement.

The problem of *presuppositions*. The second-century date eliminates the apparent predictive prophecy from Daniel (except for the allegedly bungled one in 11:40–45). One suspects that the anti-supernaturalist bias in mainstream biblical studies furnishes much of the 'push' for this view.[22] Since such criticism works 'without a God hypothesis' (von Rad), nothing is so axiomatic as that there can be no genuine predictive prophecy. But in Daniel studies the matter is often not put so baldly. Rather, in rejecting an earlier date, the question is asked why a sixth-century prophet should 'focus minute attention' on concerns of the second century (Collins). Others might say it is not a question of whether God could so predict but whether he *would* do so; such fairly long range prediction seems pointless – it does not line up with God's concern for the here-and-now situation of his people.

Two considerations must be kept in mind. One is existential, having to do with the unique and unprecedented character of Antiochus'

---

[19] See the discussion in D. S. Russell, *The Method and Message of Jewish Apocalyptic* (Philadelphia: Westminster, 1964), pp. 130–132.

[20] See Goldingay, p. 321.

[21] Alec Motyer, *Roots: Let the Old Testament Speak* (Ross-shire: Christian Focus, 2009), p. 298.

[22] One hesitates to say that the king is naked and standing in the street, but if he is, one might just as well acknowledge it. See the comments of Andrew E. Hill and John H. Walton in *A Survey of the Old Testament* (Grand Rapids: Zondervan, [3]2009), p. 570.

persecution. Robert Dick Wilson spelled this out long ago. He said that the persecution of Antiochus Epiphanes is one of the most important events in the history of God's people, ranking on a level with the call of Abraham, the giving of the Law, the captivity and the incarnation. Antiochus instituted 'the deadliest peril the church has ever confronted'; he ordered the cessation of circumcision, stopped the services of the temple, instituted pagan worship instead, set up idol altars in every city, demanded every Jew should sacrifice in line with the pagan ritual, and commanded the holy writings to be destroyed. Those refusing conformity were ruthlessly slaughtered; whole families were exterminated for the guilt of one of their number, and the chosen people were on the point of annihilation. 'There never was, before or since, such a period of desperation or despondency in the history of the church.'[23] Epiphanes was attempting the 'entire destruction of people and religion at one fell blow'. Once one grasps this, says Wilson, one can see that 'the stupendous crisis justified the prediction'.[24] God's goodness was at work, forearming his people for what they would face.

The second consideration is theological and is best spelled out in Isaiah 40 – 48. There one finds something of a rationale for predictive prophecy (in reference to Yahweh's Cyrus-plan to give Judah release from Babylon). The ability to predict accurately is a litmus test of genuine deity; hence Yahweh's challenge to pagan 'godlets': 'Tell us what is to come hereafter, *that we may know you are gods.*'[25] In contrast Yahweh declares of himself:

> I am totally God and there is none like me:
> declaring the end from the beginning
> and from ancient times what has not occurred,
> saying, 'My plan will stand
> and I will do all that I please,'
> calling a bird of prey [Cyrus] from the east,
> the man of my plan from a distant land.[26]

The argument is that 'calling it' long in advance is the way the real God tends to function and thereby provides evidence (when fulfilment comes) of his real 'god-ness'. *Would* God grant predictions several centuries beforehand? Isaiah 40 – 48 implies that that is just what we could expect.

---

[23] Though one should not forget the Haman scheme in the book of Esther.

[24] Robert Dick Wilson, *Studies in the Book of Daniel*, 2 vols. in 1 (Grand Rapids: Baker, 1972 [1917/1918]), 2:270–276.

[25] Isa. 41:23, ESV; emphasis author's.

[26] Isa. 46:9c–11b.

Some would put little stock in this argument from Isaiah 40 – 48, partly because it has been late-dated by many as has Daniel.[27] If one takes Isaiah himself as responsible for the whole prophecy, one must assume that the prophet from somewhere between 740–700 BC prophesied the rise and work of Cyrus (which took place ca. 539 BC). Which raises the usual questions: Why would there be predictions of Cyrus 150–200 years ahead of time? What good would that do? So, many take the position that there was an Isaiah Junior, whose name we do not know (hence he's dubbed 'Deutero-Isaiah'), who years after Isaiah himself, say around 540 BC or so, was responsible for Isaiah 40 – 55. This means that the predictions about Cyrus become prophecies after the fact or else made so close to the time that Deutero-Isaiah could make an educated guess at what was coming. Note what this view does. It does not merely posit a later date or a different author, but annihilates one of the major *theological arguments* of Isaiah 40 – 48; it attacks the very theology of the text. But it illustrates that the main problem with predictive prophecy is not theological or practical but presuppositional, a built-in antipathy to the very possibility of predictive prophecy. The last thing people – including some biblical scholars – want is a real God running around loose and having the chutzpah to order history ahead of time.

I have simply outlined some of the problems I have with a second-century date for Daniel. Our considerations under 'language' and 'time' suggest that the *latest possible* date for Daniel would range between 300–220 BC, and that still leaves critics with the problem of predictive prophecy. I can't claim to prove a sixth-century date, but I see too many problems with the second-century (165 BC) position, and I haven't the faith to overcome those obstacles. Given those, it seems better to me to take a 'naïve' view and posit a date of ca. 530 BC.

3. How is it packaged?

We should always ask if a writer has left evidence of any design or structure on his work. In this matter I am unable to get around the use of two languages in Daniel: Hebrew in chapter 1, Aramaic roughly chapters 2 – 7, and Hebrew in chapters 8 – 12. Chapter 7 seems the climactic piece of the Aramaic 'stories' section and yet it is not a story but a vision. So language-wise chapter 7 belongs to 2– 6 and yet category-wise, as a vision, it introduces a series of visions (8 – 12) and itself stands as the first vision in chronological sequence (7:1; 8:1; 9:1–2; 10:1). Chapter 7 then has an overlapping function in

---

[27] The matter is far more complex than I can treat here; I am merely touching on the effect the later dating of Isaiah 40 – 55 has on predictive prophecy.

the book's structure.[28] It is both climax and preface. In this section, however, I want to focus on the structure of chapters 2 – 7; the next segment will survey the import of 7 – 12.

Lenglet has proposed a *concentric* or 'chiastic' pattern for chapters 2 – 7,[29] which seems to follow accurately the emphases of the text. It may be summarized as follows:

Vision of the four kingdoms (ch. 2)
   Deliverance of three from the furnace (ch. 3)
      Divine discipline of a king – eventual success (ch. 4)
      Divine discipline of a king – eventual judgment (ch. 5)
   Deliverance of Daniel from lions (ch. 6)
Vision of the four kingdoms (ch. 7)

But there is also a *thematic* structure in 2 – 7, which develops in an ABC/ABC pattern. Let me substantiate this pattern by summarizing the key words that burden these chapters:

2:   Tell, interpret, make known, reveal
     verses 4, 5, 6, 7, 9, 11, 16, 19, 22, 23, 24, 25, 26, 27, 28, 29, 30, 36, 45, 47

3:   Rescue, save/deliver
     verses 15, 17 [twice], 28, 29

4:   'Rules' (ESV)
     verses 17, 25, 26, 32 (English) [= vv. 14, 22, 23, 29 in Aramaic]
     + 'kingdom', 'dominion' (3, 34)
     + 'King of heaven' (37)

5:   Show interpretation, make known, interpret
     verses 7, 8, 12, 15, 16, 17, 26

6:   Rescue, save
     verses 14 [twice], 16, 20, 27 [3 times]

7:   Dominion, throne(s), kingdom (ESV)
     verses 6, 9 [twice], 12, 14 [5 times], 18 [twice], 22, 23, 26, 27 [6 times]

---

[28] See J. Paul Tanner, 'The Literary Structure of the Book of Daniel', *Bibliotheca Sacra* 160 (2003), pp. 277–281; Richard D. Patterson, 'The Key Role of Daniel 7', *Grace Theological Journal* 12.2 (1991), pp. 245–261.

[29] In his article in *Biblica* 53 (1972), pp. 169–190. Many have noted it, including Baldwin, pp. 59–60.

The pattern is thematic but the emphasis is theocentric, showing the God of Judah's sorry exiles to be far superior to any would-be deities of Babylon or Persia. Hence, based on the thematic concerns of the text, we find the pattern repeated twice:[30]

ch. 2 ◄———	The God who reveals ———►	ch. 5
ch. 3 ◄———	The God who rescues ———►	ch. 6
ch. 4 ◄———	The God who rules ———►	ch. 7

Yet it gets more fascinating, for one can also argue for a *pairing* pattern in this 'story' section, that is, that each set of two chapters may be meant to complement each other. Schematically, it looks like this:[31]

2: The rule of Babylon is temporary (therefore, rejoice in the enduring kingdom)

3: But the rule of Babylon may be tyrannical (therefore, be prepared to pay the price)

4: Proud king who was humbled and feared

5: Proud king too stupid to learn

6: Fidelity suffers in Persia as well as in Babylon

7: Fidelity will suffer in the end

It is interesting that none of these three structural layouts excludes the others. All three of these could be valid at the same time, and, if so, would indicate a rather complex artistry at work in the book.[32] I know other biblical critics may pooh-pooh my inferences, but I always tend to associate sophisticated and conscious literary design with one originating, artistic mind rather than with an illusory committee making contributions over the centuries.

4. Why was it written?

To divine the purpose of the whole book we go primarily to the 'vision' section, chapters 7 – 12. Chapter 7 is again pivotal. As Fyall says, the scope of chapter 7 is the whole of human history, and chapters

[30] See my discussion in *The Word Became Fresh* (Ross-shire: Christian Focus, 2006), pp. 55–56.

[31] I do not recall if I read someone who proposed this or not. Upon reflection I believe I may have extrapolated the scheme based on some of David Gooding's work, viz., his stimulating article in *Tyndale Bulletin* 32 (1981), pp. 43–79.

[32] Some may dismiss the pairing pattern as too subjective; perhaps so, but the concentric and thematic ones are, in my view, quite solid.

8 – 12 unpack certain parts of that whole picture.[33] Chapter 2, we remember, to a certain degree parallels chapter 7. Both these chapters reveal that after the days of Nebuchadnezzar and Babylon, history – and by implication God's people – will continue under the domination of an ongoing series of political powers. To use Acts 1:6 anachronistically, the exiles may see Babylon drop into political Sheol but God would not then 'restore the kingdom to Israel'. Rather, another pagan world power would arise, and another. Hill and Walton have put it well, speaking of Daniel 2:

> [W]e see a succession of kingdoms that conveyed to the Israelites that it was not yet time for the kingdom for which they had been waiting. Certainly this would have been a disappointing message for the exiles to hear. The main significance, however, is the fact that in God's agenda, the mighty empires of the world come and go, and they will be superseded by the kingdom of God that will never be destroyed (2:44). This would give reason for continued hope.[34]

The visions seem to reinforce this point. For example, chapter 7 speaks of a 'little horn' that comes up in the course of the fourth and 'different' kingdom (7:8), that makes war on the saints (7:21) and crushes and controls them (7:25). However, the Ancient of Days intervenes, disposes of the little horn and gives the kingdom to his people (7:22, 26–27). Then in chapter 8 we meet another 'little horn' (8:9) that comes out of the break-up of the Greek kingdom (8:8, 21–22) and will ravage many of God's people (8:24–25). But the little horn of chapter 8 does not come from the final/fourth kingdom of chapter 7 but from the splintering of the Greek kingdom, which is equivalent to the third kingdom of Daniel 7:6. (This point will need to be established in detail when treating chapter 8.) This implies there will be a little horn wreaking havoc on the saints (ch. 8) before the (final) little horn does so (ch. 7). There will be a 'little horn' (ch. 8) before *the* 'little horn' (ch. 7). The little horn of chapter 8 will be a foreshadowing of the final one. Israel will face (to borrow John's lingo) antichrists before she faces Antichrist[35] and should not allow

---

[33] Fyall, p. 18.
[34] Hill and Walton, p. 574. Jesus makes a similar point in Mark 13. He refers to wars and talk about wars, nation rising against nation, kingdom against kingdom, earthquakes, famines (vv. 7–8) and yet cautions: 'but the end is *not yet*' (v. 7b). What media preachers and televangelists may cite as signs of the end are, Jesus says, simply the distressing and spectacular events that will occur in the course of this present age.
[35] Cf. 1 John 2:18.

the similarities to fool them into thinking they are dealing with the latter or that 'the kingdom of God was to appear immediately'.[36]

Chapter 9 (Daniel's prayer and its answer) carries the same message. Daniel was pondering Jeremiah's prophecy (Jer. 25:12) and thinking how the seventy years' exile might mean the 'fulfilling' (lit.) of the 'desolations of Jerusalem' (9:2). The answer Daniel received indicated that 'while the return from exile would come within seventy years of Jeremiah's prophecy, this should not be confused with the full restoration. Rather than seventy years, the required span would be seventy weeks of years'.[37]

David Gooding finds the same argument operating in chapter 11. Because the critical issues surrounding chapter 11 are complex, I will not reconstruct the planks of Gooding's argument here.[38] But his conclusion meshes with the emphasis already highlighted:

> It is a very necessary warning in advance to people who will find themselves living in momentous times not to think that they are already living in the time of the end and that the End is at hand, simply because their own times show certain features that will mark the time of the end as well.[39]

Two words of Jesus then might sum up the message of Daniel: 'the end is not yet', and 'but the one who endures to the end – he shall be saved'.[40] That is not what we usually like to hear, for we think, for example, of the planned annihilation of Christians in Somalia and Iraq, of the decades of deprivation and terror endured by Christ's flock in southern Sudan, of his servants tortured in Vietnam, and we long to tell them that the Lord has marked on his calendar a date in the very near future for their vindication. No, we have something like Daniel's book instead – a realistic survival manual for the saints.

---

[36] Cf. Luke 19:11.
[37] Hill and Walton, p. 573. Keil, p. 24, long ago detected this burden in the visions.
[38] The reader can check the appropriate section of Gooding's article, pp. 72–79.
[39] Gooding, p. 77.
[40] Mark 13:7, 13.

Daniel 1:1–21
1. There is a God in Babylon

Elisabeth Elliot was twice widowed, first by the martyr death of missionary Jim Elliot and then by the death of her second husband, theologian Addison Leitch. She tells of how helpful the Apostles' Creed was to her as she mourned the loss of Dr Leitch. She used it to answer the question: What things have not changed even though my husband has died?[1] One might imagine Daniel and friends asking a similar question after being hauled off to Babylon in 605 BC, far from Judah and all that was near and dear and clear. They might have wondered, what has not changed even though we have been carted to Babylon? And the text of Daniel 1 answers: God. God has not changed; he is still there, wherever 'there' is. Daniel 1 hammers this point home by its thrice-repeated theological note: *the Lord/God gave* (2, 9, 17; in each case the verb is *nātan*, lit., to give, which is visible in ESV but not in, e.g., NIV). Daniel will stir our souls in chapter 2 with his ringing declaration to Nebuchadnezzar: 'But there is a God in heaven who reveals mysteries' (2:28). Indeed it is the keynote of Daniel 2. But in Daniel 1 the writer makes a similar yet different point. He is saying (as 2, 9, 17) 'There is a God in Babylon'. How then do we discern his presence?

1. God is present in his sovereign role (1–2)

Verses 1–2 face us with the historical data (1), the theological explanation (2a), and what we might call the media 'take' (2b) on Judah's demise. Verse 1 seems to depict events of 605 BC after Nebuchadnezzar and his Babylonian troops had whipped the Egyptians at Carchemish. He came on into Syria-Palestine conquering and subjugating; his

---

[1] Many thanks to Bill Smith, a pastor friend, who passed on this testimony in his church's newsletter.

'siege' of Jerusalem may not have been anything prolonged. This was the first wave of Judah's exile, the one in which Daniel and friends were wrenched from home.[2]

The biblical writer insists that God exercises an *active* sovereignty in the history of his people. Why did Jehoiakim knuckle under to Babylon and why were the temple vessels pilfered? *The Lord gave Jehoiakim king of Judah into his hand.* You would never find that kind of statement in a historical work today. For one thing, we do not have the divine revelation needed to make such a statement, but neither, for the most part, do we have historians with a theocentric world view who would be willing to say – or admit – such a thing. Judah's demise is not merely the inevitable corollary of Babylon's military might. No, *the Lord gave* Jehoiakim up to Nebuchadnezzar. Right at the beginning of Daniel's book we are told that Israel's God is the Lord who directs history as he wills.

But we also meet a *faithful* sovereignty here. In beginning to give up Judah to Babylon the Lord is simply being true to his word spoken in the past, both generally and specifically.[3] In Leviticus 26, Yahweh had spelled out the blessings and curses of the covenant; he had threatened that if he met repeated rebellion in Israel he would scatter them among the nations and leave them to rot in their enemies' lands.[4] Now that was beginning. But, more specifically, Isaiah had castigated King Hezekiah when that king had been willing to join an alliance with Merodach-baladin of Babylon (ca. 705 BC), trusting in their joint political-military muscle as a way of facing the 'Assyrian Question'.

> Look, days are coming
> when all that is in your house
> and what your fathers have treasured up to this day
> shall be carted off to Babylon;
> not an item will be left,
> says Yahweh.

[2] Some charge the text with error for saying Nebuchadnezzar came against Jerusalem 'in the third year' of Jehoiakim, when Jer. 46:2 says Nebuchadnezzar's victory at Carchemish was in Jehoiakim's *fourth* year (plus Jer. 25:1 equates Nebuchadnezzar's first year with Jehoiakim's fourth year). However, Daniel likely uses the 'accession-year' system of reckoning royal reigns as was the custom in Babylon. In this scheme a partial year at the beginning of a reign was not counted; Jeremiah, however, followed the 'non-accession year' system and counted the partial first year as a year of Jehoiakim's reign. For a lucid summary and a feasible historical reconstruction, see Steinmann, pp. 80–83. On the matter of Jehoiakim's third/fourth year, cf. also Jack Finegan, *Handbook of Biblical Chronology* (rev. ed., Peabody: Hendrickson, 1998), sections 420–21, 433; same result but different process than, e.g., Steinmann.

[3] I am indebted to Iain Duguid, pp. 6–7, for pointing out both aspects.

[4] See Lev. 26:33, 39.

And some of your sons who have come out from you,
whom you fathered,
will be taken and they shall become
eunuchs in the palace of Babylon's king.[5]

Now that prediction is beginning to be fulfilled. We tend to think
of God's faithfulness in more positive terms. But sometimes it may
be a negative faithfulness. Here we meet with a *severe* faithfulness,
and yet if we keep Leviticus 26 and Isaiah 39 in view we must still
say it is a severe *faithfulness*. And if the Lord is so diligent over his
threats of judgment, surely he will treat his assurances of grace with
the same exacting care.

What is most striking, however, is that God operates by a *humble*
sovereignty. The Lord not only *gives* Jehoiakim into Nebuchadnezzar's
power but also *some of the vessels of the house of God*, so that
Babylon's king carted them off to Babylon (lit., Shinar) and placed
them in *the house of his god* (or *gods*) – in fact, he stashed them *in
the treasure house of his god* (2b). Now there is no doubt about how
the media would view this. In the Ancient Near East the fortunes of
a god and a people were viewed together. That Judah's king and
temple vessels were taken simply meant that the Lord was not able
to protect them. If the people were losers, it meant the Lord was a
loser. Much like the Olympics. If an athlete representing a nation
loses in an event, we may say his or her nation 'lost'. Kenya lost,
Germany lost, the USA lost. There is that identification.

We have a clear instance of this pattern much earlier in Israel's
history. When the Philistines captured the ark of the covenant in
battle with Israel and placed it in their shrine beside the image of
Dagon (1 Sam. 5:1–2), no interpreter was needed to explain what it
meant. Clearly Yahweh was subservient to Dagon, the victor. That
impression got reversed, however, when Dagon's image was found
face down before Yahweh's ark next day. In fact, Dagon began
'cracking up' (1 Sam. 5:3–4)!

So the Lord knew how it would 'look' when he gave his king, his
people, his temple utensils into Babylon's power. Pagans would be
singing, 'Praise Marduk, from whom all blessings flow.' Which is
why his is a humble sovereignty – because he shows here that he
is a God who wills to *suffer shame* if it might awaken his people to
their danger. We see the same tendency in Christ Jesus, who 'did not
consider equality with God as something to be used for his own
advantage' but rather 'emptied himself by assuming the form of a
slave' and 'becoming obedient to the point of death – even to death

---

[5] Isa. 39:6–7.

on a cross'.[6] Here in Daniel 1 – and picking up the later language about Daniel's resolve in verse 8 – we can say that Yahweh is a God willing to 'defile himself' if by doing so he can eventually purge his people.

Here then is God in his sovereign role, but a sovereignty not visible to the world. Only his people who know the secret of verse 2 (*the Lord gave*) will be able to see it – like the early Christians Michael Green mentions in *The Empty Cross of Jesus*: they dated the deaths of their martyrs by the appropriate year and then added, *regnante Jesu Christo*, 'in the reign of Jesus Christ'. Sometimes that is the only glue that holds one's sanity intact.

2. God is present in his silent role (3–16)

It is well that we have another 'God gave' testimony in the middle of this section (*Now God gave Daniel favour and compassions before the chief-of-staff*, 9)[7], since we are far more aware of Babylon's dominance than of God's presence. Babylon's king wanted candidates for his civil service corps from *the sons of Israel* (3), lads who were politically elite (3b), physically impressive (4a), intellectually acute and socially poised (4b). In short, they must have status, looks, brains and 'presence'. And they were to undergo a total Babylonian makeover (4c). So Daniel and his friends face *the foreign regimen*.

Verses 3–7 summarize the Babylonianization programme. These lads are to be indoctrinated into a new culture (*the literature and language of the Chaldeans*, 4c), mollified by a new luxury (5a),[8] and challenged with a new identity (6–7).[9]

---

[6] Phil. 2:6–8, HCSB.

[7] 'Chief-of-staff' is the way *God's Word* (World Publishing, 1995) renders *śar hassārîsîm*, which conveys the probable idea here. There is uncertainty about whether *sārîs* here in Dan. 1 occurs in its earlier sense of 'official' or its sometimes later one of 'eunuch' – and, if the latter, whether Daniel and his friends were made eunuchs. I doubt they were since the candidates wanted were to be excellent physical specimens 'without any blemish' (4). See Miller, p. 59, and G. H. Johnston, NIDOTTE, 3:288–294.

[8] I am not assuming that the food allotment was overly sumptuous, but it was surely one of the perks of the programme. The training may be rigorous but not harsh. Babylon is a government that provides for them and so seeks to tame them. Babylon can be kind and therefore seductive.

[9] The name changes may seem inconsequential but likely point to Babylon's design to take away every vestige of their Judah roots. They are even to think of themselves as Babylonians. The meanings of the Babylonian names are difficult and tenuous. Daniel ('God is my judge') is Belteshazzar ('May Bel [= Marduk] protect his life' [?]); Hananiah ('Yahweh is gracious') becomes Shadrach ('the command of Aku' [?], the moon god), Mishael ('Who is what God is') is Meshach ('Who is what Aku is' [?]), and Azariah ('Yahweh has helped') is Abed-nego (perhaps a corruption of 'servant of Nebo', god of wisdom). Some think the biblical writer deliberately corrupted the Babylonian names as a dig at Babylonian theology; see Steinmann, pp. 88–89, 92, for discussion.

What might the immersion in *the literature and language of the Chaldeans* involve? Probably the study of Sumerian, Akkadian and Aramaic among languages and the extensive literature written in them, including the various mythological texts, as well as historiography, astronomy, mathematics and medicine.[10] They would likely have to imbibe the 'scientific' omen texts; for example, there was a series of astrological omens in seventy-seven tablets, twenty-three of which focused on observations of the moon; then perhaps medical omens – one series ran to forty tablets; nor could they neglect dream interpretation – the longest collection runs to one hundred and ten tablets.[11] The regimen could probably prove overwhelming; after a bit one likely felt awash in Babylonian literature and lore. Which may be why Daniel chose to draw a line, why we meet *the servants' resolve*.

Verse 8 calls for special attention in our summary of verses 8–16. It opens with a use of the verb *śîm* with Daniel as subject. What is not obvious in most English translations (because we like to avoid overly-wooden translations) is that *śîm* also occurs twice in verse 7. It is a common verb, meaning to put or set. But if we get nastily literal it is easier to feel the 'edge' in verse 8a:

7a: *the chief-of-staff set names for them . . .*
7b: *so he set for Daniel Belteshazzar*
8a: *Now Daniel set (it) upon his heart . . .*

The Overseer of Babylonian Assimilation clips along in his normal fashion, imposing his Babylonian agenda on these captives – he sets names for them, sets a name for Daniel – but Daniel has his own 'setting' that he has done; he has set it upon his heart that he will not defile himself with the king's food allotment.

What was wrong with the royal food allotment? Some think the problem was *dietary* – food from the royal table likely included meats, for example, that were off limits ('unclean') for Israelites (Lev. 11:1–23). This, however, does not explain Daniel's rejection of the wine. Some think the objection was (what we would call) *religious* – the food may have been offered to idols before being taken to the king's tables.[12] But what would guarantee that the *vegetables*[13] Daniel

---

[10] D. J. Wiseman, 'Chaldea', ISBE, 1:632.

[11] D. J. Wiseman, 'Babylonia', ISBE, 1:399–400. For a sample of dream omens, see Alfred J. Hoerth, *Archaeology and the Old Testament* (Grand Rapids: Baker, 1998), p. 373.

[12] Check the description in A. Leo Oppenheim, *Ancient Mesopotamia* (rev. ed., Chicago: University of Chicago Press, 1977), pp. 187–192.

[13] The traditional 'vegetables' is a bit misleading. The two related words in vv. 12 and 16 refer to produce grown from seed that is sown and so includes not only vegetables but fruits and grains – and presumably bread made from grain. See Miller, p. 69.

requested (12) had not also been part of an idol offering? Still others hold the difficulty was *symbolic* – sharing in the king's food was a token of dependence on the king and a tacit sign of loyalty to him.[14] But even Daniel's alternative diet would have been 'government issue'; it would have been impossible to avoid indications of dependence.

We may never know, then, specifically why Daniel longed to avoid the decreed food rations. Which probably means the *defensive* view best explains his decision. What do I mean by this? Well, Babylon was simply smothering Daniel and his friends.[15] Daniel may well have thought, 'There is a real danger here; I could get sucked up into this and neutered by it all.' He recognized that if Babylon gets into you, the show is over.[16] Hence he had to draw the line at some point to preserve some distinctiveness, to keep from being totally squeezed into Babylon's mould. Walton *et al.* sum it up well:

> It is not so much something in the food that defiles as much as it is the total program of assimilation. At this point the Babylonian government is exercising control over every aspect of their lives. They have little means to resist the forces of assimilation that are controlling them. They seize on one of the few areas where they can still exercise choice as an opportunity to preserve their distinct identity.[17]

We should pause and note how the story highlights Daniel's wisdom. For one thing, it suggests Daniel is wise simply in his *recognition* of how critical this moment and matter could be. This episode didn't have 'crisis' written all over it like the raging fire of chapter 3 or the ravaging lions of chapter 6. The circumstances here are far less electrical and so all the more subtle. Sometimes 'smaller'

[14] Baldwin, p. 83.

[15] Cf. Goldingay's (p. 22) description: 'A group of young Israelites, for the moment silent, faceless, nameless, helpless objects for manipulating by the Babylonian state, are to be taken, taught, provided for, trained, and renamed in this alien environment. Trundled off to a foreign land, they are placed in the charge of a foreign official with a foreign name, are called by foreign titles, and are allocated a foreign education, foreign diet, and foreign names for themselves, to prepare them to serve in a foreign court.'

[16] I can't help but think of Leslie Nielsen's lines in one of his movies: 'It's like drinking Drano – it cleans you out but leaves you feeling empty inside.' So the impact of Babylon.

[17] John H. Walton, Victor H. Matthews and Mark W. Chavalas, *The IVP Bible Background Commentary: Old Testament* (Downers Grove: IVP, 2000), p. 731. Similarly, see Sinclair B. Ferguson, 'Daniel', in *New Bible Commentary* (Leicester: IVP, ⁴1994), p. 749, and even Calvin, 1:108.

commitments made along the way fortify faith to plant its feet when it has to meet more severe threats.[18]

However, we especially see Daniel's wisdom in his *manner* of pressing his request. Daniel broached his request to Ashpenaz (8b). Then we are assured that God caused Ashpenaz to regard Daniel with *favour and compassions* (9). Yet he denied Daniel's request (10)! He apparently felt sympathy for Daniel but did not want to risk the royal rage by countering one of the king's explicit orders. Should – due to unauthorized diet change – the king see Daniel and friends more 'haggard' than others it could be 'curtains' for Ashpenaz.[19]

Of course the favour and compassion of verse 9 might go beyond sympathy, for it may be that Ashpenaz's refusal in verse 10 is not a refusal. We can't be sure, because obviously the biblical text conveys no eye movements or tones of voice, but it is feasible to read verse 10 as a veiled invitation rather than a direct refusal, as if to say: '*I* cannot issue such an order, but then if you can manage it some other way, have at it!'[20] In any case, Daniel went down a notch on the chain of command, proposed a trial run of ten days to the steward who served them (12–13), found him agreeable (14) and – in ten days and beyond – providence favourable (15–16).[21] The arrangement became ongoing: the verbal forms in verse 16 are participles, indicating continuous action ('kept taking away' and 'kept giving them').

All this to say we should be impressed with how Daniel handled this matter. In the face of Ashpenaz's refusal (10, or at least seeming refusal), Daniel did not throw a religious hissy fit, blowing off about Babylon's heavy-handedness and 'insensitivity'. He simply looked around for the next possible step to take (11ff.) to see where that might land him. Daniel was not one of those people who believe that 'firmness of principle always involves acting stubborn and pig-headed'.[22] It's as if Daniel is fully aware that he is under *the Lord's grace*.

That grace is the undertow of the whole passage and here it 'explains' Daniel's success in verses 8–16, verses that serve as the hinge on which the story turns. Note the major flow of Daniel 1:

---

[18] See Wallace, pp. 40–41; cf. Veldkamp, p. 16: 'We should remember that the devil is an even greater danger in the world's dining rooms than in the den of lions. When we hear the sounds of the king's meal being served, when we hear the glasses clink, we should be even more on our guard than when famished lions open their mouths.'

[19] 'Haggard' comes from $z\bar{a}'ap$, which usually connotes rage (cf. BDB, 277); here and in Gen. 40:6 it seems to indicate haggard or dejected appearance.

[20] See Goldingay, p. 19, for a similar view.

[21] Though speculative, it could be that the steward was amenable to the request because he could enjoy the food meant for Daniel and friends himself. It may have been better fare than lower bureaucrats received! Cf. Baldwin, p. 84.

[22] Veldkamp, p. 19.

Subservience in Babylon (3–7)
Resistance in Babylon (8–16)
Success in Babylon (17–20)

Everything depends on the 'resistance' offered in verses 8–16, and the success of that resistance depends on the Lord's grace, as verse 9 testifies.

We need to ponder this grace. First, note that this grace is a bit surprising.[23] One doesn't ordinarily expect a Babylonian lackey to care two hoots about the concerns of foreign exiles. *But God gave.* This brings to mind Helmut Thielicke's story of how he went, on someone's advice, to the Brown House (the Nazi central office) in Munich to protest his dismissal from his university teaching position (ca. 1940). He was initially unhelpfully rebuffed, but then he noted that a young civil servant there stopped and fixed his gaze on him. He asked Thielicke if he could be of assistance. Thielicke said the young man was so kind and helpful that he told him his whole trouble. The fellow then arranged for Thielicke to see the first bureaucrat he would need to face.[24] Even if his quest was eventually futile, what a pleasant surprise this was. We would call it an oxymoron in the highest – a slice of kindness in the heart of Nazidom. How kind God is to lay down the cushions of his compassions amid the harshest of our circumstances.

Observe also that God's grace is very quiet here. In this section it is hidden away in the one-liner in verse 9. Grace is there and at work but doesn't create a stir or make a racket. It seems to work so naturally and unobtrusively. Margaret Clarkson uses a phrase that nicely captures this point in her hymn 'God of the Ages':[25] 'Quietly sovereign' – that is part of the beauty of the Lord our God (cf. Ps. 27:4). And he is present in his silent role in Babylon.

3. God is present in his subversive role (17–20)

God continues to act quietly and silently but with an additional twist in verses 17–20. Here God's work appears subversive. The text breaks down into two parts: divine gift (17), and human recognition (18–20).

Verse 17 is our third 'grace note' in the chapter: *Now as for these four lads – God gave them knowledge and skill in all literature and wisdom, and Daniel himself* [emphatic subject] *had understanding*

---

[23] Though perhaps it shouldn't be; it might be seen as an initial answer to Solomon's prayer in 1 Kgs 8:46–50; cf. Duguid, p. 14.
[24] Helmut Thielicke, *Notes from a Wayfarer* (New York: Paragon House, 1995), pp. 116–117.
[25] 'God of the Ages' (Hope Publishing/Word Music).

in every vision and dreams. Naturally this does not mean the youths do not study and toil and invest themselves in their studies. They surely do. But it means that God's goodness attends, surrounds and prospers their work and so explains their success. That success is obvious. At the end of the prescribed (re-)education they meet with the king for their oral examination interview, and he finds that these four far outstrip all the others, and so they enter the king's service. Verse 20 ratchets their commendation up a notch with a touch of what may reflect royal hyperbole: *And as for every matter of wisdom requiring understanding of which the king inquired of them, he found them ten times better than all the magicians and conjurers who were in all his kingdom.*

Now if we step back and look at all of Daniel 1, we discover an irony that is almost amusing. At the beginning of the story we find captives from a subjugated kingdom (3–4), but here these very captives stand at the head of the palace royal service corps. In verses 1–2 we read of Judah's shameful defeat, including the pillaging of her temple vessels, while here we meet the 'victory' of Judah's captives as they serve next the throne. Such a fascinating irony.

Before I moved from Mississippi, I noticed a piece in our local newspaper about a strange turn of events. The article reported that Mississippi State University was to be the recipient and repository of the official papers of General and later President Ulysses S. Grant. Grant, of course, served the north in our War Between the States (which northerners call 'The Civil War'). He may not have been the most skilled of generals but he did assume a general was to fight (some northern generals didn't understand that). And fight he did. Some of his fighting was in Mississippi itself – he reduced Vicksburg by siege in 1863. And he brought General Robert E. Lee to surrender in 1865 after beating down southern forces with the north's superior numbers and resources. Even after 150 years many southerners would still regard Grant as 'the enemy'. Which makes the irony so delicious: the caretaker and conservator of Grant's official papers is not the University of Illinois or Michigan but Mississippi State. Of all places. The south may have lost the war but has won the privilege of harbouring the papers of its enemy.

That's what we see in Daniel 1: the losers have by the twists of God's providence become the winners. It is God's subversive work. Yet we must be careful to note that God does not work this way simply to show how clever he is. Rather his work seems intended to prove beneficial toward those in Babylon. When we read Daniel 2 we see that it is because of Daniel and his friends that Nebuchadnezzar's raft of religious flunkies (magicians, conjurors, etc.) keep their heads. And in chapters 2, 3 and 4 we see how Daniel & Co. speak God's revelation and truth into Nebuchadnezzar's life. God's purpose involved more than simply the fate of these Judean exiles – they were to 'stand before governors and kings . . . to bear witness before them'.[26]

The situation is analogous to that of the little Israelite girl who served Naaman's wife.[27] What trauma and horror she must have felt when Syrian raiders wrenched her from her home, and presumably from her parents, in Israel. Serving Mrs Naaman may have placed her in more posh circumstances but the aching heart must have remained. But her natural witness in the midst of her housework exposed her genuine concern for her master's welfare and her confidence in the power of Israel's God working through his prophet. It all leads to a cleansing of disease and a confession of faith. Sometimes God may allow hardship to reach us because he wants his mercy to reach beyond us. And that may be subversive as well.

4. God is present in his sustaining role (21)

We are beyond the *God gave* notes, but one simply cannot pass up this last verse: *And Daniel went on until the first year of Cyrus the king.*[28] Sounds harmless enough, but sounds, like looks, can be deceiving.

At verse 21 the writer has obviously punched the 'fast forward' button. Who was Cyrus? He was the king of Persia who began reigning in 539 BC. Nebuchadnezzar then has passed from the scene (kings always seem to die). And what of Babylon? It fell. To whom? To Cyrus and the Persians. Do you see? Mighty Babylon of verses 1–2 (or 1–20) has fallen but God's servant continues. At that time Daniel would probably be over 80 years old.

I've a hunch, however, that the text is more than a statement about Daniel. The text is a sort of parable, as if to say: Kingdoms rise and fall, God's people go on. This text supplies anecdotal evidence of Isaiah's praise of Yahweh:

> He reduces princes to nothing,
> the rulers of the world to mere emptiness.
> Scarcely are they planted, scarcely sown,
> scarcely has their stem taken root in the soil,
> than he blows on them and they wither
> and the storm carries them away like chaff.[29]

---

[26] Mark 13:9.

[27] See 2 Kgs 5:1–3.

[28] The verse does not mean that Daniel's life only reached to the first year of Cyrus; that was not the case (see 10:1). The concern is that he outlasted Babylon, not how much further he got.

[29] Isa. 40:23–24, NJB.

So in verse 21 Babylon, the hairy-chested macho brute of the world, has dropped with a thud into the mausoleum of history, while fragile Daniel, servant of the Most High God, is still on his feet.

On 10 December 1958, boxing great Archie Moore, almost forty-three, defended his light-heavyweight title against Canadian Yvon Durelle, thirty. Durelle floored Moore three times in the first round and once in the fifth. But Moore seemed to gain strength as the fight went on while Durelle tired. In the eleventh round, Moore scored his 127th knock-out. He simply outlasted his younger opponent. And that is the little piece of eschatology that Daniel 1 wants you to get a grip on before you proceed to the rest of the book: remember that the servants of God will simply out-endure the kingdoms of this age.

The Hebrew text of verse 21 contains only seven words – seven Hebrew words packed with dynamite.

Daniel 2:1–49
2. A dream that will come true

Most of us probably try to avoid beginning a sentence with a conjunction. And I don't know exactly why – maybe someone along the way has told us it is bad form. Perhaps that is why our style-conscious modern English translations omit the conjunction at the beginning of 2:1. But it's there in the Hebrew text, and at least the AV and the ASV pick it up: *And in the second year of the reign of Nebuchadnezzar, Nebuchadnezzar dreamed dreams.* Not earth-shattering, but the tiny connective bears witness that chapter 1 is no detached episode; it is the spring that 'nourishes' the ongoing story. A little reflection shows this is so – and quite beyond the simple conjunction linking chapters 1 and 2. The temple vessels of 1:2 will form the grist for the demise of Belshazzar in chapter 5; the here-I-must-draw-the-line decision of 1:8ff. will be re-enacted in chapters 3 and 6 in face of blaze and beasts; and Daniel's skill in understanding visions and dreams (1:17) will be on display in both chapters 2 and 4. So every one of the 'stories' has its roots in chapter 1. And this usually-eliminated *and* in 2:1 bears its own faint witness to that.

1. Literary features

We can break down chapter 2 into broad chunks:

Demand and destruction (1–13).
Inquiry and supplication(14–24).
Interrogation and confession (25–30).
Dream and interpretation (31–45).
Honour and exaltation (46–49).

Now let's make some observations. In the first segment (1–13) note that as a reader you have no clue about the 'real' problem until verse 5; there for the first time you begin to think this could be a nasty business if this raft of pagan retainers has to cough up the raw material of the dream itself. But initially the reader thinks the king is the one with the problem. And then don't miss the note of irony here. The king's professionals begin with that polite courtly hyperbole, O *king, live forever!* (4) – and yet we know from the later dream interpretation that that simply will not be the case, for the king is simply another passing phase in the wobbly annals of international royal governments (39–40).[1]

We must mark also how verses 1–13 depict Babylon as a place of fear, helplessness and brutality. The fear is Nebuchadnezzar's. His spirit is *agitated* (1, 3) over his dream. 'How easy it is to terrify strong men outside of Christ!'[2] The dream itself was scary. Nebuchadnezzar was no nitwit. He knew that the massive metallic monster had to represent something (maybe his own kingdom) and he knew the stone brought catastrophe to it. He's king of Babylon and he's shaking as he unbuttons his PJs in the morning.

The helplessness belongs to the king's batch of intellectuals-at-court, who can't fathom why the king won't tell them his dream so they can consult their volumes of dream-interpretation manuals and come up with an answer. They are told to reveal both his dream and its meaning. What king ever did that (10b)? It's so arbitrary (welcome to monarchy). It was not that he had forgotten the dream – that rests on a misunderstanding (or mistranslation) of his statement in verse 5a.[3] But who knows why the king insisted they must come up with both text and interpretation? He may have suspected they were devious or phony (cf. 9b). In any case, they were non-plussed because kings get to ask the impossible. And they will die for inability to do the impossible (12–13). Nebuchadnezzar will purge the whole lot of them. That's the brutality of Babylon. Life can be fairly cushy there – until the king gets into a really foul mood. Verses 1–13 let you glimpse the Babylon behind the glitz and glamour.

Finally, notice that there is a loaded theological statement in verses 1–13; it's found in verse 11. Granted, it is perverted pagan theology, but is theology for all that. In fact, each of the five segments of chapter 2 sport a weighty theological note:

---

[1] See Steinmann, p. 115; Fyall, pp. 32–33.

[2] Thomas, p. 23.

[3] The wise men certainly didn't think the king had forgotten the dream since they kept pressing him to reveal it. Moreover, if the king was upset over the dream he must have remembered what upset him. On this matter, see Miller, p. 81, and Olyott, p. 25. Olyott notes that verse 9 assumes the king recalled the dream – otherwise he could not check the wise men for accuracy.

Verses 1–13	⟶	verse 11
Verses 14–24	⟶	verses 20–23
Verses 25–30	⟶	verse 28
Verses 31–45	⟶	verse 44
Verses 46–49	⟶	verse 47

The second segment (14–24) opens and closes with Daniel appealing to Arioch, the *chief of the executioners* (a possible rendering in 14). Daniel, as in 1:8–13, has a knack for knowing the next step. What should one do when under a decree of execution? Well, maybe speak to the executioner (14–16)! Observe the *economy* of the narrative: we are not told how Daniel knew Arioch (14), nor are we told, for example, how Daniel gained an audience with the king (16). Was this latter self-initiated? Did Arioch pave the way for him? None of it matters. Why clutter the story? But we see the *emphasis* of this section by observing what gets the most 'press' in the writer's report. That, of course, is Daniel's exclamation of praise in verses 20–23. He notes that there was a prayer meeting (18) but doesn't record any of those prayers. He simply notes the answer (19) and then gives four verses for Daniel's praise. That has to be deliberate – and justifies Steinmann's contention that Daniel's praise in verses 20–23 is the theological centre of the chapter, holding priority even over the dream and its interpretation.[4] Nebuchadnezzar's praise in verse 47 forms a later parallel and echo to Daniel's praise here. The upshot is that the pagan lackeys of Babylon will not die (24) – another instance of Abraham's seed, Daniel in this case, bringing blessing to 'all the families of the ground'.[5]

I will comment on the third segment (25–30) in connection with the theme of the chapter. Here I want to make just one observation about the dream and its interpretation in verses 31–45. (I defer most discussion of what kingdoms or empires are involved until the exposition of Daniel 7.) Notice how quickly our writer passes over the second and third kingdoms; they barely get a mention in verse 39. Primary attention then falls on Nebuchadnezzar (37–39a) and the *fourth* kingdom (40–43).

The last section (46–49) needs little comment except to note the surprise and embarrassment Nebuchadnezzar might have caused an Israelite reader (or ourselves) when he falls on his face and pays worshipful homage to Daniel (46). One can't really tone it down very much. The Aramaic verb the ESV renders *paid homage* is *sĕgid*;

---

[4] Steinmann, pp. 109, 123–125.
[5] Gen. 12:3. See Wallace, pp. 52–53. Some think that the Aramaic participle in verse 13 indicates that some of the wise men were already being executed; but the participle can also be used of incipient or anticipated action – 'about to be killed' (ESV).

it is used eleven times in Daniel 3 and always refers to 'worshiping' Nebuchadnezzar's golden image. The Hebrew cognate (*sāgad*) occurs four times in Isaiah (44:15, 17, 19; 46:6) of 'bowing down' to an idol. Obviously, verse 47 qualifies the king's obeisance somewhat – he recognizes the revelation has come from Daniel's God. But why should verse 46 really shock us? One is tempted to say: 'The guy's a pagan for crying out loud. What do you expect?'[6]

2. Controlling theme

'When tyrants suffer from bad dreams, God is at work.'[7] Nebuchadnezzar apparently agrees but does not know *how* God is at work. And so this walking paradox of power and fear wonders whether he has had a dream or a nightmare, and he won't know unless he finds out what it means. His dream turns out to be God's vehicle of communication to the pagan king. His dream actually depicts God's plan for the world. But someone must declare, reveal or make known what the dream means. That is the theme of Daniel 2 – almost, we may think, to the point of overkill. Simply consider the mass of synonymous Aramaic verbs relating to disclosing the king's dream and its interpretation:

gĕlâ, reveal	19, 28, 29, 30, 47 [twice]
hăwâ, show (ESV), declare	4, 6 [twice], 7, 9, 10 [not visible in translation], 11, 16, 24, 27
yĕda', make known	5, 9, 23 [twice], 25, 26, 28, 29, 30, 45

Add to these *'ămar* (tell) in verses 9 and 36 and, in the Hebrew section, *nāgad* (tell) in verse 2 and *yāda'* (to know) in verse 3, and one hears these 'revealing' verbs over 30 times. The keynote, then, is Daniel's testimony in verse 28: *But there is a God in heaven who reveals mysteries, and he has made known to King Nebuchadnezzar what will be in the latter days.* Which brings us to the witness of this chapter: what does God reveal to *us* in this dream?

---

[6] Anyone who still holds that the stories come from a second-century author will have a problem with v. 46, because a second-century (Maccabean) author would have had a problem with it – he would have choked and gagged over it and punched the 'delete' button. What Young wrote of v. 48 would equally apply to v. 46: 'But if these words were written at the time of the Maccabees or at any other period of *strict* Judaism, it is difficult to understand why the author, supposedly a strict Jew with an abhorrence [sic] of everything pagan, would represent his Jewish hero as receiving such honors from a pagan king' (p. 82).

[7] Luthi, p. 29.

3. Theological testimony

First, *God reveals how futile pagan religion is* (1–30). The dream comes in year two of Nebuchadnezzar's reign (1),[8] and he summons the whole range of his religious professionals – the *magicians, conjurers, sorcerers, and Chaldeans* (2).[9] More than just dream interpretation was needed; if the dream indicated adverse conditions to come, one then needed the aid of those who could cast the right spells and engage in the proper hocus-pocus to reverse or negate the threatened ills.[10] As noted previously, we don't know why the king wouldn't divulge the dream itself to these in-house interpreters. There are, however, cases of kings being suspicious of such characters.[11] Or it could be Nebuchadnezzar simply had an 'edge' about him; sometimes monarchs just like to act like monarchs because they can. Until they get cancer or acid indigestion or nausea they tend to think they are far above the common lot of humanity, who can be deleted at will. In any case, the king told these government employees to come up with the dream or become 'body parts' (5, Steinmann's translation).

The temperature is rising at court. In a moment the king will blow his top (12), but even the Chaldeans and the rest are more than a little put out at the king:

> *Nobody in the world could find out the king's trouble; what is more, no other king, governor or chief would think of putting such a question to any magician, enchanter or Chaldean. The question the king asks is difficult, and no one can find the king an answer to it, except the gods, whose dwelling is not with creatures of flesh* (10–11, JB).

Now think: Why does the biblical writer want you to hear that? Not because in helpless frustration they so much as call the king an

---

[8] The 'second year' of 2:1 poses no major rub with the 'three years' of the Hebrew lads' training in 1:5. Given the 'accession-year' pattern used in Babylon, the king's accession year would be the first year of training for Daniel and friends, his official 'first' year their second, and his 'second' their third training year. Their 'Babylonian intensive' could have been concluded by the time of 2:1.

[9] One finds a bewildering variety of renderings for these terms in English translations. See Andrew E. Hill, 'Daniel', *The Expositor's Bible Commentary*, 13 vols. (rev. ed., Grand Rapids: Zondervan, 2008), 8:61–62. 'Chaldean' here refers to 'a special class of Babylonian priest-scholar'. The point of the text is that the king called upon the full resources of the religio-scientific community. Note also 'astrologers' in v. 27.

[10] Keil, p. 88.

[11] Cf. A. Leo Oppenheim, *Ancient Mesopotamia* (rev. ed., Chicago: University of Chicago Press, 1977), p. 227.

irrational royal nut case but because their words are *a confession of the failure of paganism*.[12] Daniel himself reinforces their words in verse 27, and yet because there is a God in heaven – and in Babylon! – who reveals mysteries (28), Daniel can give thanks to him,

> *for you have given me wisdom and might,*
> *and have now made known to me what we asked of you,*
> *for you have made known to us the king's matter* (23b, ESV).

So by depicting the helplessness of paganism the writer wants to say: 'Don't you see? Paganism is nothing but a religious cul-de-sac. It can give no sure word from outside.' By contrast then – and in light of the whole chapter – he is saying that life is a dead-end street without a God who discloses what the future holds. He is telling exiled Israel that there is no need to be awed by paganism, despite its trappings and splendour, for it is nothing but empty and dark. We will come back to this matter but, for the moment, the text insists we listen to praise.

This segment of Daniel 2 dwells on both negative and positive, both on paganism that remains in the dark and on the God who brings dark things to light. In verses 17–19 the writer hurries to report the facts: how Daniel reports the danger to his three friends (17), how he urges them to prayer (18), and that God revealed to Daniel the king's dream (19). The story would flow nicely if immediately after verse 19 we read verse 24 and following. But the writer will have none of it. He's not in a hurry anymore. Rather, he pauses for praise (20–23). 'Don't rush off,' he says, 'let's take our time and hear how God is adored.'

How he is praised! Daniel blesses God for his wisdom and power (20) and for revealing *deep and hidden things* like the king's dream (22–23). And probably in response to the dream's interpretation (cf. 36–45) he praises God for his sovereignty: *he changes times and seasons*,[13] and *he removes kings and sets up kings* (political turnover is in his control). And so the narrative is pushing us to praise. By taking the time to spread out Daniel's praise on your Bible page the text is warning us not to rush from our solution (19) to the next item on our list (24). No, it is time for worship instead. Kent Hughes tells of how Spurgeon was in the process of explaining the gospel to a woman who was on the edge of entering the kingdom when she burst

[12] Similar to the 'digs' at Egyptian paganism in Genesis 41:8, 15, 24.
[13] 'In other words, God determines when in history events are to take place and how long each process or phase in history is to endure' (Archer, p. 43). Note that Daniel's praise speaks *of* God in the third person in vv. 20–22 and *to* God in the second person in v. 23.

out with, 'Oh, Mr Spurgeon, if the Lord saves me, he shall never hear the end of it!'[14] That should be our attitude – and even the way Scripture is written is designed to reinforce that pattern. Here in Daniel 2 it's as if the Holy Spirit reaches out an invisible hand from the Bible page, grabs you by the collar, and whispers, 'Now what should you say to this? Is Daniel the only one who owes praise?'

Let's go back to the futility of paganism. Remember the contrast: pagans driven by fear (1) and darkened by ignorance (10–11, 27) versus a God who reveals and discloses what is coming both in the muck and climax of history (28).[15] By and large, men and women today stand on pagan ground; they have no sure light on the future, no idea where human life and history are heading.

Peter Moore describes the impressive sunken garden in front of the Beinicke Rare Book Library on Yale University's campus. It is meant to simulate the universe. A large marble pyramid stands in one corner, symbolizing time. Another corner sports a huge doughnut shaped structure standing on its side. It signifies energy. In a third corner is a huge die perched on one tip as if ready to topple any which way. It is the symbol of chance. This, Moore says, is the world view of modern man: 'a self-existing universe consisting of energy, time and chance.'[16] And those in Babylon, ancient or modern, don't know which way the die will fall. Chance is opaque. It is the world of whatever.

Bible Christians think the Yale garden is a lie. They hold that there is a God who knows and orders the course of history down through the rise and rubble of nations until the days when he sets up *a kingdom that shall never be destroyed* (44). This is no brilliant insight of theirs; they only hold this because there is a God in heaven who reveals mysteries – and has done so. He has given them revelation material like Daniel 2. But we who hold this kingdom-view can easily forget how unbearably sad Joe and Jane Pagan might be, for they go out their front door in the morning and have no idea where history is heading, or if it is. Maybe it's all too cerebral; but I can only say

---

[14] R. Kent Hughes, *2 Corinthians: Power in Weakness* (Wheaton: Crossway, 2006), pp. 97–98.

[15] V. 28 specifies that God has made known to the king 'what will be in the latter days' (ESV). The phrase (lit., 'the end of the days') occurs 14 times in the OT with context deciding the sense, whether the future in general (e.g., Gen. 49:1; Num. 24:14; Deut. 4:30) or what some might call a more 'last days' ('eschatological') future (cf. Isa. 2:2 and Mic. 4:1; Ezek. 38:16; Hos. 3:5). Alec Motyer says it indicates 'the undated future, neither necessarily far nor certainly near' (*The Prophecy of Isaiah* [Downers Grove: IVP, 1993], p. 54). Here the phrase is 'exegeted' by 'after this' in v. 29, i.e., it seems to refer to all that is post-Nebuchadnezzar (see Baldwin, p. 91). See also Laird Harris, TWOT, 1:34. For a contrary view, Steinmann, p. 129.

[16] *Disarming the Secular Gods* (Downers Grove: IVP, 1989), p. 59.

that if I didn't believe Daniel 2:44, I couldn't find the energy to place one foot in front of another.

To have a God who reveals mysteries, however, does not mean we have a God who unveils everything. He doesn't show us which stocks will profit or whether you can avoid cancer till you're eighty-nine, or whether one's nation will still exist twenty years hence. He only reveals what we need to have. And yet Daniel's praise helps us here, because he assures us that even what God *doesn't* tell us he knows: *he knows what is in the darkness* (22). You can walk into the future with a God like that – who shows you that history is going toward his unshakable kingdom and who assures you that even though you have many personal uncertainties you follow a God who knows what is in the darkness. So you can keep going with hope and without fear.

Secondly, *God reveals how fragile human power is* (31–43). In this segment Daniel recounts the king's dream to him (31–35) and then proceeds to its interpretation (36ff.).[17] In the interpretation major attention falls on the first and the fourth kingdoms. In the first case, with Nebuchadnezzar, Daniel presses home the source of human authority (37–38). Twice we meet the loaded verb *has given*; if Nebuchadnezzar has kingdom, power, might and glory and if he rules over humans, beasts and birds, it is only because the God of heaven has given them all to him.[18] In short: 'the only reason you are on that throne is because the God of heaven has placed you there.'

The second point of emphasis is the *fourth kingdom* (40–43). Here Daniel depicts the weakness of human strength. This kingdom combines massive strength with disturbing weakness, crushing power with failing cohesion. What a rickety base for the whole monstrosity of human kingdoms to rest upon![19]

But probably the most telling jolt comes in verse 39, where Daniel delivers what seems to be an almost passing blow on human pride. You won't feel it in the esv, for that translation has buried the opening form in the Aramaic text far down in the sentence. Literally, verse 39

[17] Daniel as dream-interpreter before Nebuchadnezzar is often compared to Joseph in the same role before Pharaoh in Genesis 40 – 41. As Archer (p. 42) points out, Daniel's task was far more arduous – Joseph never had to come up with the contents of the dream itself.

[18] Even Antichrist cannot chew through that leash of divine sovereignty – note the fourfold *edothē* ('it was given') in Rev. 13:5–7.

[19] It doesn't matter what form the 'clay' is in – it's still a 'no go'. In v. 33, the word for 'clay' (*ḥăsap*) seems to refer to a finished product, i.e., pottery (see Lucas, p. 64). Clearly that would be brittle (v. 42). In vv. 41b and 43a 'clay' has the word *ṭînā'* added, which refers to wet or soft clay (cf. esv). Even at that stage the clay and iron don't hold well. On v. 43 and the mixing 'by the seed of men', or possibly, 'in marriage', see Harman, pp. 68–69.

begins, *But after you . . .* (NKJV). Now that's a striking thought! One wonders if it stuck in Nebuchadnezzar's mind. Such a simple yet powerful assumption in those words: *after you*! Nebuchadnezzar's kingdom will not last. Kings and kingdoms, presidents and dictators, democracies and tyrannies and monarchies come and go and enter the landfill of history.[20]

Several years after Estonia regained its sovereignty after the 1991 Soviet collapse, the town of Tartu decided to auction off its statue of Bolshevik leader Vladimir Lenin, setting the starting price at $15,000. That statue had decorated a town square in Soviet years. Time was when Tartu would not have dared to do that. But even Lenin is subject to a divine 'after you' – and so his statue becomes nothing more than the centrepiece for a municipal fund-raiser.

How then are the various 'audiences' of Daniel 2 meant to respond to this dream and its interpretation? What about Nebuchadnezzar himself? Surely he was to acknowledge that his kingship was a gift from the God of heaven, that his own kingdom was but a passing episode, that he simply belonged to the 'chaff regime' (cf. 35) – this could be the beginning of repentance. I agree with Joyce Baldwin: 'This is just what Nebuchadrezzar [sic] did not do. He asked no questions either about the future or about Daniel's great God. Relieved that he was the head of gold and that his fears were ground-less, he concerned himself with the present, and with the man who had met his need.'[21] He confesses Daniel's God is a *revealer of mysteries* (47), but at this point such revelation got no traction in the king's mind.

What of Israel? What were exiles and those who would become exiles to understand from this revelation? They should at least see that the kingdom of God (in the v. 44 sense) is not going to come as soon as Babylon passes off the political scene.[22] How often God's people have to be saved from the 'if only' heresy, whether it is 'if only Babylon bites the dust, then . . . ' or something else. Daniel 2 is not trying to rob Israel of her hope but wants her to have a true and realistic hope and so says: it will yet be a long historical road before the kingdom of God comes. What to do then? Iain Duguid suggests that verses 48–49 may hold an answer:

It is not coincidental that the chapter ends with Daniel and his friends promoted to responsible positions within the Babylonian

---

[20] What seems an empire was merely an episode; Fyall, p. 36.

[21] Baldwin, p. 94. The king's name may be spelled both Nebuchadnezzar and Nebuchadrezzar; both are found in the Bible; cf. D. J. Wiseman, *Nebuchadrezzar and Babylon* (Oxford: Oxford University Press, 1991), pp. 2–5.

[22] See 'Why was it written?' in the Introduction for more detail, pp. 24–26.

system. . . These men didn't isolate themselves from the kingdom of this world as they waited for God to establish his kingdom; rather, they poured themselves into seeking the welfare of their temporary home in Babylon.[23]

We are to serve where we have been placed within the fading kingdom as we go on waiting for the final kingdom (cf. Jer. 29:5–7).

How does this part of the text address contemporary believers? I think it addresses both our understanding and our fears. Let's expand first on the 'understanding' component.

One can count scholarly noses over whether we are to see a degenerative principle implied in the sequence of gold-silver-bronze-iron plus clay (32–33). Some think that over-reads the symbolism (Lucas, Goldingay). But it is difficult to avoid the inference. Hill observes of the statue: 'its splendor dissipates (from gold to iron and clay) but its hardness increases (from gold to iron).'[24] Not only is the second kingdom said to be *inferior* to Babylon (39; however that is conceived), but the focus on the scary paradox of the *fourth kingdom* (strength and weakness) indicates a descent toward fragmentation. This is saying something important to contemporary readers about the pattern of human history: on the whole history degenerates; it carries its own germ of disintegration that becomes increasingly apparent. There is then no 'progress' gene implanted in history's womb that ensures some sort of infallible upward movement. Some may complain that this destroys optimism. Only empty optimism. True optimism comes from an indestructible kingdom (44–45) not from a defunct but deified historical process. You cannot write 'history' with an upper case 'H' and think that it will save anything.

But then this dream interpretation also speaks to us in our fears. It says to us: Don't be impressed with human political power, no matter how 'iron-ish' it appears; it is all so fleeting; do not fear it. Daniel 2 says, Look at it square in the eye and repeat after Jesus: 'You would have no authority over me at all unless it had been given you from above.'[25]

Third, *God reveals how firm his kingdom is* (44–45; cf. 34–35). The description of the *stone*-kingdom is brief, but it is everything the kingdoms of this age are not. It is first, *indestructible* (*the God of heaven will set up a kingdom that shall never be destroyed*, 44a); second, *final* (*nor shall the kingdom be left to another people*, 44b); third, *overwhelming* (*It shall break in pieces all these kingdoms*

[23] Duguid, p. 42.
[24] Hill, p. 67.
[25] John 19:11.

and bring them to an end, 44c; cf. 35a); and fourth, *supernatural (a stone was cut from a mountain by no human hand*, 45a; cf. 34; all quotes ESV).

Perhaps one could add a fifth mark of this 'fifth' kingdom: *paradoxical*. The language of the text here in Daniel 2, concise as it is, seems to imply both an initial and a consummated form to this kingdom. On the one hand, it begins as a mere stone *cut out without hands* (34, NKJV), which indicates 'the obscurity and apparent weakness of its origin'.[26] It is inaugurated (*the God of heaven will set up a kingdom*, 44a) *in the days of those kings*. I take this to be a reference to rulers of the just-discussed *fourth kingdom* (40–43). If that fourth kingdom should prove – at least partially – to be Rome, then this 'setting up' would fit nicely with the initial coming of the kingdom of God in Jesus' preaching (Mark 1:14–15) and works (e.g., Luke 11:20). Moreover, that the stone that struck the image *became a great mountain and filled the whole earth* (emphasis mine) may imply a distinction between 'small beginning' and 'final dominance'. And yet that final cataclysmic phase takes centre stage here. 'But when God's time comes, his kingdom requires the destruction of earthly kingdoms rather than his working through them. They are God's will for now, but not for ever; and when his moment arrives, his kingdom comes by catastrophe, not by development.'[27]

This solid assurance of the victory of God's kingdom is meant to bring a contagious certainty to the people of God, people so often squashed under the arrogant heels of earth's kingdoms and rulers. Such an immovable dogma puts iron in their intestines and nerve in their spirits as they walk through the disappointments of life and the reverses of history. They never totally despair because they know that Jesus Christ is not only the 'faithful witness' and the 'firstborn of the dead' but the 'ruler of kings on earth'.[28]

The Roman and Christian-hating Emperor Julian (AD 332–363) was mortally wounded in a war with the Persians. While Julian's expedition was in progress, one of Julian's followers asked a Christian in Antioch what the carpenter's son was doing. The Christian replied, 'The Maker of the world, whom you call the carpenter's son, is employed in making a coffin for the emperor.' Within days news came to Antioch of Julian's death.[29] That is where Daniel 2 leaves us. Jesus has a coffin for every empire and emperor; the only true security is in the kingdom of the carpenter's Son.

[26] Ferguson, p. 64.
[27] Goldingay, p. 59.
[28] Rev. 1:5.
[29] John Whitecross, *The Shorter Catechism Illustrated from Christian Biography and History* (repr. ed., London: Banner of Truth, 1968), p. 46.

Nebuchadnezzar did not forget his dream. And you must not forget it either; don't forget what the God of heaven reveals to you through this dream, for this is a dream that will come true.

Daniel 3:1–30
3. Saints in the hands of a saving God

In the late 1930s, in the heyday of Joe Stalin-adulation in the Soviet Union, Stalin's name was mentioned in a provincial meeting. This 'triggered' a standing ovation and a standing dilemma – for no one dared be the first to sit down. Finally, an elderly man, unable to stand any longer, took his seat. They noted his name and arrested him the next day.[1] He had failed to worship the idol long enough. Or there was Paul Schneider. He stood lined up with other prisoners at Buchenwald concentration camp. It was 20 April 1938, Hitler's forty-ninth birthday and, in tribute, the prisoners were ordered to remove their berets and venerate the Nazi swastika flag. At once all whipped off their headgear. But guards observed one man who would not 'bow' to the swastika – Paul Schneider. They beat him, twenty-five lashes with an ox-hide whip. That was only the first ox-hide treatment – because he refused to worship the idol.[2]

Rulers – especially autocrats – seem prone to dabble in religion, and Nebuchadnezzar is no exception. His effort to use religion as political cement brings on this story of saints in the hands of a saving God, and we will consider the concern, shape and testimony of this story.

1. Concern and shape

Daniel 3 begins abruptly: *Nebuchadnezzar the king made an image of gold'* (1a). *Image* (Aram., ṣĕlēm) immediately conjures up the 'image' in the king's dream in chapter 2, where the word appears five times (31 [twice], 32, 34, 35). Here in chapter 3 the word occurs eleven times (of twelve) of Nebuchadnezzar's monstrosity (1, 2, 3

---

[1] Robert Conquest, *Stalin: Breaker of Nations* (New York: Viking, 1991), p. 213.
[2] Don Stephens, *War and Grace* (Darlington: Evangelical Press, 2005), p. 59.

[twice], 5, 7, 10, 12, 14, 15, 18). This tempts one to assume a connection.[3] Perhaps like this: In spite of the ominous 'after you' of 2:39, Nebuchadnezzar determines to make his 'head of gold' (2:38) era of human history as permanent as possible; indeed, he will embody his own regime in a massive image and will require religio-political homage of his deified dominion, a kind of worship of 'the spirit of Babylon'.

This means that the story is first-commandment material (Exod. 20:3). The way is then clear, if costly, for God's people. The writer holds before you this episode because he wants you to make the same response as Daniel's friends: I will believe and obey the first commandment even if it kills me (and it may). That is the concern of the story.

As to the shape of the story, Daniel 3 seems to follow a chiastic or x-pattern. Ernest Lucas has helpfully worked this out; I will follow his break-down but with some changes in terminology.[4]

King's decree: dedication of image (1–7)
    Accusation: 'rebellion' (8–12)
        Royal rage – opportunity (13–15)
            Answer: confession (16–18)
        Royal rage – punishment (19–23)
    Deliverance: evidence (24–27)
King's decree: vindication of friends (28–30)

This careful (but by no means stodgy) literary pattern argues first, for the *unity* of the story (i.e., artistic compositions come as wholes at one time – they are not the chance product of bits and pieces layered over centuries) and second, highlights the *focus* of the story – clearly verses 16–18 serve as the 'hinge' of the whole account; this is the stand the writer wants his hearers/readers to take. Now to the witness of the story.

2. Testimony

The witness of the chapter arises from its three primary themes – pressure, obedience, and fellowship.

a. The power of pressure (1–15)

Nebuchadnezzar's image was meant to dominate. Any humongous monstrosity ninety feet high by nine feet wide (60 × 6 cubits) would

[3] Cf. George M. Schwab, *Hope in the Midst of a Hostile World* (Phillipsburg: Presbyterian and Reformed, 2006), p. 47.
[4] See Lucas, p. 86.

do so.[5] Some guess that a reasonably high pedestal may have been included in the height measurement, offsetting perhaps a tendency to tipsiness. No one knows for sure where the plain of Dura was – possibly a location a few miles south of Babylon.[6] The dedication service required the attendance of the whole range of civil service employees (2) and the homage paid was tantamount to a pledge of loyalty to the state. No one, of course, was required to give up his/her deities of choice; one only had to, as it were, burn his pinch of incense to the king's god and regime and then go happily back to his favourite religious superstition. The image does not seem to represent Nebuchadnezzar himself, for the three friends seem to take it as representing his *gods* (18; or 'god', NJPS); yet behind his gods/god stands the power of the king and the state, so it is difficult to avoid the spectre of statist religion here. The stakes are now higher for Daniel's three friends. In chapter 2 their danger arose from an occupational hazard; in chapter 3 it comes via an assault on first-commandment loyalty.

It will be useful to *analyze the pressure* Daniel's friends faced. First, it came from *authority*. In verses 1–7 we meet with *Nebuchadnezzar the king* six times (NASB preserves this more literal rendering) – almost as if to overstress the king's authority, whereas 'Nebuchadnezzar the king' only appears twice (9, 24) in the rest of the chapter. The pressure comes from feeling the sheer weight of Nebuchadnezzar himself.

Second, the pressure came from *conformity*. The raft of civil service folks are *gathered* (2–3), told (4–5) and threatened (6). *Therefore . . . all the peoples, nations, and languages fell down and worshipped* (7, ESV). Just like that. The praise band plays (7a),[7] and the crowd gets its back sides in the air and its noses in the sand and enjoys job security. They felt they had no choice. They 'had' to do it. There's a tremendous invisible coercion that comes from being among a whole mob of flattened worshipers.

Pressure may be intensified from *malice* (8–12), when one may know that enemies already have a vested interest on one's downfall. The men who accused Daniel's friends were *Chaldeans*, whether ethnic Chaldeans or more particularly professional astrologers it

---

[5] About 27 x 2.7 m in metric measurements.

[6] So Miller, p. 111. Miller points out that since it was in the 'province' of Babylon, a location within the city walls is unlikely (though D. J. Wiseman suggests it may have been by the fortified city wall – *duru*; see *Nebuchadrezzar and Babylon* [Oxford: Oxford University Press, 1991], p. 111). Miller also thinks the distance south of the city would have provided desired secrecy until the great unveiling.

[7] On Nebuchadnezzar's orchestra, see the study by T. C. Mitchell and R. Joyce in *Notes on Some Problems in the Book of Daniel* (London: Tyndale, 1965), pp. 19–27. The *sûmpŏnĕyâ*, which ESV renders 'bagpipe' (cf. vv. 5, 10, 15), may refer to a 'drum' (note HCSB); see discussion in Steinmann, p. 173.

may be hard to determine. They *maliciously accused* (ESV) *the Jews,* a lovely idiom which literally reads, 'they ate their pieces'. Their envy is apparent in verse 12: *certain Jews whom you have appointed over the affairs of the province of Babylon* – no reason why those appointments couldn't have gone to Chaldeans. But they stress the personal affront the Judeans pose to the king. These Jews, they allege, thumb their noses at the king's order. In the last line of verse 12, *your gods* and *the image of gold* are in emphatic position before the verbs: *your gods they will not serve and the image of gold you set up they will not worship.*[8] They cast everything into a mould of sheer defiance of the king.

Finally, pressure mounts from *intimidation* (13–15). There is something withering about the towering rage of a monarch anyway, but all the more so when he says there should be three words that should move you: burning fiery furnace. The prospect of roasting tends to motivate. In light of these various considerations perhaps we can appreciate the power of the pressure they faced.

Now, I think, we must go back over verses 1–15 to consider how to *neuter the pressure.* The text says nothing directly on this score but only suggestively. Yet it seems clear that the narrative speaks in a mocking manner, that our writer has dipped his pen in the ink of sarcasm.

Notice the vicious verbs our writer uses. The very first line tells of the image the king *made* (*'ābad*), and Nebuchadnezzar himself uses the same verb in verse 15. In fact, for an Israelite, Nebuchadnezzar's statement in that verse (*Now if you are ready . . . to fall down and worship the image that I have made*) sums up the theological asininity of the whole affair. To worship what someone made! But a reader almost ducks under the machine-gun-like occurrences of the verb *qûm* ('set up'); it appears nine times (1, 2, 3 [twice], 5, 7, 12, 14, 18), always in reference to the image the king had *set up.* Swipe the uses of that verb with your orange highlighter, then go back over the text – see if it doesn't seem as if a kind of cumulative mockery is at work. The image is a 'set up' job, as we say. The writer is telling you that it's no more divine than your knee replacement.[9]

The writer is probably mocking as well when he describes all the pomp of the occasion. He seems to tell the story with such deliberate repetition – the extended lists of the 'brass' attending (2, 3; cf. 7) and the four-fold itemizing of Nebuchadnezzar's orchestra (5, 7, 10, 15). By the way he writes up the story the writer turns the pomp into

---

[8] Note that the narrator himself does not report that the three men refused the image worship; he allows their enemies to supply this datum.

[9] Cf. my comments in *The Word Became Fresh* (Ross-shire: Christian Focus, 2006), pp. 16–18.

pomposity and coats the dignity with derision. The occasion is clearly impressive, yet in the writer's hand subversively ludicrous. It reminds me of Presbyterian missionary Don McClure's report of a worship service among the Shulla people in the Sudan. McClure said that one of the missionary women had discarded an old corset in the trash. But apparently one of the Shulla men had done some rummaging. He came into the meeting 'with great dignity', wearing the corset on his head with the rest of his body completely in the buff. He thought he exuded gravitas, but McClure couldn't help thinking that the fellow simply had a used-up woman's girdle on the wrong end of things![10]

Now I think there is that kind of 'double take' in Daniel 3. But how does this offset the pressure on the three friends or on God's harried people in similar circumstances? Well, by being both solemn and sarcastic the writer is saying: This *is* a fearful trial, but can you see, in another vein, what a farce it is? A god that's made? An image 'set up'? That may not take away all the trembling but at least you know there is no truth in it. So by his humour the writer tries to be helpful. How farcical this is shows how empty it is – and so no need for (utter) terror.

In mid-1938 Hitler paid a visit to Italy, hoping to cement an alliance. Mussolini entertained him royally, subjecting him to various displays of Italian military 'might'. But the crowds had a sort of sullen apathy toward the German leader. Hitler spent four hours in Florence but must have been dismayed when it became clear that the cheers rending the air were fictitious; they were crowd effects from some Italian movie and were played by a bunch of amplifiers from open windows.[11] It was a sign that something was wrong, that there can be great power and real emptiness side-by-side.

That is what our writer wants us to see. If once you see the farce, the emptiness behind the façade of power, then you will be less likely to be intimidated by the pagan pressure. The matter the friends face is deadly serious; but the manner in which the story is told is subtly humorous; and the humour is intended to help you stand against the pressure. Holy laughter (Veldkamp) helps you to endure, especially if you see the real weakness behind the veneer of power.

b. The obstinacy of obedience (16–18)

When the three men answer the king, they so much as say, 'You might just as well save yourself the orchestra fee.' It is admittedly a

---

[10] Charles Partee, *Adventure in Africa* (Grand Rapids: Zondervan, 1990), pp. 100–101.
[11] Richard Collier, *Duce!* (New York: Viking, 1971), p. 142.

marvel that they stood their ground when they had multiple reasons for compromise. For example, they might have reasoned that they must hold on to their government posts at all costs because exiled Judah needed friends in high places. Who knows what might come on their own people if pagan scoundrels filled their positions? How could they act as buffers for Israel if they burnt to a crisp (cf. Calvin)? Then again the king *was* giving them a second chance (13–15). Even in his fury he must have retained some liking for them and their service thus far.[12] There is a certain kindness even in the king's anger. Would it not seem the pinnacle of ingratitude to – as it were – spit in his eye? Or they might have appealed to the official-versus-personal argument, as gobs of politicians do. They could engage in this 'moment of silence' before Nebuchadnezzar's golden mummy-on-its-feet, but it would only be an empty ritual – they wouldn't mean it; it would simply be something their employment demanded of them; they would do it in their 'official' capacity even though 'personally' opposed to it.[13]

But they let none of such considerations fuzzify matters. Their answer focuses on the ability and pleasure of God. Some of our translations are not so accurate in verse 17; they render the opening clause, *If it/this be so* (as ESV; cf. 'If that is the case', NKJV), probably meaning, as the NIV blatantly paraphrases (picking up on 15), 'If we are thrown into the blazing furnace'. But the friends are probably not picking up on the king's furnace threat but on his god-question in the last of verse 15.[14] And, in any case, a better rendering of verse 17 is:

If our God exists whom we are serving, he is able to deliver us from the burning fiery furnace – and from your hand, O king, he can deliver.[15]

This part of their answer deals with the ability of God; they are not so certain about his pleasure: *But if not . . .* (18a). They are sure of God's ability (17), they are not so sure about his purpose (18a). It's

---

[12] These three hold-outs were leaders in the home province, which may have given the king added provocation and embarrassment. Hence the second opportunity may be all the more remarkable. See Baldwin, p. 103.

[13] Cf. Veldkamp, p. 63. They might also have questioned where the king would get honest and dependable advisers if they themselves did not ensure their own tenure. But they backed away from all such attempts to play God.

[14] Nebuchadnezzar's question reeks of not only scorn but of self-deification – he assumes that in this matter he is above any god, imagined or real.

[15] On the conditional clause, 'If our God exists', see Archer, p. 54, and Steinmann, p. 181. The last verb in v. 17 could have either an affirmative (he will deliver) or a potential (he can deliver) sense; contextually, I prefer the latter (cf. HCSB).

as if they said: 'We don't know what our God will do, O king; you may turn us into puddles of carbon; but in one sense it doesn't matter; the bottom line is that we will not serve your gods or worship your image.' So they were unsure of God's circumstantial will (whether they escape) but were sure of God's revealed will ('You shall have no other gods besides me')[16].

Observe how the three men did not lose sight of the crucial matter. What matters for them is not deliverance but obedience. That's what the narrative says over and over. The verb for *worship* (Aram., *sĕgid*) appears eleven times in this chapter (5, 6, 7, 10, 11, 12, 14, 15 [twice], 18, 28), while *serve* (*pĕlaḥ*, in the sense of 'serving' a deity) occurs five times (12, 14, 17, 18, 28). A total of sixteen usages hammers the point home: what really matters is not security but worship. And the three friends never forget this (18).

These men give us then a full-balanced picture of faith: faith knows the power of God (he *is able*, 17), guards the freedom of God (*but if not . . .*, 18a), and holds the truth of God (*we will not serve your gods*, 18b). There are some in our day, however, who would not be entirely happy with this 'faith'. In their view, faith involves being far more cocksure about God's ways. Their kind of 'faith' is allergic to any uncertainty about details. If they could re-write the chapter, they would have the friends declare: 'Nebuchadnezzar, we are going to *call down* God's deliverance; we, O king, are going to *bind* the fire.' But Bible faith doesn't do that. Faith does not predict God's ways; it simply holds to God's word (in this case, Exod. 20:3); faith obeys God's truth, it does not manipulate God's hand; faith is not required to plot God's course but only to obey God's command. Faith's finest hour may be when it can oppose Nebuchadnezzar's three words (burning fiery furnace) with three of its own: '*But if not.*'[17]

The real miracle of Daniel 3 has already happened. Walter Luthi was right: 'That there are three men who do not worship in Nebuchadnezzar's totalitarian state, is a miracle of God. The miracle of the confessing Church. That the three were not devoured by the fire is no greater miracle. Suppose the fiery furnace *had* consumed them. The real miracle would have happened just the same.'[18]

---

[16] Exod. 20:3.

[17] God's tendency is to provide for and cushion us with his grace. And yet it is the case that he does not always grant us a job that is satisfying, nor the spouse that we have long prayed for, nor the children we so ardently desire. It is at this point that Geoff Thomas levels a searching application: 'Indeed, every Christian has to face up to the alternative possibility, that "even if he does not deliver us" we will still do his will – serving Christ for loss, serving Christ for loneliness, serving Christ for death. We don't have to be rich; we don't have to marry; we don't have to become parents; we don't have to live; but *we have to obey*' (pp. 41–42; emphasis his).

[18] Luthi, p. 50

c. The flames of fellowship (19–30)

Deliverance nears as the heat rises. Nebuchadnezzar is about to receive the answer to his question of verse 15 – *Who is the god who will deliver you?* 'Deliverance' is the keynote of the story (note the use of *šêzib, deliver*, in 15, 17 [twice], and 28; and a synonym *něṣal* in 29); and the story of deliverance breaks down into four sections:

'Committal', (19–23)
Surprise (24–25)
Evidence (26–27)
Confession (28–29) – note that in 29b the king answers the very question he posed in 15[19]

The worst seemed to have happened – the 'burning fiery furnace' (used eight times in the chapter). But now the shock (24–25). Nebuchadnezzar has to check to see if his contacts are in. He mentions a matter of maths (four men, not three), of freedom (unbound and walking around), of security (not hurt), and of identity (the appearance of the fourth is *like a son of gods*). Who is this last guest? In verse 28 the king identifies him as an angel sent by the God of the three men. Nebuchadnezzar's phrase, *a son of gods*, shows the king thought him to be a divine or heavenly being. But we cannot allow a polytheist to be our decisive theological guide. Could this be a manifestation of 'the Angel of Yahweh', perhaps a pre-incarnate manifestation of Christ?[20] I think likely so, but I cannot prove it decisively from this text.[21] Here, in any case, is 'the fourth man' who is both the companion and protector of his servants.

As believers today appropriate this account they must remember that the miracle in Daniel 3 is a token and not a blueprint,[22] that is,

[19] Baldwin (p. 105) draws attention to the terms for the friends' wardrobe in v. 21. English translations of the first three terms are guesses but even ancient Greek translators had fits with them, which may well indicate that the story is significantly earlier than the second century or the translators would have known the meaning of the terms.

[20] On the Angel of Yahweh, see J. Barton Payne, *The Theology of the Older Testament* (Grand Rapids: Zondervan, 1962), pp. 167–170; and on the issue in v. 25, see discussion in Steinmann, pp. 193–195.

[21] For some reason, this section of Dan. 3 makes me think of Mark 6:45–52: Jesus on the mountain to pray, the disciples in a boat on the sea, labouring against a wind storm. Then 'about the fourth watch of the night he came to them, walking on the sea' (v. 48b; that is the sort of thing Yahweh does [Job 9:8; Ps. 77:19; Isa. 43:16]). But how would early Christians hear a story like that? Would they not take it as showing them that there is no barrier that can keep Jesus from coming to them in their troubles? Not a sea – nor, as in Dan. 3, a furnace.

[22] Fyall, p. 59, makes this helpful distinction.

it is a sample of the way Christ preserves his people but not a guarantee of his dramatic deliverance in every case. Still Christ's flock are strangely comforted here. Christ did not keep them out of the furnace but found them in it. He does not always shield you from all distresses and dangers, but it is in the loneliness, in the betrayal, in the loss that the Fourth Man comes and walks with you. He has the knack of both exposing you to, yet keeping you through, waters and rivers and fire (cf. Isa. 43:2–3) – and operating rooms and funeral parlours and an empty house. The Fourth Man can always find his people.

This furnace story tells of deliverance but it is about worship. Daniel 3 means to tell me that the only matter that matters is that I keep the first commandment even if it kills me. And now that we live in post-empty-tomb time there is added reason to remain faithful. Os Guinness tells of one of the periodic efforts to wipe out religious belief in the former Soviet Union. The Communist Party sent KGB agents to the nation's churches on a Sunday morning. One such agent was struck by the deep devotion of an older woman who was kissing the feet of a life-size carving of Christ on the cross. He asked her, 'Babushka [Grandmother], are you also prepared to kiss the feet of the beloved general secretary of our great Communist party?' 'Why, of course,' she shot back. 'But only if you crucify him first.'[23] So we can meet 'burning fiery furnace' with three other words: old rugged cross.

[23] In Os Guinness and John Seel (eds.), *No God but God* (Chicago: Moody, 1992), p. 112.

Daniel 4:1–37
4. The tree decree

I could scarcely believe what I was reading. But the Associated Press had no reason to lie. Here was a newspaper clip about a woman employed by the University of Illinois at Chicago who ate dirt. Not always. Time was when she craved Argo Starch, but the starch-makers began producing it in a more refined form and so, to obtain the proper 'crunch' she wanted, this woman had turned to dirt. It's an eating disorder called geophagia, and the article assured readers that the practice was dying out. But one could sympathize with my near unbelief: this was the twenty-first century and I was reading about people who ate dirt.

So what about kings who eat grass? You may read Daniel 4 and get to verse 33 and exclaim, 'Surely you don't expect me to believe this actually happened? It sounds like the stuff of fairy tales.' Like eating dirt, however, there's a name for it – a form of deviant behaviour called boanthropy. One imagines oneself a cow or bull and acts accordingly. Old Testament scholar R. K. Harrison felt privileged to have observed an actual case of boanthropy in a British mental institution in 1946. He saw a man in his early twenties, in fine bodily health but decidedly anti-social, who spent whole days from dawn to dusk outdoors on the institutional grounds. He was limited in his ability to care for himself, so someone always washed and shaved him. They gave him water from a clean container so he wouldn't drink from mud puddles. But as he wandered over the grounds he would pluck up chunks of grass to eat; he never ate institutional cuisine with other inmates.[1] I cite this one sample not to convince you that the Bible is true (there is no *proof* in such an analogy) but to keep you from impulsively saying the Bible is stupid.

[1] R. K. Harrison, *Introduction to the Old Testament* (Grand Rapids: Eerdmans, 1969), pp. 1115–1117.

Tracing the literary shape will help mentally organize a fairly long narrative. It develops like this:[2]

Opening testimony: proclamation, first person (1–3)
Report of content of dream, first person (4–18)
Report of interpretation of dream (19–27)
Report of fulfilment of dream (28–33)
Closing testimony: restoration, first person (34–37)

Observe that Nebuchadnezzar states the upshot of the whole episode at the very beginning; speaking of the *Most High God* he says:

His kingdom is an everlasting kingdom,
and his dominion endures from generation to generation (3b).

This is the conviction the king reached at the end of it all, but he sets it down here right at the first. He puts the conclusion in the introduction. Sometimes the Bible does this. Psalm 73 is a case in point. It's not a narrative (as Dan. 4), but the pattern is the same. Asaph begins with his conclusion: 'Surely God is good to Israel, to those who are pure in heart.'[3] Then he drags his reader through all the trauma and distress and anger he waded through before he found that conclusion reaffirmed. That is what the king does here: verses 1–3 declare where he came out, and verses 4–37 are essentially flashback, telling how he came to reach that conclusion.

Note also the three major 'report' sections (4–18, 19–27, 28–33) and how the reigning idea of the chapter occurs three times (toward the end of each section): *the Most High rules over the kingdom of men and gives it to whomever he wishes* (17, 25, 32; see also 26). The associated ideas of kingdom, dominion and *King of heaven* (3, 34, 37) reinforce this theme. The stress then in Daniel 2 is that God reveals, in chapter 3 that he rescues, and in chapter 4 that he rules. Daniel 4 hammers home the point that *God rules the kingdom of men and human rulers serve only at his pleasure.*

1. A huge gift (19–27, in light of 4–18)

We can summarize the witness of Daniel 4 under three ideas, the first of which may be called a huge gift.

This time (unlike ch. 2) Nebuchadnezzar freely tells his dream (10–17). He dreamed of a 'world tree' (6) that seemed to have

---

[2] I have followed the versification scheme used in most English translations; what is 4:1–37 in standard English versions is 3:31 – 4:34 in the printed Aramaic text.
[3] Ps. 73:1.

universal scope (11) and pack benefits for all – *beasts, birds,* indeed *all flesh* (12).[4] All for nothing apparently. For a heavenly messenger comes down with orders to chop down the tree. A thorough job it is – branches whacked off, leaves stripped, fruit scattered, while beasts and birds skedaddle (14). Orders are for the *stump and its roots* to be left. Although one could translate verse 15b impersonally (*let it* [i.e., the stump] *be wet with the dew of heaven*), it becomes clear that the stump represents a person when 15c and 16a speak of its/his *portion* and *mind* (lit., 'heart'). Even without interpretation it's a scary dream with an obvious catastrophe at the heart of it.

The setting of the dream is instructive. Nebuchadnezzar claims he was *at ease* and prospering, then had this dream *that frightened me* and *the visions of my head terrified me* (4–5). How easily peace can be shattered. But in the king's case, if fear ruins peace, fear at least has power – *so I made a decree* (6). (One wonders how often fear explains the exercise of power.) Power can get help, and so all the wise men of Babylon come running (6–7). But futility is often brother to power, and once more, as in Daniel 2, all the paid pagan professionals could not interpret the dream (7). One wonders if fear partly explains their inability. Surely they could divine that the dream suggested something calamitous, likely for Nebuchadnezzar; perhaps they thought it safer for their heads not to bear ill news. Still, beyond such general prognostication, they could not nail down the details. And the writer's purpose here (as in 2:10–11) is to underline the failure of paganism, to say 'there is no light there – all the brew of paganism leads into a tragic cul-de-sac'. *At last Daniel came in* (8a). Here is God's gift to the pagan king, the conduit of light in the midst of his darkness and fears. Daniel is the kindness of God to Nebuchadnezzar in giving him truth and clarity in his dilemma.

But he is far more. He is not just God's kindly light, he is the model servant (19–27). Notice the tense and yet proper combination of compassion and truthfulness in Daniel. His compassion for the king is clear in verse 19. When he hears the dream, he is *appalled* and his thoughts *terrified* him (the latter is the same verb used of the king in 5b). He does not fear for his own life but for the judgment coming on the king. Daniel could wish what the dream depicts would fall on Nebuchadnezzar's *enemies* (19c). He has a genuine compassion for this pagan monarch and can take no pleasure in this 'severe' word he must pass on to him – and yet he does not hold back from speaking that truth plainly (22–26). He relates clearly the identity of the tree (20–22), describes in the dream's terms the destiny decreed for him

---

[4] Note the 'birds' in the branches of such 'trees' – the 'Assyrian' tree of Ezek. 31:6 and the messianic one in Ezek. 17:23 (cf. also Matt. 13:31–32).

(23–25), and leaves him with a ray of hope (26). Daniel displays both a reticence of love and a compulsion of truth.[5]

Andrew Bonar used to tell how a Grecian painter had produced a marvellous painting of a boy carrying on his head a basket of grapes. The grapes were so well done that when the picture was put up in the forum for folks to admire, the birds pecked the grapes, imagining they were real. The painter's friends congratulated him, but he did not seem satisfied. When asked why, he replied, 'I should have done a great deal more. I should have painted the boy so true to life that the birds would not have dared to come near!'[6] The perfect painting would have forced the birds to be paradoxical – both eager and fearful. And that is the proper balance one meets in the Lord's true servants: a love-driven sadness that cringes to speak the hard word of God, yet a God-honouring obedience that speaks it anyway.

And yet Daniel offers more. He not only speaks with compassion (19) and candour (20–26) but also offers counsel (27). Nebuchadnezzar has not asked for this last. But here Daniel is at his prophetic best. This exilic functionary tells the ruler of the world what he should do:

> *Therefore, O king, let my counsel be acceptable to you, and break off your sin by (doing) righteousness and your iniquities by showing favour to those who are miserable – perhaps there may be a lengthening of your prosperity* (27).

The word for 'prosperity' here is cognate to Nebuchadnezzar's term in verse 4 for being *at ease*. Daniel is holding out the possibility (and only that – note the *perhaps*) that the king's 'ease' or prosperity might continue and he avert the judgment threatened in the dream.

Such a possibility is perfectly in line with the divine design in prophecy. Yahweh had said through Jeremiah that if a nation or kingdom heard of Yahweh's design to wipe it out and those people turned from their evil, then Yahweh would back off bringing the judgment he had announced (Jer. 18:7–8). The 'repentance' involved may even be shaky. After King Ahab and his beastly wife had spilled the blood of Naboth and his boys and had annexed Naboth's property for the crown, the prophet Elijah had blistered Ahab with Yahweh's intent to wipe out his household (1 Kgs 21:20–22; 2 Kgs 9:25–26). Ahab was deeply moved and depressed by this word of judgment (1 Kgs 21:27) and Yahweh told Elijah that because of such repentance – temporary though it might be, he would delay the judgment for a generation (21:29). So with Josiah, king of Judah, in

---

[5] Calvin's remarks (1:270) are very instructive here.

[6] Marjory Bonar (ed.), *Andrew A. Bonar: Diary and Life* (Edinburgh: Banner of Truth, 1960), p. 466.

2 Kings 22:8–20. There was nothing that could take Yahweh's scheduled disaster against Judah off the calendar, but because Josiah had humbled himself in repentance that slated calamity was put off until after Josiah's time. In short, judgment may not be cancelled, but it may be postponed if the threat of judgment is received in humility and penitence.

That, I think, is what Daniel's advice offers to Nebuchadnezzar. It may be, if only the king responds rightly, that the judgment might be delayed and the king's ease and prosperity could continue. What Daniel sketches is not some personal plan of salvation for Nebuchadnezzar but a sample of vocational repentance. The king is a self-indulgent autocrat who surely knows what his *sin* is and that *doing righteousness* means ceasing such practices; and he could surely show favour and bring relief to those subjects in his kingdom who found themselves on the bottom of life's pile. If he only responded rightly to this dream and its interpretation, who knows but that the God of heaven might delay that sentence? What high privileges Nebuchadnezzar received: God gave him revelation (the dream-plus-interpretation), admonition (27) and opportunity (29).

It's a 'huge gift' when the God of heaven clearly makes known his word – even his severe word – to you. But be advised that he may not do so through some premier servant with the status of Daniel. It may be through the pastor of your church, who labours hard in the study and preaching of the word. You may or may not have a close personal relationship with him; you may even dislike some things about him. But if he seeks to lay bare the word of God for your good week by week, you have been given a huge gift. And sometimes, of course, there is no human 'vessel' involved, but the Holy Spirit himself speaking to you in the Scriptures exposes and decimates your pride.

2. A big point (17, 25, 32)

With our computers we find it so easy to express emphasis – we can easily place some clause or sentence into italics or bold print (even in the 'typewriter age' we could underline or print something in all caps). But biblical writers had to use other strategies in order to stress a point, and one such was repetition. As noted earlier, toward the end of each report section (4–18, 19–27, 28–33) the writer includes a note indicating the purpose of Nebuchadnezzar's coming humiliation: that *the living* or the king might *know that the Most High rules the kingdom of men and gives it to whom he will* (17, 25, 32). That's the writer's way of using bold print. That is the big point of the chapter.

This lesson had already been taught to Nebuchadnezzar, had he been listening. Behind the subtle but ominous 'after you' in 2:39 there was a clear implication that Nebuchadnezzar was but a passing phase in the scheme of human kingdoms. Then the king's in-your-face arrogance breaks out in 3:15 when he defiantly demands of Daniel's three friends, 'Who is the god who will deliver you out of my hands?' And the appearance of 'the fourth man' evaporated the royal cockiness (3:25ff.). Now in chapter 4 the prophesied humiliation takes place. But not immediately – mercy loves delays. Nevertheless, after twelve months Nebuchadnezzar is clearly full of himself (30) and God turns him out to pasture (31–33).

It is not as though the king is making an empty boast when he exclaims, *Is this not Babylon the great, which I myself have built as a royal residence by the might of my power and for the glory of my majesty?* (30, NASB). As he scans the panorama of the city he can spot all kinds of achievements. Stephen Miller's summary nicely captures how impressive Babylon was:

Babylon was a rectangularly shaped city surrounded by a broad and deep water-filled moat and then by an intricate system of double walls. The first double-wall system encompassed the main city. Its inner wall was twenty-one feet thick and reinforced with defense towers at sixty-foot intervals while the outer wall was eleven feet in width and also had watchtowers. Later Nebuchadnezzar added another double-wall system (an outer wall twenty-five feet thick and an inner wall twenty-three feet thick) east of the Euphrates that ran the incredible distance of seventeen miles and was wide enough at the top for chariots to pass. The height of the walls is not known, but the Ishtar Gate was forty feet high, and the walls would have approximated this size. A forty-foot wall would have been a formidable barrier for enemy soldiers.[7]

[7] Miller, p. 140. Cf. also Paul Ferguson's graphic introduction to his article, 'Nebuchadnezzar, Gilgamesh, and the "Babylonian Job"', *Journal of the Evangelical Theological Society* 37/3 (1994), pp. 321–331: 'Nebuchadnezzar stood on his palace roof, which had been made of cedar from the forests of Lebanon. Stacked all around were over fifteen million bricks, each containing his name and royal titles. He was surrounded by six walls and a 262-foot moat.' He continues: 'He had forgotten that all the bricks were made of mud. He had also forgotten the affirmation made at his accession that all he possessed came from one deity. He had not remembered that his father had represented himself on a monument as the "son of nobody," helpless without his god. He had failed to notice two streets below him called "Bow Down, Proud One" and "May the Arrogant Not Flourish." He did not even recall that one of the names of his palace was "The Place Where Proud Ones Are Compelled to Submit"' (p. 321).

The Ishtar Gate was on the north side – it led into Procession Street (62 feet wide, 1,000 yards long[8]) paved with imported stone. A bridge (400 feet long[9]) spanned the Euphrates between the east and west sectors of the city. Nebuchadnezzar enjoyed at least three palaces there and had constructed the famous 'hanging gardens', apparently so his wife (Amytis) could enjoy a taste of her native Media which she had left for the flatlands of Babylon.[10] No wonder it all had Nebuchadnezzar talking to himself (30).

Some may caution us not to read Nebuchadnezzar's boast as so much blatant arrogance,[11] but the last line of the chapter claims to carry the king's own evaluation: *and those who walk in pride he is able to humble* (37b, ESV).

Now let us close in on the lesson, the big point, that *the living* and Nebuchadnezzar in particular were to absorb. We will focus on verse 17, which is the fullest statement of it. *The living*, the text says, are to know *that the Most High rules*, that is, that Israel's God is sovereign. His is a *present* sovereignty – *the Most High rules*. 'Rules' is not a verb as such but an adjective. The stress, however is different from the dream interpretation in chapter 2. There, after a sequence of earthly regimes, the God of heaven 'will set up a kingdom that shall never be destroyed' (2:44). But 4:17 does not depict a rule that is to come but one that operates even now. God's rule will come (ch. 2) but that does not mean God is not king now (4:17).

The Most High also exercises a *concrete* sovereignty – he rules *the kingdom of men*. Nothing ethereal or fluffy about that. As Ronald Wallace has said, God rules 'down here', not merely 'up there'. 'It was in *the kingdom of men* that he wanted his will done – in Babylon!'[12] He rules the kingdom of men: smelly, sinful, selfish, scheming men. There's nothing more 'down to dirt' than that. In our darker moments we may lose sight of this comforting assurance.

Further, God's sovereignty is *particular* and *free*: he rules the kingdom of men *and gives it to whomever he wishes*. It is particular in that 'not only kingdoms but individual kings are shown to be under the control of Daniel's God'.[13] He not only directs the general destiny of nations but appoints specific rulers to their places over them. And does so freely, giving such place to *whomever he wishes*.

---

[8] 19 m wide, 914 m long.

[9] 122 m.

[10] For summaries, see Miller, pp. 140–141; Alfred J. Hoerth, *Archaeology and the Old Testament* (Grand Rapids: Baker, 1998), pp. 374–378. For details, see D. J. Wiseman, *Nebuchadrezzar and Babylon* (New York: Oxford University Press, 1991), pp. 50–80.

[11] Wiseman, pp. 98–99.

[12] Wallace, p. 82 (emphasis his).

[13] Baldwin, p. 107.

No one coerces or manipulates his choices. No one, à la verse 35b, plays parent to God and slaps his hand as though he had made a mistaken move.[14]

God also operates with such a *fascinating* sovereignty: he not only gives the kingdom of men to whomever he wishes but also *sets over it the lowliest of men*. 'Lowliest' does not mean what we may sometimes call moral scumbags (though sometimes that may be the case) but primarily those of low or obscure status. Isn't it precisely here that we open up our 'conundrums of history' file? How often we wonder how a certain man or woman came to national leadership. Who would have ever guessed? All of which shows how *interesting* God is, and so should prove fuel for worship.

The text, however, seems to push us even further – that the Most High holds an *exclusive* sovereignty. Remember that Nebuchadnezzar and his ilk were not hard-hearted secularists but religious pagans. As such they already believed that the god raised the human king to leadership where he functioned as the god's viceroy and representative.[15] Nebuchadnezzar then already believed that Marduk (or Nebo) rules the kingdom of men and gives it to whomever he wishes. But, as Eugene Merrill points out, Daniel 4 slams this belief:

> Because these kings and their subjects thought they were called to their office and given its privileges and responsibilities by their own gods, Daniel's assertion that the God of Israel was in fact the originator and grantor of human authority was a tacit denial of any perceived role for the gods of the nations.[16]

It seems to me then that this keynote of Daniel 4 (17, 25, 32) is sabotaging the pagan kingship theology. It is rather the Most High, Israel's God, who gives kingship even to pagan kings. It is a dig at the false claims of Babylonian religion.

What then are the implications of this 'big point' for us? First, there is a personal one: you must grasp the supremacy of Israel's God and submit to his sway. Walter Kaiser tells of the funeral of Louis XIV. He had requested that at that service in the cathedral of Notre Dame all would be darkened except the one candle on his casket at the front. But when the court preacher Masillon got up to give the funeral oration, he walked over to the casket, snuffed out the light, and began his message with the words: 'Only God is great!

---

[14] On the image in v. 35b, see Young, p. 113 (drawing on Keil), and Leupold, p. 203.

[15] See Bertil Albrektson, *History and the Gods* (Lund: CWK Gleerup, 1967), pp. 42–52.

[16] Eugene H. Merrill, 'A Theology of Ezekiel and Daniel', in *A Biblical Theology of the Old Testament*, ed. Roy B. Zuck (Chicago: Moody, 1991), p. 389.

Only God is great!'[17] And that is what we need to go around muttering to ourselves. Nebuchadnezzar II and Louis XIV are not the only ones who need this. For we are all a bunch of Nebuchadnezzar clones, wanting to call our own shots, to direct our own show (puny as it is) and seldom – except in a rare moment of sanity – stopping to consider how asinine our passion for self-deification is.[18]

Then there is a 'political' implication. If verse 17 is true, you must not be overly-impressed by human governments nor awed by human rulers. Human governments are interim arrangements that God appoints to fill space until the power and glory of Jesus' kingdom. Human rulers, tyrannical or democratic, are God's lackeys who have tenure only at his pleasure.

3. A small mercy (34–37)

This section relates the mercy of the king's restoration, a mercy that was implied in the *until* of verse 32 (*until you know that the Most High rules*). When the *seven times* (16, 25)[19] have passed, the *stump* will be restored. So Nebuchadnezzar returns to sanity, and most of this section reports the truth that sanity declares (34–35, 37). Notice the way the king puts the matter in verse 34: *my reason returned to me, and I blessed the Most High, and praised and honoured him who lives forever* (ESV). Note the first *and* and its logical import. Reason returns and so he blesses the Most High. That is what sane people do – they offer adoration to the God of heaven. Truly rational people talk like this; they confess the supremacy of *the King of heaven*.

But there is something in this restoration-section we dare not miss. Did you notice that twice Nebuchadnezzar says, *My reason returned to me* (34, 36)? I have called this section 'a small mercy', not because the return or the gift of reason is actually a small matter but because we ourselves tend to regard it as small – if we regard it at all. When did you last give thanks for this mercy?

I like Luther's 'Small Catechism' because in it he keeps me from escaping this 'basic level' of thanksgiving. When he deals with the first article of the creed ('I believe in God the Father Almighty, Maker of heaven and earth'), he asks, 'What does this mean?' His answer is couched in terms of a male householder in Reformation

---

[17] Walter C. Kaiser, Jr, *Micah-Malachi*, The Communicator's Commentary (Dallas: Word, 1992), p. 192.

[18] Cf. Veldkamp, p. 74.

[19] Commentators are divided over the 'seven times'; some think they must equate to seven years; others hold that the year-view claims more than can be justified from the phrase.

times; if you try to de-genderize it, you ruin it. So here is what the creed means:

> I believe that God has created me and all that exists; that he has given and still preserves to me body and soul, eyes, ears, and all my limbs, my reason and all my senses; and also clothing and shoes, food and drink, house and home, wife and child, land, cattle, and all my property; that he provides me richly and daily with all the necessaries of life, protects me from all danger, and preserves and guards me against all evil; and all this out of pure paternal, divine goodness and mercy, without any merit or worthiness of mine; for all which I am in duty bound to thank, praise, serve, and obey him. This is most certainly true.[20]

There it is with eyes and shoes, among all the ground-level stuff of life – 'my reason and all my senses'. Hardly a *small* mercy, but I may make it such by not regarding it as the gift I should.

The inauguration on 20 January 1969 had been a full day for the Nixon family. They were back at the White House after Mr Nixon had taken the oath of office and before they toured the various inaugural balls that evening. It was after dark when Pat Nixon phoned the White House chef. She indicated that most of the family would like steak in the upstairs dining room and then added: 'I'd just like a bowl of cottage cheese in my bedroom.' That threw the kitchen into a tizzy. They had all kinds of prime fillets, had stocked up so much that the pantry seemed like a grocery store. But not a spoonful of cottage cheese. So the head butler, in a White House limousine, sped around Washington until he found an open delicatessen with a supply of cottage cheese.[21] It's woefully easy to ignore the common, cottage-cheese-level matters. But we mustn't do it when they are gifts of the Most High God. *My reason returned to me.*[22]

[20] Philip Schaff, *The Creeds of Christendom*, 3 vols. (reprint ed., Grand Rapids: Baker, 1990), 3:78.

[21] J. B. West, *Upstairs at the White House* (New York: Coward, McCann & Geoghegan, 1973), pp. 355–356.

[22] Whether Nebuchadnezzar was really 'converted' remains a perennial question. Much depends on how his words in v. 8 are taken. Remember v. 8 is part of his 'report' after and in light of his restoration. On this verse, see Fyall, p. 63, and Lucas, p. 100. Another problem: some scholars who date Daniel to the second century BC think that the royal illness depicted really belonged to Nabonidus, a later king of Babylon (556–539 BC) and that Dan. 4 juices up the story around the figure of the more famous Nebuchadnezzar. Some think that the discovery of the very fragmentary 'Prayer of Nabonidus' in Cave 4 at Qumran in 1955 strengthens this possibility. It does only if one is prone to swallow critical camels. On the matter, cf. the extensive excursus in Steinmann, pp. 215–228; and briefly, Edwin M. Yamauchi, 'Nabonidus', ISBE, 3:469–470.

But don't forget the big point. The kingdom of men does not belong to any who can make the best boast. No, God has super-exalted One to whom he has given the kingdoms of this world, One who, being in the form of God, took no advantage of his equality with God but emptied himself and became obedient to the point of death, even death on a cross.

Daniel 5:1–31
5. The strut stops here

It was there in the morning newspaper: more than one hundred robins had dropped from trees and were found dead on sidewalks and front porches of Santa Rosa, California. They all had purple stains on their beaks, which fact led one ornithological official to charge the fallen fowl with drunkenness. Apparently they had overdosed on alcohol after eating berries that had fermented on the branch because of unusually cold weather. And after reading the first verse of Daniel 5 we may assume that that is the problem here – nothing but a royal debauch featuring the triple trouble of wine, women and worship. But we soon realize the real trouble was not alcohol but arrogance (22–23), a bit of royal 'struttery'. And the God of heaven wiped it out in an evening's work.

1. Historical backdrop

But we're getting ahead of ourselves. Daniel 5 begins with the words *Belshazzar the king* and we readers are a bit surprised to find the writer has suddenly dropped Belshazzar into our laps. We have just come from four chapters of hearing of the famed Nebuchadnezzar and all too abruptly we are staring Belshazzar in the face. Who is he? Where did he come from? We need to play some historical catch-up.

Nebuchadnezzar died in 562 BC, after a reign of forty-three years. In less than another twenty-five years all was lost. Evil-Merodach (561–560), Nebuchadnezzar's son, followed his father on the throne. He, however, was apparently assassinated by his brother-in-law Neriglissar, who had a tenure of about four years and was succeeded by his son, Labashi-Marduk. This poor creature was 'liquidated' within a month and one of the conspirators, Nabonidus, became king (555–539 BC). It seems that Nabonidus did not have designs on the throne himself but may have been placed there as a 'compromise candidate' by the conspirators. Some think that Belshazzar, Nabonidus' son, was the real mover behind the conspirators. In any case, Nabonidus had a religious or 'faith' problem. He was a passionate devotee of the moon god Sin, to such a degree that he alarmed the Babylonian clergy, for he seemed intent on prying Marduk loose from his supremacy in Babylon. This may have led to a 'relocation programme' for Nabonidus – he spent the next ten years at Taima/Tema, an oasis in the North Arabian desert, five hundred miles from Babylon. His son, Belshazzar, functioned as *de facto* king in Babylon, operated in a more pro-Mardukian manner, and thus kept the local clergy from revolt.[1] Which is why we are suddenly staring Belshazzar (553–539 BC) in the face at Daniel 5:1.[2]

2. Literary features

It is surprising when 'the narrative leaps from the reign of Nebuchadrezzar to the very end of the Babylonian empire', to the last night on which its last ruler was killed.[3] But that's fair, for our narrator is not giving us a history of the Babylonian empire but a tract for nourishing Israelite faith. We know that, but sometimes must pinch ourselves to remember it. So there is an *abruptness* about the narrative here. It takes but eleven Aramaic words and one verse to plunk us down among Belshazzar's banquet tables. The preceding narratives in chapters 2, 3 and 4 all seem to give us a certain 'warm-up' and ease us as readers into their particular stories or dilemmas. Not so here. And the ending (30–31) is equally abrupt. Chapters 2, 3 and 4 all end with some 'confession' by Nebuchadnezzar (2:46–47; 3:28–29; 4:34–37), but there is none of that at the end of chapter 5.

---

[1] For this background, see Paul-Alain Beaulieu, 'King Nabonidus and the Neo-Babylonian Empire', in *Civilizations of the Ancient Near East*, 4 vols. (New York: Charles Scribner's Sons, 1995), 2:972–977; Bill T. Arnold, 'Babylonians', in Alfred J. Hoerth, Gerald L. Mattingly and Edwin M. Yamauchi (eds.), *Peoples of the Old Testament World* (Grand Rapids: Baker, 1994), pp. 64–66; and Eugene H. Merrill, *Kingdom of Priests* (Grand Rapids: Baker, 1987), pp. 475–478.

[2] The mention of Belshazzar may carry critical implications for dating at least ch. 5. Time was when Belshazzar was touted as a figment of the writer's imagination, a bit of sheer fiction. Subsequent discoveries (from 1860 on) have dispelled that fiction about a fiction. However memory of Belshazzar seems to have vanished by the time of Herodotus (fifth century BC) and Xenophon (fourth century BC). If that is so, how would an alleged second-century (Maccabean) writer dredge up a memory of Belshazzar? But someone writing ca. 530 BC would not have that problem: the memory of Belshazzar would still be 'live' before his descent into the bowels of historical limbo. Cf. Miller, p. 150, and Steinmann, p. 260.

[3] Baldwin, p. 119.

We only read that *Belshazzar the Chaldean* was eliminated and *Darius the Mede* was enthroned.

Now impressions are simply impressions, and here one has no firm basis for divining a biblical writer's attitude. But it seems to me (and I confess this *is* subjective) that the writer had a certain sympathy and patience for Nebuchadnezzar but that the clipped and abrupt style of chapter 5 suggests a certain hostility and animosity toward Belshazzar.

The narrator also engages in *suppression* of information. This is not a chargeable offense but a literary technique that excites surprise at the end. At the beginning of chapter 5 readers have no inkling that this royal carousing is much different than any other or that this night will be much different from any other – except perhaps that the debauch was very well attended. To be sure, we are soon into a scary, first-class crisis, but the story itself begins innocently enough. Only at the end are we hit with the fact that on 'this very night' Belshazzar's soul was required of him (cf. Luke 12:20) and that Babylon dropped through the trapdoor into the nether regions of history. The effect is very much like the story of Micah and his Levite in Judges 17 – 18. Over two chapters we hear of a certain Levite who becomes personal chaplain and priest to Micah and his perverted collection of images at his 'house of gods'. A contingent from the tribe of Dan passes by Micah's establishment and pilfers all his deviant religious parapher-nalia – and hires his Levite priest with the offer of a more lucrative 'call'. Only at the very end of the story does the writer divulge the nameless Levite's identity – none other than Jonathan, the grandson (or direct descendant at least) of *Moses* (Judg. 18:30)![4] The shock was saved for last. We have the same device here in Daniel 5.

Besides literary devices certain literary *themes* are prominent in chapter 5, one of which is *revelation*. Indeed that is the dominant concern of the chapter. Everything hinges on whether someone can show (Aram. *ḥăwâ*, 7, 12 [twice], 15), make known (*yĕda'*, 8, 15, 16, 17) or interpret (*pĕšar*, 12, 16; plus cognate noun nine times) the mysterious writing. Chapter 5, then, parallels chapter 2, where every-thing rested on *revealing* what was unknown or undisclosed.[5]

Chapter 5 also concludes another theme that has been flitting through the book to this point. One could call it the 'wobbliness' of Babylon. This theme makes its debut in 1:21, that innocuous but ominous little note about how Daniel 'continued on' to the first year of Cyrus. It is a subtle but telling indicator that Babylon had bitten the dust before the end of Daniel's life. Then in chapter 2 Daniel

---

[4] On the text, cf. my *Judges: Such a Great Salvation* (Ross-shire: Christian Focus, 2000), p. 201n.
[5] See the comments on the 'packaging' of Daniel in the Introduction, pp. 22–24.

makes clear in his interpretation of Nebuchadnezzar's dream that the Babylonian regime is but a passing phase of world history and only part of the political prelude to the kingdom of God. In chapter 3 God neuters the decree of Babylon's king before his very eyes and in chapter 4 drives him right off of his throne into the pasture. In chapter 5 Babylon's tenure comes to its last night – not a surprise to those who've laid hold of the prophetic word (e.g., Isa. 21:1–10; Jer. 51:34–37, 54–57). Babylon seems to be overpowering, but the steady testimony of Daniel 1 – 5 is that Babylon is simply tenuous. This theme reaches its proper climax at the end of chapter 5.

Finally, note how the writer depends on *speeches* to carry the weight of the narrative. After he sets the stage in verses 1–9, the writer reports the speeches of the queen mother (10–12), Belshazzar (13–16) and Daniel (17–28). They constitute the bulk of the account.

3. Theological witness

If the Medes and Persians were outside the city (cf. 29–31) we might wonder why Belshazzar and the rest were partying with such gusto. Apparently they felt secure enough: the city was virtually impregnable to assault;[6] it was overstocked with provisions (Herodotus); the Euphrates flowed through the city – no worries about water supply. Perhaps the Babylonians were celebrating an annual festival.[7] Why cancel it simply because of a horde of Medes and Persians outside the walls? Who would have thought the devious enemy would divert the course of the river into a basin by means of a canal and so lower its level to thigh-depth where it flowed through the city and allow Persian commando units to enter under the walls and begin a surprise attack?[8] But the concern of the text is not about Babylonian debauchery or Persian trickery; its testimony is that *God levels human arrogance.* We can trace this theme by following the main movements or scenarios of the story.

First, we see *human defiance met by divine opportunity* (1–9). But how do we know it was 'defiance'? Belshazzar ordered the gold and silver vessels Nebuchadnezzar had taken from Yahweh's temple (see 1:2) to be carted in so he, his cronies and ladies could use them for imbibing. Was that so all-fired bad?[9] Yes, according to Daniel's interpretive word in verse 23: *but you have lifted up yourself against the Lord of heaven* (ESV). That's what Belshazzar and his crowd were

[6] See the description of Babylon's defensive system in the previous chapter, p. 64.
[7] See Miller, p. 152.
[8] See Herodotus, *Histories*, 1:191.
[9] As Wallace (p. 95) nicely put it: 'Why should God make such a fuss about the use of a set of golden cups from a temple he seemed to have deserted . . . '

doing when they used the temple vessels for their wine and sang doxologies to non-gods that couldn't even hear the praise. 'It was a sign indeed that he believed that this God, whose vessels he was abusing and whose name he was insulting, had now in Babylon no reality or power. Belshazzar had counted him out.'[10] And the imagery involved surely supports such an inference. We may put it crassly: contempt for God's 'stuff' is the same as contempt for God himself. If you arrive, let's say, at your office and find that your desk, chair, filing cabinets, briefcases, coffee-maker, computer, pictures and knick-knacks are all sitting in the hall outside your office door, you immediately get the point. It's not merely that your stuff is out but that *you* are out. So Belshazzar's demeaning of Yahweh's vessels was his way of demeaning Yahweh. Belshazzar was not simply a drunken slob but a profane slob.

God brought him to almost instant sobriety, however. Belshazzar came unglued – he was seeing the fingers of a man's hand writing on the palace wall. He became deathly pale, his thoughts *terrified* him, and his lower body lost all strength.[11] The clear sight and sheer spookiness of those writing fingers produced paralyzing terror (5–6).

Where does one turn in such moments? Why, to religion, of course. Or at least that's what Belshazzar did. He turned to his 'faith'. He hollered for *the conjurers, the Chaldeans, and the astrologers* (7) to come in and interpret the mysterious text. So these losers came traipsing in again (cf. 2:2, 10–11, 27; 4:7). Once more they fail (8) and Belshazzar's alarm only intensifies (9). This is sometimes God's pattern – to aggravate our helplessness by exposing the uselessness of our favourite props, even our favourite religious props.[12] You may have your own paganism of choice – occultism, pluralism, macho-ism, feminism, agnosticism, moralism – and they will prove as petrifyingly useless as the Babylonian variety.

The human defiance is quite clear, but you may wonder where the divine opportunity appears. Precisely here, at the end of verse 9! God has frightened Belshazzar; religion has failed him; he is reduced to a shivering, sniffling mess with no supports whatever. He is therefore on the edge of the abyss of hope, is he not? He is the object

---

[10] Wallace, p. 96.

[11] Some think that 'his limbs gave way' (v. 6, ESV), lit., 'the knots of his loins were loosed', may refer to his losing control of bladder or bowels. See references in Lucas, p. 121. If so, it wouldn't be the last time a monarch suffered such embarrassment; see Otto Scott, *James I: The Fool as King* (Vallecito: Ross House, 1976), p. 211.

[12] Note how this will be so at the last day (Isa. 2:20–21); on the other hand, the same concern drives Paul to be sure he has a God-given righteousness as his recourse and refuge (Phil. 3:9).

of God's terror, but in one sense it is a *kind* terror. God does Belshazzar the favour of leaving him without any recourse, in utter helplessness – and hence with a huge opportunity. Whenever God brings a man to the end of himself, smashing all his props and wasting his idols, it is a favourable moment indeed. If he will but see it.

In *Diary of Kenneth MacRae* Iain Murray writes of the circumstances that seemed to drive MacRae to seek Christ. Leading up to 1908 (when he was 25), MacRae had experienced some 'broken plans and grievous disappointments'. Murray then adds: 'With Augustine he would later be able to say, as he thought of that time, "I had been undone if I had not been undone. I had been ruined if I had not been ruined. God orders lesser afflictions that we may escape greater." '[13] Belshazzar was on the precipice of deliverance but did not recognize it.

Secondly, note that *human desperation is met by divine foolishness* (10–16).

There was such mayhem and ruckus coming from the banquet hall that the queen mother[14] intruded on the scene. Everything in the story depends on her intrusion.[15] Without her counsel Belshazzar would have been left staring at the wall or watching his body quiver. The role of the queen mother here in Daniel 5 is like that of Nabal's unnamed servant in 1 Samuel 25:14–17 and of Mrs Naaman's Israelite servant girl in 2 Kings 5:2–3. These are all minor, unnamed characters and yet the whole sequence of events in each case depends upon their words.

Belshazzar summons Daniel and makes his 'pitch' to him (13–16). Belshazzar was not entirely ignorant of Daniel, for he knew something of Daniel's pre-Babylon circumstances (13), something the queen did not (explicitly) mention.[16] Moreover, 8:27 implies that Daniel was serving in some bureaucratic capacity as recently as the third year of Belshazzar (8:1).[17] He may have been relegated to a minor role; apparently he was not among the movers and shakers in the government. So Belshazzar knew of Daniel; it seems that what he didn't know or had not remembered was Daniel's indispensable

[13] Iain H. Murray (ed.), *Diary of Kenneth MacRae* (Edinburgh: Banner of Truth, 1980), p. 10.

[14] If Belshazzar's queen was included among his 'wives' (v. 3), she was already present. Most commentators agree that the queen of v. 10 is Belshazzar's mother, wife of Nabonidus. Her argument from history (vv. 11–12) suggests she had been around a while.

[15] David A. Dorsey maps out Dan. 5 as a chiasm with vv. 10–12 being the turning-point, when Daniel is remembered; *The Literary Structure of the Old Testament* (Grand Rapids: Baker, 1999), p. 261.

[16] Keil, p. 186.

[17] Archer, pp. 71–72.

interpretive service to Nebuchadnezzar. However, Belshazzar does not seem to be seeking information when he asks if Daniel is *that Daniel who is one of the captives from Judah* (13, NKJV). There is likely a bit of a dig, a put-down, in the words.[18]

Now it is precisely here, in the overlap of the queen's counsel (10–12) and the king's offer (13–16)[19] that we see the writer's irony. The name 'Daniel' occurs five times in two verses (12–13). He is Belshazzar's sure help (12) and yet he is one of the captives from Judah (13), a servant of the God Belshazzar has defied. The king has despised Daniel's God (2–4) and demeaned Daniel's status (13) and yet Daniel is the only one who can help. Normally Belshazzar would dismiss such a 'loser'.

William Barclay tells a story about T. E. Lawrence, who was a close personal friend of Thomas Hardy, the poet, and who would frequently visit Hardy and his wife. During the time Lawrence was serving as an aircraftsman in the Royal Air Force he sometimes came to visit the Hardy home wearing his aircraftsman's uniform. On one such occasion his visit overlapped with a visit of the Mayoress of Dorchester. The latter took it as an affront that she had to meet a common aircraftsman – she had no idea who the aircraftsman was. In French she told Mrs Hardy that never in all her born days had she had to sit down to tea with a private soldier. No one said anything – until T. E. Lawrence responded in perfect French: 'I beg your pardon, Madame, but can I be of any use as an interpreter? Mrs Hardy knows no French.'[20] Someone she had disdained was the only one who could help her.

That is the case in Daniel 5: the only help for Belshazzar was a cast-off Jew whose God he despised. The same is true for you. You hear that in 1 Corinthians 1:22–24:

> Jews demand signs and Greeks seek wisdom, but *we* [emphatic] preach Christ as the Crucified One – a scandal to Jews, foolishness to Gentiles, but to those who are called, both Jews and Greeks, Christ the power of God and the wisdom of God.

There the apostle is speaking of the only way to keep from perishing (1 Cor. 1:18); and the only way heaven's help comes to perishing

---

[18] See Lucas, p. 131, citing D. N. Fewell, *Circle of Sovereignty* (Nashville: Abingdon, 1991), p. 91.

[19] Belshazzar's offer to be 'third ruler' (v. 16, ESV; see also vv. 7, 29) was the best he could do; since Nabonidus and Belshazzar essentially functioned as co-kings, 'third' was the next highest. For discussion, see Steinmann, pp. 268–269.

[20] William Barclay, *The Gospel of John*, 2 vols., The Daily Study Bible (Philadelphia: Westminster, 1956), 1:224–225.

people is through a crucified Messiah. For Jews those last two words were a contradiction in terms, since Deuteronomy 21:23 told them that one hanged on a tree was cursed by God.[21] To speak of a crucified Messiah was like saying 'clean filth' or 'delicious vomit'.[22] A damned Messiah couldn't be a saving Messiah; he must be mighty, not mangled. And the Greeks had the same mind-set: God must fit into their expectations to win their vote. For the Jews, the Messiah must be mighty; for the Greeks, he must be slick. Jews want strength, Greeks style. Jews are interested in power, Greeks in packaging; Jews focus on force, Greeks on finesse. For the Jews, the cross lacks 'punch'; for the Greeks, it lacks sense. Jews demand signs, Greeks seek wisdom, Americans want therapy, 'but *we* preach Christ as the Crucified One'.[23] Divine foolishness in face of our desperation. You are not so different from Belshazzar: a cast-off Jew of the God you have despised is your only hope.

In the last section we see *human denseness met by divine judgment* (17–31). And Daniel did announce the judgment of God on Belshazzar in verse 25–28. He interprets the writing on the wall, which seems to consist of terms designating weights (the mina, shekel and half-mina), but which Daniel interprets via word-plays as indicating that God has got Belshazzar's number (26), that he is a light-weight (27), and his kingdom will split (28). In short, 'You are finished, flimsy and fractured.' And that night the Persians entered the city.

All this, however, is only the end of Daniel's answer to Belshazzar. It was, of course, what Belshazzar was interested in knowing (16). But Daniel did not simply give the king the answer he wanted. Notice that the majority (17–24) of Daniel's words are essentially a prophetic denunciation of Belshazzar; the king did not ask for this! He simply wanted the wall writing interpreted. But Daniel will not simply spit out the meaning – Belshazzar must *understand* why the interpretation will be so severe.

[21] In Deut. 21:22–23 the one who had committed a capital crime was first executed then hanged on a tree. The hanging was not the means of death but the aftermath of death. P. C. Craigie makes an important point: 'The body was not *accursed of God* . . . because it was hanging on a tree; it was hanging on a tree because it was accursed of God. And the body was not accursed of God simply because it was dead (for all men die), but it was accursed because of the reason for the death. To break the law of God and live as though he did not matter or exist, was in effect to curse him; and he who cursed God would be accursed of God'; *The Book of Deuteronomy*, New International Commentary on the Old Testament (Grand Rapids: Eerdmans, 1976), p. 285.

[22] Cf. the comments of Gordon Fee, *The First Epistle to the Corinthians*, New International Commentary on the New Testament (Grand Rapids: Eerdmans, 1987), p. 75.

[23] 1 Cor. 1:23.

Verses 17–24 function a good bit the way Judges 6:7–10 does in the Gideon narrative. Judges 6 begins by relating how the Midianites and others came trucking through Israel year after year, pilfering and picking the land clean and bringing Israel nearly to its last gasp (6:1–6). When Israel cries out to Yahweh, 'Yahweh sent a prophet'. It is almost comical. It's as if your lawnmower won't start so someone sends you a manicurist. What good can that do? So Israel wants relief from pressure, and they get a revelation from Yahweh, a word rehearsing his grace and charging them with infidelity.[24] They want deliverance; Yahweh wants them to understand why they are in a situation requiring deliverance. They want a pacifier, he wants perception. Daniel 5 is similar. Belshazzar didn't ask for a history lesson (17–24), he just wanted the mystery solved (16); but *understanding* was needed. It is this patient way that we usually love to short-circuit. Relatively speaking, then, verses 17–24 are more important than verses 25–28.

After Daniel repudiates the king's rewards (17), he launches into his address to Belshazzar (18–23). It begins with an emphatic, *You, O king* (18a). This 'you' is not reflected in English translations, probably because it simply seems to hang there; but Daniel picks it up again when he gets to his 'application' in verse 22, *'And you, his son . . .'* In verses 18–21 Daniel reviews a history lesson about *Nebuchadnezzar your father* (18).[25] Daniel speaks of the gift he received (18–19a), the power he exercised (19b), and the loss he incurred (20–21). The verb *gave* in verses 18 and 19a is very significant. *The Most High God gave . . . kingship and greatness and glory and majesty'* (18, ESV) to Nebuchadnezzar. He gave him *greatness* (19a). Here, as throughout Scripture, the axiom of Jesus holds sway: *'You would have no authority over me at all unless it had been given you from above.'*[26] It was because of this gift that Nebuchadnezzar enjoyed the privileges of immense power: for example, *whomever*

---

[24] Judg. 6:8–10.

[25] Nebuchadnezzar is called the 'father' of Belshazzar by the narrator (v. 2), the queen mother (v. 11, three times), Belshazzar himself (v. 13), and Daniel (v. 18). We know historically that Nabonidus was Belshazzar's actual father. But father-son terminology operates with a good deal of flexibility. 'Father' can denote an ancestor (BDB, p. 3) or even a predecessor. Many cite Shalmanezer III's Black Obelisk on which he calls Jehu, king of Israel, the 'son of Omri'. Omri was actually the father of Ahab (1 Kgs 16:29) and the originator of a dynasty that Jehu wiped out (cf. 2 Kgs 10:11). Yet the Assyrian king (who likely had intelligence of Jehu's anti-Omride, anti-Ahab leanings) calls him 'son of Omri', i.e., his successor. In the same way 'father' can indicate predecessor and that is likely the sense in which Nebuchadnezzar was Belshazzar's 'father'. Some scholars suggest that Nabonidus actually married a daughter of Nebuchadnezzar so that Belshazzar would actually be the great king's grandson. However, there is no conclusive evidence to support that view.

[26] John 19:11, emphasis author's.

he wished, he executed; whomever he wished, he kept alive (v. 19b, NKJV). The sense is not that Nebuchadnezzar acted in a terribly oppressive way but simply that he acted in a typically royal way. That is the way mighty kings function. But then Daniel alludes to the time Nebuchadnezzar began to strut and swagger in his royal britches, to the episode reported in Daniel 4, *when his heart was lifted up, and his spirit was hardened in pride* (20a, NKJV). He seemed to lose it all: *he was deposed, they took his glory from him*, and *he was driven* from human association (20b–21a). Daniel details the beasts and grass and dew. His dwelling, he says, was *with the wild donkeys*. Maybe Belshazzar would get it: God can take an arrogant ruler and essentially make an ass out of him.

But, no, Belshazzar did not get it. That's Daniel's point in verses 22–23.[27] Here Daniel begins his 'application' by picking up the *You, O king* of verse 18a in his *And you, his son* (22a). Here he accuses Belshazzar of being totally dense: you *have not humbled your heart, though you knew all this* (22b). His problem was not ignorance but insolence. He both opposed (23a) and refused to acknowledge (23b) *the Lord of heaven*. By desecrating the temple vessels he thumbed his nose at Israel's God (23a) and by singing doxologies to the sightless, heedless, witless bastard deities of Babylon he has denied honour to the God who gives him the breath to utter such damnable praises (23b). It's Romans 1:21 before Romans 1:21 was written. Human denseness (22–23) is about to be met by divine judgment (25–31).

Pay attention to what Belshazzar teaches you: having clear information does not guarantee the right response. He *knew all this* but did not humble his heart (22). So having good data does not necessarily bring about required change. Yet Western culture assumes that it will. Political and social gurus preach the information fallacy constantly. In my own country the knee-jerk reaction to any social problem seems to be, 'Well, we must *educate* people . . .' This often means we throw money at it, construct a bureaucracy to oversee it, and try to fund it in some budget. But it's all built on the assumption that education will bring transformation. 'If people only know what happens when they don't use seat belts, then . . .' 'If youth only know what drugs will do to them, then . . .' But Daniel's point is – Belshazzar knew and it didn't matter.

Joe Kennedy, Jr, oldest son of Joseph P. Kennedy and older brother of JFK, was slated for a bombing run of 12 August 1944. Joe Jr was to fly a PB-24 Liberator, a plane designed to be loaded with high

---

[27] There are something like fourteen occurrences of 'you/your' in vv. 22–23 (NKJV); Ferguson, p. 122.

explosives then directed to its target via remote control after the pilot and co-pilot had bailed out. Before the time to depart, an electronics officer warned Joe that the remotely controlled electronic device that was to detonate the explosives was faulty. That meant that almost anything – radio static, a jamming device, turbulence – could set off an explosion before the pilot crew could bail out. The officer urged Joe to abort the mission. Kennedy ignored the warning and flew anyway. The plane blew up at 6.20 pm over England. Both Kennedy and his co-pilot were blown out of the sky.[28] He knew; he was told; but it made no difference.

Truth is important, but we must have power to receive and welcome the truth, to respond to it properly. Yahweh's promise to exiled Israel recognizes this:

> I shall give them a single heart and I shall put a new spirit in them; I shall remove the heart of stone from their bodies and give them a heart of flesh, so that they can keep my laws and respect my judgments and put them into practice.[29]

Bible-believing churches and fellowships rightly place a premium on the place and ministry of the word. But we must be awake to the peril of having the word without the Spirit. We must plead that the Spirit of God will cause the word of God to be obedience-producing and life-transforming, for when truth does not humble us (22) or lead us to worship (23b) we are simply Belshazzar clones.[30]

The transition from Belshazzar the Chaldean to Darius the Mede took only a night (30–31).[31] We must not think, however, that

---

[28] Ronald Kessler, *The Sins of the Father* (New York: Warner, 1996), pp. 284–285.

[29] Ezek. 11:19–20a, NJB.

[30] Sometimes readers wonder why Daniel accepted his short-tenure honours in v. 29 when he had flatly refused them in v. 17. Probably he had no choice but to accept them, because Belshazzar had no choice but to dispense them. Not only did Daniel not care a whit for them, but Belshazzar probably hated conferring them on Daniel after the latter had rebuked the king with the words of vv. 17–28. However, Belshazzar was in a Herod Antipas situation (see Mark 6:26). Herod did not want to execute John the Baptist, but he had gone on oath publicly and so to save face and preserve reputation he had the prophet's head presented to the frivolous filly who had demanded it. Belshazzar was under similar pressure to keep his word.

[31] Ink continues to flow over the identity of Darius the Mede. No shame comes from admitting the problem. But we should not say something utterly foolish, like Norman Porteous when he pontificates: 'This Darius is almost certainly a figment of the writer's imagination' (*Daniel*, Old Testament Library [Philadelphia: Westminster, 1965], p. 83). Baldwin (p. 125) far more sensibly notes that the words 'being about sixty-two years old' supply the sort of detail that 'implies the existence of a particular person and not just a vague memory'. Suffice it to say that at this point I find D. J. Wiseman's suggestion that Darius the Mede is another name for Cyrus to be the most satisfying option. This requires one to translate the conjunction in 6:28 as 'even'

this account is merely about Belshazzar; it's about Presbyterians and Baptists and Anglicans and Pentecostals who have hidden Belshazzar-attitudes and who have never listened to the testimony of Belshazzar's predecessor: 'those who walk in pride he is able to abase' (4:37). But what really haunts us here is that little phrase, *that very night* (30). It suggests that Belshazzar joins the ranks of King Saul and Judas Iscariot[32] – and the rich man in Luke 12:20 – in sharing the hopeless darkness outside of God's truth.

instead of 'and' (a perfectly legitimate procedure; note the same usage in 1 Chr. 5:26, another king-with-two-names text), so that Daniel prospers 'during the reign of Darius, even the reign of Cyrus the Persian'. Interestingly enough, Cyrus was about sixty-two at the conquest of Babylon. See, among others, D. J. Wiseman, in *Notes on Some Problems in the Book of Daniel* (London: Tyndale, 1965), pp. 9–16; the excursus in Steinmann, pp. 290–296; and the lucid summary in Miller, pp. 174–177.

[32] 1 Sam. 28:25b; John 13:30.

Daniel 6:1–28
6. The night the lions were fasting

Daniel 6 *begins* with a miracle: a squeaky clean politician (3–4)! His colleagues and enemies (the terms overlap) had done a security check on Daniel and had scoured government files but came up with nothing. *They were unable to find any ground for complaint or bit of corruption because he was faithful; neither negligence or corruption was found in him* (4b). No disappointing omissions, no tainting commissions. He was what Paul (in 1 Tim. 3:2) would call 'without reproach' (Gk *anepilēmptos*), referring to a church leader whose reputation and conduct gave 'nothing for anyone to grab hold of'. That is Daniel. And his fellow bureaucrats hate him. His sterling character forces them to resort to 'Darius Appreciation Month' in order to eliminate him.

Daniel 6 is a literary parallel to Daniel 3.[1] Both are stories of God's deliverance. Chapter 6, however, is not repetitive but supplementary. Chapter 3 had shown how fidelity could be costly under Babylon. But Babylon has fallen (5:30–31) and now Persia runs the world. And so chapter 6 is saying, new circumstances do not always give you the relief you crave; you may face the same essential troubles. Bob Fyall nails it: 'It [chapter 6] is a necessary reminder that the life of faith must be lived to the very end and that earlier victories and rescues cannot be taken as guarantees of absence of future crises.'[2] Now, on to the lions.

1. The art of story-telling

Though we are primarily concerned with the teaching of the chapter, we should not neglect its technique; sometimes we can rush to the applications of a narrative and ignore its art. The primary mark of this narrative is its *economy*. The narrator is so stingy with details; there is such a restraint about the whole account.

---

[1] See discussion in Introduction on 'How is it packaged?', pp. 22–24. See also Lucas, p. 145.

[2] Fyall, p. 86.

For example, the narrator does not explicitly say why the other bureaucrats wanted to demote and eliminate Daniel. One can infer from verse 3 that they were envious of Daniel's success, but we don't know that they were privy to Darius' plan to place Daniel *over the whole kingdom*. Racial or 'anti-Semitic' motives may have played a part (13). But we don't clearly know, and the writer is content to let us guess. Perhaps one must assume that it doesn't really matter if we get to the bottom of that.

Note also how the narrator does not divulge the whole plan of Daniel's enemies in verse 5. He simply indicates that they realize that any successful trap will have to involve Daniel in an either-or faith decision (and they knew he wouldn't fudge about holding to Yahweh). Instead, our writer lets you hear their whole scheme only when they announce it to the king in verse 7–8. No need to inform readers ahead of time; they can pick it up when it's sprung on Darius. In this way the writer avoids unnecessary repetition.

In similar fashion the writer refuses to relieve tension after verse 17. He could have written, 'Now that night God sent an angel . . .', but he doesn't. He allows you to wait until, with Darius, you hear Daniel's own report in verses 21–22. Had he provided a 'reader's aside' after verse 17 he would have ruined the suspense he wanted to maintain. Once again, less detail is more telling.

Then there is the restraint we observe in Daniel's own words in verses 21–22. This is the first and only time Daniel actually talks in the story. And it is important to see that he doesn't say much. As far as his deliverance goes all we have is verse 22a: *My God sent his angel and shut the lions' mouths, and they have not harmed me.* No details, no elaboration, no satisfying curiosity. Quite different from the apocryphal tale of 'Daniel, Bel and the Snake' (second/first century BC), where the prophet Habakkuk is transported from Judea to the lion pit with stew and bread for Daniel's pit fare. But the biblical writer won't 'go there', as we say. Verse 22 is enough for him – supernatural, to be sure, but not sensational. He discloses the essential but covers over the curious. One tends to trust a writer like that.

2. The testimony of the story

I simply want to break down the story into its main segments; the teaching of each segment can be summarized by a biblical citation.[3] What then is the testimony of Daniel 6?

[3] Both John Goldingay (p. 124) and David Dorsey (*The Literary Structure of the Old Testament* [Grand Rapids: Baker, 1999], p. 261) sketch out respective 'chiastic' structures for Dan. 6; these are interesting, but I think a sequential treatment of the text better for purposes of exposition.

a. The world hates you[4] *(1–9)*

Darius the Mede apparently retained Daniel (cf. 5:29) in the higher echelons of his administration. Daniel was one of three *overseers* (ESV: *presidents*) to whom various satraps were to report, an arrangement designed so that the king *might suffer no loss* (v. 2b, ESV). One assumes this means primarily 'loss' of state revenue. Here at least is one constant, unchanging reality amid all the flux and upheaval of history: governments are huge repositories of waste, graft and corruption. That Daniel excelled the other overseers and the satraps may indicate he was especially effective in preventing the king from 'suffering loss'. Which may explain the hostility against Daniel – he was an unrelenting whistle-blower. Whatever the details, Daniel was impeccable (4b) and 'hate-able'. It is a tribute to Daniel's character that his enemies savvied that they could only send him up the river if they resorted to some religious ruse (5), and their scheme takes for granted Daniel's unbending fidelity – they simply know he will not turn aside from worshiping his God.

So they *came thronging in* (NJPS) to the king (6; also 11, 15) with their proposal.[5] They pressed the king to authorize a statute *that whoever makes petition to any god or man for thirty days, except to you, O king, shall be cast into the den of lions* (7b). This is a bit tricky to understand: does no petition even to any *man* mean that a fellow couldn't ask to borrow his neighbour's garden hoe without going through the king? That would be both ludicrous and inefficient. Hence it makes more sense to confine the scope of the proposed law to 'religious' requests and to understand 'man' as alluding to 'the priests through whom petitions were mediated to the gods'.[6] So for thirty days there was one representative of the gods and one mediator between gods and man, Darius the Mede.

All this was rather heady stuff. These men give Darius the impression that this is the darling idea of the whole civil service – overseers, prefects, satraps, counsellors and governors; there is such *unanimity* behind it. And not a little *flattery: except to you, O king*. There is something intoxicating about being the sole channel to the gods, a sort of surrogate deity, even if the term expires in thirty days.[7]

---

[4] John 15:19.
[5] The verb is *rĕgaš*; its Hebrew cognate appears in Ps. 2:1 of nations 'raging'. It seems to carry a connotation of tumult, disturbance and conspiracy. For usage in Qumran materials, cf. DCH, 7:418.
[6] Miller, p. 180.
[7] Cf. Goldingay (p. 128): 'In Persia the king was not regarded as divine in the Egyptian sense, though in court ceremonial people did obeisance before him as one would to a god, and the general idea that the king is a manifestation or representative of deity and a key mediator with deity appears in Persian writings.'

Moreover, the king surely saw (and his lackeys may have stressed it) the *utility* of this proposed decree. It would prove excellent socio-political cement, especially at a transition-point of power from Babylon to Persia; it would 'make a statement' about the dominance of Persian power. Of course, Darius' visitors argue for the ultimate *authority* behind this decree; they want it published in writing *so that it cannot be altered – in accordance with the laws of the Medes and Persians, which cannot be repealed* (8, NIV). This measure both underscores how seriously the government regards the law and also – for the conspirators – will cut away any 'wiggle room' for the king and will force him to abide by it.

Let us back away and look at verses 1–9 as a whole. This section carries a two-pronged message for Israel's exiles: see how gracious God is in giving you favour among your captors and even with kings, therefore, don't despair; and see how *costly* it may prove to remain faithful when you are favoured, therefore, don't make an idol out of human favour. One never knows when the Tuesday morning may come when one must let go of human favour to stay faithful to God. And this dilemma (if it is such) comes from the animosity that men have for God's servants. That was the case under Babylon (the furnace episode, ch. 3) and now in Persia. It matters not where you are – 'The world hates you'. There *is* an explanation for it (John 15:19) but when it occurs it may seem so inexplicable.

Charles Schulz's very first 'Peanuts' cartoon shows a boy and a girl sitting on some steps by a sidewalk. Another boy approaches them in the distance and boy says to girl, 'Well! Here comes ol' Charlie Brown!' Charlie passes in front of them and the same lad says, 'Good ol' Charlie Brown – Yes, sir!' After Charlie passes beyond earshot both boy and girl look after him, and boy says, 'Good ol' Charlie Brown . . . how I hate him!' So out of the blue. But a fact all the same. So Daniel 6 admonishes God's people: Don't think that Daniel's is an exceptional situation; it is rather an exemplary one; this is the way it is with God's servants in this world.

b. Pray for the peace of Jerusalem[8] (10–11)

In verse 9 Darius had walked right into the conspirators' trap, and in verse 10 Daniel placed his head in their noose. Things could hardly look better if you were among Daniel's would-be liquidators. But before we bring on the lions, let's camp out at verse 10 (ESV), where Daniel provides us with a superb tutorial on prayer.

---

[8] Ps. 122:6.

First, we should notice *the focus of prayer: he went to his house where he had windows in his upper chamber open toward Jerusalem.* Why toward Jerusalem? Daniel is simply praying as Scripture directed, in line with Solomon's prayer in 1 Kings 8:46–51.[9] When Israel is captive in a foreign land, they are to pray toward their land, the city Yahweh had chosen, and the house Solomon had built for Yahweh's name. That is why Daniel's windows are open toward Jerusalem. This is not superstition or mere nostalgia. You can find a sample of the kind of prayer Daniel was praying in 9:3–19 (note the date – 9:1!). His concern was for the welfare of God's people and so the big burden of his prayers was for the repentance and sanctification and prosperity of the church. I am not saying that Daniel did not include on this occasion a petition to face the lion-threat with fortitude, but such matters were not the usual content of his Jerusalem-centred prayers.

Christians frequently can find themselves in a similar position. Sometimes we discover that our prayers are dominated not with our own concerns but with the troubles and traumas of God's people, perhaps those in our local fellowship. One can hardly be a breathing member of a local congregation without realizing there are folks there who have had to wade through ongoing trouble – and so you find yourself preoccupied in prayer, pleading that God would show them glimpses of his warm mercy in their thick darkness. The more we learn of the church worldwide and the suffering of Jesus' sheep in many lands at the hands of the Christ-haters of this age, we find ourselves pleading that the Lord would keep them steadfast and in his time place them in the safety for which they long (cf. Ps. 12:5). Bringing our own needs before the Father is perfectly right, but we are not long in the Christian life when we discover that (as in Daniel's practice) intercession is a huge component of our prayers.

Secondly, we see clearly *the defiance of prayer: When Daniel knew that the document had been signed, he . . . prayed . . .* I wonder what Daniel's calculations would have been had he been a typical, pragmatic American: 'I have no choice; the law is the law; I am forced to cease prayer; otherwise . . . ' Nor is it only Americans. I recall being overseas (where, the veil of charity refuses to reveal) and hearing from a married couple why they had not been in morning worship that day: their young daughter had been invited to the birthday party of one of her friends. So they were 'forced' to miss worship. Nothing about a courteous phone call, indicating

---

[9] See the excellent comments of Duguid (pp. 96–97) in this connection. One might say that as Lev. 26 and Deut. 28 'control' Old Testament prophecy, so Solomon's prayer in 1 Kgs 8 controls Old Testament piety.

they would drop off a gift on Saturday but that as the party conflicted with their Sunday worship, their daughter would not be able to attend the party. But no; there was this 'have to' mode of thinking.

Actually, the premier moment in the whole story is right here, when Daniel prayed *anyway*. As Veldkamp says, 'The great miracle of grace in Daniel 6 is that Daniel, the man of prayer, was able to go on praying.' Let him explain:

> This shows us that the dangers we don't see are generally much greater than the dangers we do see. When we watch Daniel being lowered into the lions' den, we hold our breath in fear and anticipation. Yet, by that point the danger has already been overcome and the great fight has been fought. It is indeed a wondrous miracle that God preserves one of His children in the lions' den, but it is no less a miracle that God's gracious hand saved Daniel when all of Babylon [sic] – goaded on by satan – attempted to pry apart those two aged hands tightly clasped in prayer.[10]

Daniel was able to see the actual issue. He knew he was not facing a minor religious inconvenience (just wait thirty days until the current prayer ban is lifted). It was actually a matter of whether he would keep the first commandment (Exod. 20:3; same issue as in ch.3). Daniel faces a king who is 'god-keeper for a month' and the politicians who pushed the provision through, and prays to Yahweh anyway. Prayer is the way he keeps the first commandment; by prayer he goes on worshiping the true God anyway, and so prayer is here an 'idol-busting' activity. And the most tempting idol was not Darius' quasi-divinity, it may likely have been Daniel's own security. Daniel had to answer the question: What matters most – the worship of God or my safety? His response shows that he so much as said, 'I must not make an idol of my own safety and so by prayer I destroy that idol.'

Third, Daniel's fidelity teaches us about *the consistency of prayer: He got down on his knees three times a day and prayed and gave thanks ... as he had done previously.* Daniel's ongoing practice of prayer does not seem to have been a difficult decision for him (Veldkamp). We read of no inner turmoil or anguish. Indeed, his enemies didn't expect him to flinch at all about continuing his usual practice (5)! But that's just it, isn't it? It was his *usual* practice and sometimes that can grease the gears for a crisis.

[10] Veldkamp, p. 122. Cf. similarly Olyott (p. 80): 'the real den of lions was Daniel's bedroom'; and Thomas (p. 108): 'The great battle took place there – not in the lions' den, but at the open window looking to God.'

Ronald Wallace makes a perceptive observation in this regard:

> There is no doubt that what kept Daniel when his trial came was this rigid uninterrupted habit. He had disciplined himself to it day by day for years, and at the hour of crisis the very momentum of the custom itself would have been enough to keep him faithful to it, even if there had been at the moment no living inspirational incentive.[11]

We may quibble on a detail or two, but Wallace's point stands. We find it easy to debunk habit – habit can degenerate into lifeless routine and can murder spontaneity. But, as Jay Adams (I think) once said, a train's habit is to be confined to its tracks and therein consists its usefulness and safety. So we see with Daniel: consistency assists courage, and discipline feeds faithfulness. In the crisis Daniel's habit set him free to be faithful.

Finally, Daniel exhibits *the posture of prayer: He got down on his knees.* Such posture is an outward sign of an attitude of submission and self-humbling. Admittedly, outward gestures can be empty, but we usually assume otherwise. Should someone stand in front of you with his/her tongue sticking out, thumbs in ears, wiggling fingers, you likely read it as blatant defiance rather than meaningless aerobics. In short, in this case, knees 'speak'.[12]

Of course, Bible people know that knees have a future. The day will come when 'every knee' will bow to Jesus Christ, the crucified Monarch (Phil. 2:10 in context, which Paul got from Yahweh's own sworn oath in Isa. 45:23), and, if that is the case, we should be getting into practice. Our knees then should have more of a work-out (providing we are physically able) in both private and public worship. Some will, however, nay-say this, holding that the heart attitude is what matters in worship. And they are both right and wrong. Allen and Borror dare us to try the attitude-only approach in marriage. Does a husband try to say that his love for his wife is given only by a heart attitude, that there is no need for physical expressions of his love?[13] A fellow like that deserves a skillet to the brain to get him to think properly.

Kneeling in prayer is not a matter of indifference – it reminds you of your *true position.* It's as if you say, 'I am a servant. He is the King. I do not live in a democracy but under a monarchy. He is not my

---

[11] Wallace, p. 112.

[12] Not that kneeling is the only posture for prayer: it can be standing (1 Kgs 8:22), sitting (2 Sam. 7:18), or stretched prostrate on the ground (Mark 14:35).

[13] Ronald Allen and Gordon Borror, *Worship: Rediscovering the Missing Jewel* (Portland: Multnomah, 1982), p. 131.

errand boy. I never present my demands. I am always a beggar at the throne of grace, and, though it is a throne of grace, I never forget it is a *throne.*'

c. Put not your trust in princes[14] (12–18)

The conspirators 'have the goods' on Daniel (11) and now go to the king (12). They don't blurt out their case against Daniel immediately. Rather they allude to the edict: 'Wasn't there something about a thirty-day ban on prayer . . . ' In this way they sucker Darius to re-assert the irrevocability of the recent ordinance (12b). Darius never saw it coming. Now they press their case, which is racially driven (at least in part), for they refer to Daniel as *one of the exiles from Judah.* He is a captive, a foreigner, one who doesn't really belong. Their case against him is that his offense is both hostile and habitual: hostile, because he *pays no attention to you, O king,* i.e., by his disobedience Daniel is personally defying the king himself and not merely trampling on a law;[15] habitual, because Daniel prays *three times a day,* i.e., his offense is no momentary, forgetful lapse but a persistent and ongoing practice.[16] Now it becomes clear that the king is pro-Daniel, but a day's efforts are futile (14) and Daniel's accusers hold Darius' feet to the legal fire.[17] So Daniel goes to the lions (16a).

Note what happens at verses 16 and following. The writer fixes all our attention on the king. The whole focus in verses 16–20 is on the anguish of the king rather than the trauma of Daniel. The writer keeps us in suspense – along with Darius – about Daniel's fate until verse 21. It is a tad strange: Daniel is thrown to the lions and we only hear about the king and *his* agonizing night. Why is this the case? If we go back to verse 12 and work forward we can see how the writer depicts the king. He shows us the royal naïveté (12), compassion (14) and helplessness (14b, 16–20).[18] I think that depiction is intentional: as if to say, rulers may not be personally hostile to you, but, even if they favour you, you dare not pin your hopes on them, for they can prove as helpless as anyone else. It's the writer's way of preaching Psalm 146:3–4.

Oddly enough, Darius' words in verse 16b seem to underscore

---

[14] Ps. 146:3.

[15] They argue with a right principle even if they twist its application: defiance of a law is essentially defiance of the law-giver (see 2 Sam. 12:9–10).

[16] Cf. Steinmann, p. 318.

[17] 'Said' in v. 15 (English) is a participle: 'they kept saying to the king', i.e., keeping the pressure on; see Steinmann, p. 310.

[18] See the fine observations in Lucas, pp. 149, 154; e.g., 'There is also an element of ridicule in the picture of the king that is presented here. The one who is put on a (semi-) divine pedestal is at the same time shown to be naïve and conceited, and therefore open to manipulation by his courtiers' (p. 149).

this very point – that Daniel's God is the only one who can – and will – deliver him. Many translations take Darius' statement as a sort of desperate prayer or wish (NASB, NKJV and NJPS are exceptions). But his words are not a wish but an affirmation: *Your God, whom you serve continually – he will deliver you.* In the Aramaic the emphatic pronoun and final verb are clearly a declaration. Most expositors apparently cannot bring themselves to think that Darius could or would actually express himself so vigorously, but his early trek to the lions' den in verse 19 supports his 'faith'; he would not have bothered if he were sure Daniel had been mauled.[19]

Our writer, then, is doing a little 'preventive theology' in this section. He seems to say to Israel: 'You may have rulers or others in high places who are well-disposed toward you; but don't rest in them as your trump card, for even they for all their apparent power can prove as helpless as Samson without hair.' He is trying to bash idols before they become idols.

d. Salvation belongs to the Lord[20] (19–28)

This section breaks down into three thematic segments:

Intervention (19–23)
Retribution (24)
Proclamation (25–28)

In the 'intervention' section we run into the irony that not only did the king fast (18) but so did the lions (22). Verses 21–22 deserve special attention because they contain the only words Daniel speaks in the whole narrative. This fact may give them particular weight. And his words are brief – only the barest expression of God's intervention and Daniel's innocence. No dwelling on lion behaviour or the smell of the pit or the emotional state of Daniel. *My God* [emphatic subject] *sent his angel and shut the lions' mouths* (22a). That's all anyone needs to know. The careful scrutiny given Daniel at his de-briefing (23b) confirmed the truth of his testimony.

Vindication for Daniel involves retribution for his enemies (24). 'The dark side to Daniel's deliverance is the judgment that falls on those who had sought to destroy the kingdom of God.'[21] In Israel

---

[19] Cf. Steinmann, p. 320; and Fyall, p. 89.
[20] Jon. 2:9.
[21] Ferguson, p. 141. On this pattern, cf. Marten H. Woudstra, *The Book of Joshua*, New International Commentary on the Old Testament (Grand Rapids: Eerdmans, 1981), pp. 315, 333, and my *The Way of the Righteous in the Muck of Life* (Ross-shire: Christian Focus, 2010), pp. 46–48, 87–91.

wives and children would have been spared the punishment of the head of the household (Deut. 24:16; unless, of course, they were accomplices, cf. Josh. 7:24–25). But this was Persia, and all of them were given to the lions.

Now comes the climax of the chapter: Darius' proclamation in praise of Daniel's God (25–27). Who knows? Darius may have directed Daniel to ghost-write the proclamation for him and simply initialled his approval. In any case, he declares he is the *living God* with the everlasting kingdom who does saving wonders in his world, especially in protecting his servant in a reeking Persian lion pit. *He delivers and rescues* (v. 27a, NASB, ESV) sums it all up.

Verses 25–27 re-establish a pattern in the Daniel narratives. We missed this kind of ending in chapter 5 – Belshazzar most likely lacked the inclination for it, even if given the time. But we recall the 'confessions' or proclamations of the Nebuchadnezzar chapters (2:47; 3:28–29; 4:34–37); now with Darius we meet one of these again (6:25–27). All these come at the end of their respective narratives and have a climactic air about them. Their recurrence and placement imply the weight they pack. They are narrative flashes of standard Old Testament doctrine. One finds the latter in texts like Psalm 102:15,

> And nations will fear the name of Yahweh,
> and all the kings of the earth (will fear) his glory,

or Psalm 138:4–5:

> All kings of earth will praise you, Yahweh,
> when they have heard the words of your mouth,
> and they will sing of the ways of Yahweh,
> for how great Yahweh's glory is!

The Psalm texts tell us how it will be, while the 'confessions' of Nebuchadnezzar and Darius in Daniel give us foretastes of that coming homage. And it is crucial not to belittle or despise the foretastes.

Stan Telchin and his wife Ethel were shocked one Sunday night when a daughter called from university to tell them she had believed in God and that the Bible was his word – and that 'Jesus is the Messiah'. The Telchins went into a tailspin. They were Jewish, and Stan, in his rage, threw himself into proving his daughter wrong. As if possessed he read and read. He too came to accept the Bible as God's word and to believe at least that the Hebrew Bible did contain many prophecies about the coming Messiah. He and his wife began to attend a messianic Jewish congregation. He still was not a believer in Jesus. During this time he decided to attend a conference for messianic Jews held at a college in Pennsylvania. Here he met Lillian, an elderly disabled woman. Stan admitted to her that he was not a 'believer'. She had him read Exodus 20 to her and then point-blank asked him, 'Who is your god?' The following morning Stan went to breakfast and someone (not knowing he had never confessed Christ) asked him to give thanks for the food. He did so – and closed his prayer, 'in the name of Jesus, the Messiah'. Speaking with Lillian the day before he realized he had come to that conviction.[22]

I suppose someone could say that those closing words to Stan's prayer were just a formula, a customary way of closing off a set petition. But it was nothing of the kind. True, it was only the conclusion of a prayer, only a mere seven words. But those words were indicative of far more, of a revolution of mind and soul. Those 'mere' words were pointers to a whole new submission to Jesus as king.

We could, of course, regard these 'confessions' of Nebuchadnezzar and Darius with a jaded attitude, as royal formalities lacking much significance. But we daren't do that. Even if they are not full-blown exclusive recognitions of Daniel's God, they are clear pointers to the homage that earth's politicians and even despots will offer at the last. When we wade into chapters 7 – 12 we may realize how much we need this assurance.

[22] See Scot McKnight, with R. Boaz Johnson, 'From Tel Aviv to Nazareth: Why Jews Become Messianic Jews', *Journal of the Evangelical Theological Society* 48/4 (December 2005), pp. 779–780.

Daniel 7:1–28
7. Is history all beastly?

Now we are walking into the 'apocalyptic' section of Daniel; it seems so baffling that some readers simply drop out. But (and some may accuse me of sexism) I would argue from my own experience that such a reaction is completely unreasonable. I speak of understanding those of the female gender. If before marriage you (I speak here of males) imagine you have begun to understand the female, you are incredibly naïve; if after marriage you think you can divine the female, you are clearly deluded; if after years of happily married life you dream that at last you can fathom the female persona, you are utterly hopeless. And yet . . . none of that kept you from marriage. Neither should the mysteries of Daniel 7 – 12 keep you from ploughing on through the book.

There's a little game that sometimes get played. Someone mentions 'apocalyptic', and you instinctively know that you should wrinkle your brow, narrow your eyes and nod somewhat knowingly as if you've some understanding of what the term means. But scholars have their own problems deciding what makes apocalyptic 'apocalyptic', i.e., what special marks a chunk of biblical literature has to have to be dubbed apocalyptic. Roughly, I would say that biblical apocalyptic is a sort of prophecy that seeks to enlighten and encourage a people despised and cast off by the world with a vision of the God who will come to impose his kingdom on the wreckage and rebellion of human history – and it communicates this message through the use of wild, scary, imaginative, bizarre and head-scratching imagery.[1]

---

[1] See Duguid, p. 107 – the best summary of biblical apocalyptic I have seen; see also Elliott E. Johnson, *Expository Hermeneutics: An Introduction* (Grand Rapids: Zondervan, 1990), pp. 165–168; D. Brent Sandy and Martin G. Abegg, Jr, in D. Brent Sandy and Donald L. Giese, Jr. (eds,) *Cracking Old Testament Codes* (Nashville: Broadman & Holman, 1995), pp. 177–196.

Daniel 7 provides us with a kind of overview of history. That may be a turn-off for some. We're used to hearing someone say, 'I don't like history' (probably had a poor teacher). But, fact is, you have to live in the stuff, so you need to know what it will be like, and, if you are one of God's people, how you will endure and how God will keep you. So pay attention to Daniel 7, where you get a load of history in its reality and hope. The chapter breaks down into three sections.

1. Clear realism: the fearful face of history (1–8)

Daniel had this vision in the first year of Belshazzar (1a), which could be as early as 553 BC (though others prefer 550). The *four winds* were churning up the ocean and four beasts appear in sequence. The first is *like a lion* (4) with *eagles' wings*. However, it loses those wings; they are *plucked off* and then it stands *on two feet like a man* with a man's *mind*. The *lion* suggests ferocity, but the eagle-to-human pattern is difficult. The lion is usually identified with Babylon and many interpreters look at the 'human' component in view of Nebuchadnezzar's restoration from beastly existence in Daniel 4 – it may suggest a certain humaneness that came to characterize the regime. Instead of a humanizing tendency, however, the image may imply imposed limitation. Babylon always had pretensions to divinity, but its power too is human; that power (*eagles' wings*) is forcibly removed. 'Though it appeared to be the kingdom of the gods, Babylon was as frail as any other human kingdom.'[2]

The second beast is *like a bear* (5), raised up on one side. The *three ribs* in its mouth tell us it was not fasting, and the order, *Rise, devour much flesh*, suggests that rapacity drove this regime. The third is *like a leopard* (6) with *four wings* and *four heads*, which imply both swiftness and universality (four heads suggest all four directions). The fourth beast is like nothing we can imagine – there is no 'like' in verse 7. The difference is that it is *different* (7, 19, 23). From verse 7 one could say this beast is *different* in the terror it inspires (*terrifying and dreadful*, ESV), in the havoc it wreaks (*devoured and broke in pieces and stamped what was left with its feet*), and in the power it possesses (*ten horns*).[3] One is tempted, from verse 8, to add a fourth mode in which this beast is different: in the ruler it produces. Called *a little horn*, he is obviously a mighty, dominant ruler who combines intelligence (*eyes like the eyes of a man*) and arrogance (*a mouth speaking great things*), always a poor combination.

---

[2] Willem A. VanGemeren, 'Daniel', in *Evangelical Commentary on the Bible*, ed. Walter A. Elwell (Grand Rapids: Baker, 1989), p. 596. Calvin's view was similar.

[3] 'Ten horns, five times the natural two, represent pictorially the extraordinary power of this beast' (Baldwin, p. 140).

A brief tangent is necessary. How are we to identify these four 'beasts'? What kingdoms do they represent? The dominant view among Old Testament scholars is that they represent Babylon, Media, Persia and Greece respectively; however, historically they have been identified as Babylon, Medo-Persia, Greece and Rome. (There are, of course, variants to these main views.) I think the 'historical' view correct in the main. This means that here in chapter 7 the 'bear' (5) denotes Medo-Persia (i.e., the Persian empire). The book of Daniel always seems to keep the Medes and Persians together as a unit, not splintered into segments. In chapter 8 Daniel has a vision of a ram and a male goat. In the interpretation of the vision the ram with the two horns is specifically identified as representing the kings of Media and Persia (8:20). In chapter 6 Darius' decree operates 'according to the laws of the Medes and Persians' (8, 12, 15) that couldn't be changed. And Daniel tells Belshazzar that the kingdom is 'given to the Medes and Persians' (5:28). The book of Daniel seems to know no Medes except those who are linked with Persians. It is true that Darius is himself called a Mede (5:31), but he was not ruling over Media or over the Medes. Moreover, Steinmann notes:

> The Medes had been subsumed under the Persians eleven years before Babylon was conquered by Cyrus the Great. Cyrus had combined the Median and Persian kingdoms in himself, since he was of Persian royal descent on his father's side and of Median royal descent on his mother's side, and he solidified this with the defeat of the Median king, his grandfather Astyages, in 550 BC.[4]

Both usage and history then argue against trying to sliver off Media from Persia and insert it as a separate kingdom in the line-up of Daniel 7. In my view, therefore, the kingdoms are Babylon (lion), Medo-Persia (bear), Greece (leopard) and – presumably – Rome.

I say 'presumably,' because that is the most natural identification for post-Daniel folks to make: Rome was the next dominant empire after Alexander's Macedonian-Greek regime. But I am a bit chary about identifying the fourth beast in Daniel 7 with historical Rome. The writer seems to bend over backwards to say the fourth beast cannot be categorized. To be sure, all the 'beasts' are *different* from each other (3), but the fourth beast is in a class all by itself, *different* from the preceding three (7), *different* in its viciousness and voraciousness (19), *different* apparently in the scope of its domination (23), just as the 'little horn' that comes from it is *different* from

---

[4] Steinmann, pp. 148–149.

rulers that precede it (24). He is saying, 'The fourth kingdom is like nothing you've ever seen before.' Veldkamp explains:

> To use non-metaphorical language, we could say that the fourth empire to be established on this earth will be a true universal empire that will make all other empires look pale and insignificant by comparison. This empire will conquer all other kingdoms and states, whether they be great or small, neutral or belligerent. It will be an empire without parallel in power and ruthlessness [and, we might add, in persecution, 21, 25].[5]

I would prefer, then, simply to dub the fourth beast the 'different' kingdom and understand it as the last human kingdom, the one in which human evil and rebellion will reach its apex.

However, the writer is not merely inviting you to interpret details; rather, he wants verses 1–8 to make an overall impression on you. He wants them to scare you; he wants you to 'register terror' as you see these gross and frightful creatures.[6] He seems to be teaching us something about the overall pattern of history. He is certainly not blabbering blithely about 'progress' in history. Rather he seems to imply that, on the whole, nations and kingdoms are out for conflict and conquest and control, that empires are bent to dominate and devour, no matter how many people they mangle or how much misery they inflict. Some may say that the view of history is so dark here 'because this is apocalyptic' and it tends to be pessimistic toward the present order. No, biblical apocalyptic is all for proclaiming genuine hope but refuses to do so by ignoring or denying the evil regimes that clutter human history. It is as if the writer invites us to incorporate the doctrine of total depravity into our politics.[7] The kingdoms of this age seem to seize on *Arise, devour much flesh* (5) as their mantra.

Sometimes one must descend to particulars to feel the point; generalizations have no 'edge'. The last century provides too many samples. Turkish government troops had already killed up to 100,000 Armenians in 1895–6. Then in 1915, the Turks accused the Armenians of assisting Russian invaders and so 24 April was set as Armenian liquidation day. As many as 600,000 died that day, many under great cruelty, like having their heads placed in vises and squeezed until

[5] Veldkamp, p. 165.
[6] Cf. Baldwin's perceptive comments (pp. 138–139) on the emotional reactions the reader is meant to have.
[7] For a succinct explanation of 'total depravity', see my booklet, *The House that Jesus Built* (Ross-shire: Christian Focus, 2007), pp. 12–13, under the heading 'Sinners are perfectly sinful'.

they collapsed. When Koreans protested Japanese tyranny in 1919, men and boys had their fingers passed over red hot wires, toenails were ripped from flesh with pincers; some were flogged, repeatedly, until, taken to hospital, big slabs of gangrenous skin had to be cut off. Then there was that Black Friday during World War II when Japanese troops went through Alexandra Hospital in Singapore, bayoneting all patients, doctors and nurses, and then tied hundreds of Chinese hand to hand and massacred them on the beaches.

Sometimes the brutality can be laid at the feet of a single dictator. In 1932 Joseph Stalin demanded grain deliveries from the Ukrainian peasantry, quotas that were larger than the total crop. The demand was ruthlessly enforced, and at least five million, more likely seven million, simply starved to death. And in the 1970s Idi Amin carried out his own style of carnage in Uganda: sledge-hammering prisoners, so that execution cells were littered with human eyes and teeth; bodies floating down rivers; civilians who happened to belong to the 'wrong tribe' screaming in agony as their sex organs were ripped away.[8]

These examples are not really exceptional; such episodes pervade history. Nor does one have to dig deeply to come up with cruelties perpetrated by the more 'refined' Western democracies. Daniel's vision is telling us that history *is* beastly; it is scary. He wants us to hold a clear realism about life in this world.

Some time ago Dave Harvey published a book on marriage. The title was *When Sinners Say 'I Do'*. So refreshing to see that clear recognition right in the title: marriage may prove wonderful, but don't forget what kind of people are in it. And verses 1–8 are saying to us, now don't be naïve about human history; don't be so gullible as to think that some new regime or new ideology or new party will instigate some form of cosmic therapy. At the close of *The First Salute*, her book on the American Revolution, Barbara Tuchman makes a very perceptive comment: 'Revolutions produce other men, not new men.' And the fearful face of history seems to confirm that.

2. Heartening secret: the firm kingship of heaven (9–14)

When our boys were small they had in their 'biblical library' collection a little book about Jonah – it had pictures and the printed story, plus a companion cassette tape with Burl Ives reading the story. As the sailors debate what to do with Jonah, the sound effects on the tape intensify, so that Mr Ives has to raise his voice to read above

[8] See James and Marti Hefley, *By Their Blood* (Grand Rapids: Baker, ²1996), pp. 94, 342–343, 459; Ernest Gordon, *To End All Wars* (Grand Rapids: Zondervan, 2002), p. 51; Robert Conquest, *Stalin: Breaker of Nations* (New York: Viking, 1991), p. 163.

'the storm'. When, however, they chuck Jonah overboard, the 'storm' suddenly ceases and Mr Ives reads on in a normal voice in that great calm. The transition here in Daniel 7 from verse 8 to verses 9–14 is equally abrupt. At the end of verse 8 we brace ourselves to hear more of this *little horn*, to soak up a bit more terror. Instead, we suddenly cut from the little horn and fourth beast and we find ourselves watching a throne and judgment scene. It's as if the text says, 'Don't over-angst about that little horn; instead glue your eyes on this.'

The transition at verse 9 is not only purposefully abrupt, but the whole structure of verses 9–14 seems designed to diminish the place of the little horn and fourth beast. Each segment of this section is introduced by *I was looking* (9, 11 [twice], 13).[9] The three 'scenes' are simply:

The Ancient of Days (9–10)
Little horn/beast(s) (11–12)
One like a Son of Man (13–14)

Verse 11 suggests the seemingly effortless manner in which the little horn and (fourth) beast are dispatched. Yet the 'sandwich' structure reinforces this minimizing effect, for it's as if the little horn and its beast are scrunched and squeezed between the Ancient of Days (9–10) and the Son of Man (13–14). The literary envelope seems to make the little horn truly 'little'! So if you understand verses 9–14 correctly, you will know that the Bible is trying to thrill you by placarding where the power and glory, justice and kingship really reside.[10]

[9] The clause occurs nine times in the chapter (also in vv. 2, 4, 6, 7, 21, in addition to those cited). The Aramaic is the same in each case but English versions tend to vary the rendering.

[10] On the puzzling v. 12, I think Baldwin (p. 142) has said all that can safely be said: 'Two points are clear: (i) whoever the original beasts stood for, their kingdoms continue to have a recognizable identity, and (ii) history has not yet come to an end, despite the intervention of God's judgment, though *a season and a time* implies a limited future.' This section also packs implications for a 'critical' matter. Note how v. 11 specifies that not only the little horn (by implication) but the (fourth) beast is totally eradicated. Hence it will exercise no further power. Those who hold that the fourth beast is Greece (and its split-offs like Syria and the Seleucid dynasty) identify the 'little horn' as Antiochus Epiphanes. But that makes Dan. 7 a false prophecy. After Antiochus bit the dust the Seleucid dynasty still continued and Syria still made trouble for Judea. Yet v. 11 predicts that the beast would be completely eliminated in a decisive and presumably total judgment. If Antiochus is the little horn here, the 'prophecy' is plainly in error. I suppose an Antiochus advocate could say, 'Well, yes, the "vision" was proclaimed in 167 BC before the Antiochus scourge had been resolved and so the writer could not provide a prophecy after-the-fact (at which he was fairly accurate) but had to try his hand at predictive prophecy and so obviously missed it.' But then the problem begins. If the readers of a second-century Daniel knew that 'little horn' here was code

But to the details. What is it in this part of Daniel's vision that heartens the Lord's pressured people? Two scenes, two facts. The first is: *The Ancient of Days holds court* (9–10). Be careful you don't imbibe the wrong impression here. One 'advanced in days' is how one would describe an aged man. But don't look at this through the eyes of a youth-obsessed Western culture – get yourself back to, well, Israelite culture. This title for God then means that he is grand, not that he is frail; it imports ideas of dignity, not of senility. Contextually, it is telling: the vision has just rehearsed a sequence of 'beastly' kingdoms (1–8) but *the Ancient of Days* has obviously been there long before a space was cleared on the plain of history for any of them.

What does this scene intend to convey? First, *sanity: the Ancient of Days took his seat* (9a). 'Human kingdoms are always caught up in feverish activity, military or diplomatic', but he 'is never taken by surprise, never undecided, never in a panic about his world'.[11] He sits; he does not stew. Next, *fury: his throne was flames of fire, its wheels burning fire; a river of fire was flowing and coming out from before him* (9c–10a). From the first of redemptive history, fire signals Yahweh's presence (Gen. 15:17; Exod. 3:2; 13:21; 19:18), even his presence in judgment (Lev. 10:1–2; Num. 11:1–3; 16:35). Here in Daniel 7 the fire suggests the fury of God in judgment, but it is a *just* fury, for *the court sat, and the records were opened* (10c); it was all 'by the book'. Finally, *majesty: a thousand thousands served him, and ten thousand times ten thousand stood before him* (10b). Daniel tries to wring something like infinity out of the multiplication table in order to express the innumerable host that acknowledges the supremacy and splendour of the Ancient of Days.[12]

The second scene and fact is· *The Son of Man has the kingdom* (13–14). More precisely, Daniel saw *one like a son of man* to whom was given *dominion and glory and kingdom*. One *like a son of man* is one who appears as a human, as a man, in Daniel's vision. He may prove to be more than human but in Daniel's vision he appears as a human. The *dominion/kingdom* terminology is concentrated here in verse 14 (see also 6, 12, 24, 27 [twice] for 'dominion'/*šolṭān*, and

---

for Antiochus Epiphanes, would they not be perturbed by the fact that, after his demise, his regime was still pestering Judea, contrary to v. 11? Why should they receive Daniel as Scripture when it obviously contained such botched prophecies? For this argument, see Young, p. 153.

[11] Ferguson, p. 155.

[12] Ferguson (p. 156) suggests what this scene may have meant to Daniel: 'In a new way, Daniel, who had so often dared to stand alone, must have realized, "I am not alone." Myriads of others served the Lord with him. He was an earthly outpost of the heavenly garrison.'

also 18 [twice], 22, 23 [twice], 24, 27 [4 times] for 'kingdom'/*malkû;* this picks up the keynote of Daniel 4.[13]

What are we to make of this figure? He seems to stand in contrast to the first three *beasts*: they are *like a lion, like a bear, like a leopard* (4, 5, 6) while he is *like a son of man,* a human likeness over against beastly ones. Further, all four beasts come up out of the roiling sea (3). He is from another world. This implies he is a *divine* figure. J. A. Emerton is frequently cited:

The act of coming with clouds suggests a theophany of Yahweh himself. If Dan. vii.13 does not refer to a divine being, then it is the only exception out of about seventy passages in the O.T.[14]

Moreover, verse 14 asserts that *all peoples, nations, and languages* are to *serve* him. The Aramaic verb is *pĕlaḥ,* used nine times in the book of Daniel (3:12, 14, 17, 18, 28; 6:16, 20; 7:14, 27) and always of 'serving' or paying reverence to deity or a purported deity.[15] Hence NIV rightly renders the verb as 'worship' here – which indicates we are dealing with an *individual* figure here and that *one like a son of man* is not merely verbiage referring to a corporate entity like the saints of the Most High (cf. 22, 27).

He is also a *royal* figure. If he is given and has a kingdom (14), he must obviously be a king. If he, to some degree, stands in opposition to four beasts who were *four kings* (17; perhaps viewed as founding monarchs of their respective kingdoms), then he must be a king as well.[16] If the ten horns of the fourth beast are kings, and the little horn as well (24), then surely the *one like a son of man* must be at least as much.

Jesus had no qualms about confessing his own identity from Daniel 7. When the high priest illegally placed Jesus under oath and demanded he declare if he were 'the Messiah, the son of the Blessed One', Jesus replied: 'I am, and you [plural = Caiaphas and his cronies]

[13] See 'How is it packaged?', Introduction, pp. 22–24.

[14] Cited in Collins, p. 290. Note a sample of texts in which cloud(s) are associated with the presence and/or coming of God: Exod. 16:10; 19:9; 24:16; 34:5; Num. 11:25; Pss. 97:2; 104:3; Isa. 19:1; Nah. 1:3. Cf. E. J. Young, 'Daniel's Vision of the Son of Man', in John H. Skilton (ed.), *The Law and the Prophets* (Phillipsburg: Presbyterian and Reformed, 1974), pp. 434, 444.

[15] Against Montgomery, 7:27 is not an exception. A number of versions (e.g., ESV) translate 27b 'their kingdom . . . and all dominions shall serve [*pĕlaḥ*] and obey them'. The pronouns are singular, however: 'his' and 'him'. ESV and others take 'people' (the people who are the 'saints') as the antecedent of these singular pronouns and so in translating render the singular pronouns as 'their'/'them'. Nothing wrong with that as such, except that 'Most High' is a nearer antecedent and the singular pronouns more naturally refer to him. Cf. Miller, p. 217n.

[16] Cf. Young, 'Daniel's Vision', p. 449.

will see the Son of Man, sitting at the right hand of Power and coming with the clouds of heaven.'[17] Jesus' reply combines the witness of Psalm 110:1 and Daniel 7:13–14; the 'sitting' of Psalm 110 refers to his ruling and waiting; the 'coming' of Daniel 7 to his arrival as judge. Incredible as it seems, the time will come when Caiaphas and company will see the Son of Man not as a prisoner in their dock but as judge at his assize.

I want to come back to the function of verses 9–14 in their context. They seem designed to hearten the beleaguered people of God. The fourth beast and little horn are no more than introduced (7–8) when we meet the swift shift of verses 9–14. There's much more to tell of the fourth beast and little horn (cf. 19–27), but the text insists we forget about that for the present and focus on the Ancient of Days and the Son of Man, who will easily dispose of the little horn in his time. The text is saying to you: 'Here, you must see this scene [9–14] behind the "seen" [7–8]: the majestic Judge [9–10] and reigning King [13–14] have mortgaged none of their sovereignty over history and its scourges.' Seeing this secret behind history may not keep God's people from pain but should keep them from panic; we may still be fearful but should not be frantic.

A rough analogy may help us appreciate this point. During World War II the Germans were quite confident of the unbreakability of their Enigma code. But British mathematicians and scientists cracked it with their own Ultra system. Then they had to keep secret about how they knew German secrets. But what a boon it was! For example, in March 1941 Ultra decoded plans of the German Luftwaffe and the Italian navy to assault British convoys in the Mediterranean. British ships set out from Alexandria, Egypt, to meet the threat. To keep the Germans from thinking the Brits had cracked an Enigma transmission, the Royal Navy commander sent out a Sunderland flying boat on a reconnaissance; it was within sight of the Italian fleet so that the latter surmised the Brits had accidentally 'discovered' their location. The British then essentially blew the Italian fleet to bits and sent the remnants packing back to Naples.[18] Just because the British had Ultra did not mean they could forget the war. But it had to be a real morale booster for England's leadership that they could know what was going to happen ahead of time. That is the effect verses 9–14 should have on God's servants. They say to hard-pressed saints, 'Here's what is going to happen – heaven's kingship is firm; it may not eliminate suffering, but it will give sanity.'

[17] Mark 14:62.
[18] William B. Breuer, *Secret Weapons of World War II* (Edison: Castle Books, 2005), pp. 63–64.

3. Coming test: the final conflict of suffering (15–28)

This segment is an expansion of the vision given so far. Or, one might say the vision is still in progress and Daniel takes the opportunity to interrogate one of the visionary bystanders (16a), who in turn gives a concise (17–18) and then expanded (23–27) explanation. It may help to set out the passage visually:

Daniel's distress (15)
　Request for clarity (16a)
　Summary explanation (16b–18)

　Desire about details (19–20)
　Additional vision report (21–22)
　Detailed explanation (23–27)
Daniel's distress (28)

The passage strikes three keynotes which we can dub clarity (16b–18), severity (19–25) and victory (26–27).

Verses 17–18 then are a basic explanation of the vision. So we have no excuse for claiming we don't know what the vision means. If one is fuzzy about details, we at least know this much. The *four great beasts are four kings* (17)[19] and the *saints of the Most High* will both *receive the kingdom and possess [it] forever* (18).[20] That is the gist of it. This may be apocalyptic, but that's reasonably clear. Can't read verses 17–18 and say we don't know what Daniel's vision is about.

Having said that, there is something unclear in all this clarity. There is dispute over who are the *holy ones* [traditionally, *saints*] *of the Most High* (18a). Some hold they are heavenly beings not earthly people, angels and not believers.[21] I take the term as referring to God's faithful people on earth, at this point the faithful in Israel. Verse 25 relates that the little horn will *wear down the holy ones of the Most High and will seek to change times and law*. If, as Montgomery holds, the *times* were the 'calendar feasts of the church', one has a hard time imagining what direct relevance that would have to angels (if they are the *holy ones*). Moreover, in verse 27 we have a

---

[19] As noted before, perhaps the four kings are viewed as founding monarchs of the kingdoms. In any case, verse 23 shows that the beasts also represent kingdoms as well as kings.

[20] The Aramaic in verse 18 actually says they will possess the kingdom 'to forever and to the forever of forevers'. Such emphasis obviously shows the writer really does mean *forever*.

[21] Both Collins (pp. 312–318, pro-angels) and Steinmann (pp. 366–370, pro-people of God) have extensive discussions.

reference to the *people of the holy ones* [or, saints] *of the Most High.*
Angel advocates hold that this could mean the people who 'belong
to' or are 'associated with' the holy ones/angels. But as Steinmann
notes,[22] the traditional text at least has a disjunctive accent on the
word *people*, which indicates that those who passed down the text
took *holy ones* as in apposition to 'people': *to the people, [that is,]
the holy ones of the Most High.* These *holy ones* are God's believing
people living on earth.

Verses 19–25 highlight the 'severity' theme. Daniel's curiosity
fastens on the fourth beast (19), the *ten horns on its head* (20a), and
the *other horn*, the 'little' one, with eyes and mouth (20b).[23] He then
inserts a new bit of his vision; we may have surmised it but did not
explicitly know it: he saw the little horn making war on the saints
and overpowering them (21).

Daniel's interpreter than expands on the fourth beast-kingdom
(23–25). He says it will exercise *worldwide domination: it will devour
all the earth and trample it down and smash it to pieces* (23b). Its
savagery will be universal. Yet this regime will suffer *internal fragmentation: ten kings will arise, and another will arise after them . . .
and he will put down three kings* (24). Evil can never manufacture
enough glue to keep itself together; it has no lasting cohesion, the
dissension always seems to surface. The iron and clay (2:41–43) just
can't seem to bond.[24] The evil regime may crush with vicious power,
but that power always seems to have cracks in it. Then, at least in its
little-horn-phase, this kingdom will inflict *hate-driven persecution*
on the people of God: he *will wear down the saints of the Most High*
(25a), something which verse 21 has already prepared us to hear. This
persecution strangely and comfortingly and ultimately rests in God's
decision, for the saints are *given* into the little horn's hand (25b),
meaning 'given by God' (see Rev. 13:5, 7, 15, NASB). They are so *given*
for *a time, times, and half a time*, which may indicate a definitely

---

[22] P. 369.

[23] Some see a kind of three-stage history of the fourth kingdom in these three
components; see Young, pp. 148–149, but especially Olyott, pp. 95–96, for a lucid
and satisfying exposition. Stephen Miller also reminds us that 'the little horn' did not
remain 'little': '"Little" refers to the horn's size at the beginning. That it grew is
indicated by the expression "came up" [v. 8], and its increase in size beyond the
original ten horns may be assumed by the fact that it overpowered ("uprooted") three
of them and by the statement in v. 20 that it "looked more imposing than the others"
[NIV]' (p. 202).

[24] See Rev. 17:16 for a picture of this. There are scads of historical instances. Think
of the 1939 non-aggression pact between Hitler and Stalin; yet by 1941 not only was
Hitler going to attack the USSR, but – if some historical sleuths are to be believed –
the Soviets were already planning to attack German troops; cf. Edvard Radzinsky,
Stalin (New York: Anchor Books, 1997), pp. 452–456.

limited and perhaps relatively brief period – from a Lord who delights to 'shorten the days' (cf. Mark 13:20).

Victory then follows (26–27). Dominion, glory and a kingdom were given to one *like a son of man* (14), so what would be more natural and proper than that *the kingdom and the dominion and the greatness of the kingdom under the whole heaven* (ESV) should be given to the people, to the saints of the Most High?[25] So the servants have no kingdom apart from their King, and the King does not reign without his servants. Jesus just cannot stand being separated from his people.

What then is 'the little horn' of Daniel 7? It seems to me that Daniel's vision presents him as the last leader of earth's final kingdom. Would this matter to 500s BC Israelites? I think so. The 'beast' vision with its emphasis on 'No. 4' would tell them that their trauma will not cease when Babylon falls or Persia allows them to return to Israel. Indeed, time will come when a future regime and ruler will make Nebuchadnezzar and Cyrus look like kindergarten truant officers. It's no wonder Daniel's thoughts terrified him (28). In my view, the one Daniel calls the little horn here in chapter 7 is the one Paul calls the 'man of lawlessness' in 2 Thessalonians 2:1–12 and whom John would call the Antichrist (1 John 2:18). Jesus will handle him (2 Thess. 2:8). But before this final conflict of suffering, even now across the world, various little-horn-types mash and mangle Jesus' people. And how can they endure? What keeps them from caving in?

I like the story Faith Cook tells of Ruth Clark, the housekeeper and cook for Vicar Henry Venn (d. 1797) and his household. Ruth was converted during her years of service with the Venns. After Henry Venn's death, his married children provided and cared for her. Declining health and then being hit by a speeding horse and carriage brought Ruth near her end. One of the Venn daughters asked Ruth whether she had any doubts as earthly life was coming to a close. Ruth confessed she had 'no rapturous feelings' but still no fears or doubts, and then she explained: 'He that has loved me all my life through will not forsake me now.'[26] Must that not always be our assurance: that the Lord who has made us his people will surely keep us through the worst we have to face? Or, as Walter Luthi put it:

> But we know of the Son of Man, who is at the same time the Head and Shepherd of the fellowship. The shepherd sees the lion coming, and the bear, and the leopard, and the Fourth Beast, and does not flee.[27]

[25] See J. A. Motyer, 'Messiah', *New Bible Dictionary*, 3rd ed., p. 759.
[26] Faith Cook, *Lives Turned Upside Down* (Darlington: Evangelical Press, 2003), pp. 119–128.
[27] Luthi, p. 104.

Daniel 8:1–27
8. Why is a two-bit king so all-fired important?

In one of Charles Schulz's 'Peanuts' cartoons Linus informs Lucy: 'When Juliet asks, "O Romeo, Romeo, wherefore art thou Romeo?" she is not wondering where he is; rather, she is commenting on the fact of his being named Romeo!' Lucy, with a hopelessly baffled look, then asks herself: 'Now that I know that, what do I do?' She apparently did not consider that a particularly vital piece of information. A reader might feel the same about Daniel 8. Here Daniel foretells the rise of a relatively obscure king from a split-off of the Greek empire who will cause havoc for Israel. But why bother to spill a chapter's worth of ink on that? The overall break-down of the chapter is rather straightforward; it tells of Daniel's vision:

Setting (1–2)
Contents (3–14)
Interpretation (15–26)
Impact (27).

But the question remains – why all the fuss over a relatively obscure king? The implied response Daniel 8 gives is that *it's important for God's people to know and prepare for what they will have to face*, not only near the end (ch. 7) but also along the way (this chapter). It seems to me that the message of the chapter orbits around two basic contentions the text suggests.

1. God steadies his people to walk through the course of history (1–8, 20–23)

Daniel's vision came about 550 BC (the third year of Belshazzar, v. 1; some would prefer 547), two years after the vision of chapter 7 (7:1).

The more natural reading of verse 2 does not understand that Daniel actually *was* in Susa but that in his vision he *saw* himself there, by the Ulai canal.[1] Susa (= Shushan) was 220 miles east of Babylon, 150 miles north of the Persian Gulf (in what is today southwestern Iran).[2]

We can summarize the first part of Daniel's vision with the help of the 'glossary' of verses 20–23. The *ram* signifies *the kings of Media and Persia* (20). Its *two horns* evidently come up in sequence, the latter one higher than the other, suggesting Persian dominance. This ram is conquering and unconquerable (4) – until the Greek *goat* ploughs into the Persian ram, smashing and mashing it (5–7, 21). The goat operates in blitzkrieg style, so fast that he doesn't touch the ground (5). The *huge horn* (5, 21) symbolizes the first king of the goat-empire, who proves to be Alexander the Great. But he receives no tenure – he is *broken* (d. 323 BC) and his empire gets parcelled out to four other *horns* (8, 22), just as, after twenty years of turmoil, four of Alexander's generals dominate a segment of his kingdom: Cassander over Macedonia and Greece, Lysimachus over Thrace and Asia Minor, Seleucus over Syria and Mesopotamia, and Ptolemy in Egypt.

Some observations. Notice that Daniel's vision depicts *a turbulent and extended time of history*. Think of verse 4 (the dominance of the ram). Joyce Baldwin says that 'nearly two hundred years of history and political aggrandisement' are summed up in that verse.[3] Of course, Daniel could not have known at that time how much chronology was scrunched into that vision. But surely he realized that in one empire battering another into oblivion and that empire in turn disintegrating into chunks of its former greatness meant he was looking at quite a sequence of years. Moreover, this segment of history is anything but peaceful and calm. These are times of conquest and upheaval and demise. Nations seem to be both furious and fragile. And this is where the people of God have to live; this history is their address.

Daniel's vision also portrays *an instructive and humbling history*.

---

[1] A lot of 'seeing' goes on; in 1–3a the verb *rā'â* (we are back to Hebrew in chs. 8 – 12) occurs six times (translated 'appeared', 'saw').

[2] See Pierre de Miroschedji, 'Susa', ABD, 6:243–244, for the strategic position of Susa in the Persian period. Here, still under the Babylonian regime, Daniel speaks of Susa 'in the province of Elam', which as Gleason Archer (p. 19) explains, may be one of those fascinating fingerprints left by a sixth-century BC writer: 'From the Greek and Roman historians, we learn that from Persian times Susa, or Shushan, was the capital of the province of Susiana; and Elam was restricted to the territory east of the Eulaeus River. Nevertheless we now know from cuneiform records that Shushan [Susa] was part of the territory of Elam back in Chaldean times and before. It is very striking that Daniel 8:2 refers to "Susa in the province of Elam" – an item of information scarcely available to a second-century B.C. author.'

[3] Baldwin, p. 156.

Reading verse 4 gives us the impression that the Persian ram is impervious and untouchable. So we are shocked when we see the king of the hill become street dirt (7). That won't happen to the goat kingdom, at least not in the same way. It's just that great horns are mortal (8) – so a ruler can die and the whole enterprise fall apart. The text implies that superpowers are not really safe places. They may get knocked off or simply peter out. They are such tenuous affairs. One can get a micro-cosmic taste of this in the aftermath of the Nuremberg trials in 1946. After the executions of Nazi celebrities on 16 October, fourteen bodies, including those of Goering (who had 'cheated' by managing suicide), Ribbentrop, Keitel, Rosenberg, Frank, Streicher, Jodl and Seyss-Inquart, were delivered to a Munich crematorium. That same evening a container holding the amassed ashes was driven through the rain into the Bavarian countryside. After an hour's drive the vehicle stopped and the ashes were poured into a muddy ditch.[4] Five or six years before, these men could dominate and intimidate. That night a drizzle washed them away.

This sort of history, then, *calls for a sober and durable discipleship.* Here is Daniel, in Babylon, aware that the seventy years of Israel's exile are coming closer to a close (see 9:1–2), and yet there is this vision of Persian and Greek empires and split-offs from the latter. So it becomes clear that when the years of exile cease and Israel is back in *the glorious land* (9), they will have to plod through a long stretch of this troubled stuff we call history. Getting back to the land will not mean that the kingdom of God will immediately appear. John Walton has put it well:

> In the meantime the Israelites were to live out their faith in a Gentile world under circumstances that would make it more and more difficult to do so. They had to count on the sovereignty of God to sustain them generation by generation, crisis by crisis. They also had to trust the power of God to control the flow of world empires as they rose and fell. God's agenda is never in jeopardy; nevertheless, they were to be prepared for the long term.[5]

Even Christ's people today are not exactly thrilled over that word. We tend to prefer a quick-fix approach rather than the long view of discipleship. Not only Daniel 8 but Jesus himself has taught us better. He said we will 'hear of wars and rumours of wars', that 'nation will rise against nation, and kingdom against kingdom'; but these are not

[4] Anthony Read, *The Devil's Disciples: Hitler's Inner Circle* (New York: W. W. Norton, 2003), pp. 922–923.
[5] Andrew E. Hill and John H. Walton, *A Survey of the Old Testament* (Grand Rapids: Zondervan, ³2009), p. 573.

the sign of the end,[6] they are simply the way things will be in the present age. And it is in and through these bumps and jumps and lumps of history that we are to prove faithful.

2. God forearms his people to face the crises of history (9–19, 23–26)

a. The locus of the focus

I 'interrupted' Daniel's vision in order to deal with the import of the first part of it, but it continues in verses 9–19, with its focus on *a single horn* that *comes forth from littleness* (9), a king (in view of v. 8) who will rise from small or obscure beginnings. That soon changes; the verb root 'to be great' (*gādal*) occurs once of Persia (4), once of Greece (8), but four times of this *horn* (9, 10, 11, 25). Whether translated 'be/become great' or 'make oneself great', the 'great' verb reeks of arrogance.[7] In that arrogance he opposes God (*the prince of the host*, 11), eradicates God's worship (11b–12),[8] and crushes God's people (10, 12a).[9] Interestingly, Daniel, as an exile in Babylon, might find a little back-handed encouragement in this vision: he was seeing a future situation in which Israel *was* back in the land and worshiping at God's (re-built) sanctuary. But there was the downside and the mystery: the horn *will throw truth to the earth and shall act and succeed* (12b). Why do tyrants get to walk all over God's people?

---

[6] Mark 13:7–8.

[7] See Steinmann, p. 394, for discussion.

[8] 'The regular offering [*tāmîd*] was suspended' (v. 11, NJPS). The *tāmîd* was the 'burnt offering' of a lamb sacrificed morning and twilight daily (see Exod. 29:38–42; Num. 28:3–8). Some commentators see a part-for-the-whole pattern here: the fate of the *tāmîd* signals the abolishment of the whole God-ordained system of worship.

[9] The 'host' the horn assaults in v. 10 (some of which it throws down and tramples) is clearly a heavenly host/army, yet vv. 12a and 13b seem to indicate a very earthly 'host', the people of God, which v. 24 seems to confirm. Perhaps the 'host' of v. 10 consists of celestial counterparts of the earthly host of vv. 12 and 13. Cf. Goldingay (p. 221): 'Antiochus was not literally fighting angels; rather, that was the significance of his attack on people and sanctuary. The visible realities such as the Jewish people and the Jerusalem temple had a transcendent significance that Antiochus denied. When believers are hurt, heaven is hurt.' Verse 12a is a bit of a conundrum: 'and a host will be given (up) along with the regular offering on account of transgression/rebellion'. One can find a raft of differing renderings. Whose 'transgression' or rebellion is meant? Some (e.g., Duguid, Miller, Keil) think Israel's, others (e.g., Fyall, Collins) the little horn's. I lean to the latter on the strength of v. 13, where the 'transgression' making desolate clearly refers to the imposition of the little horn's bastard liturgy.

b. How long?

But the 'why' question is not in the text. Instead, the question is 'How long?' One angel asks of another, *For how long is the vision of the regular sacrifice and the transgression that desolates, the giving over of both sanctuary and host to be trampled?* (13). The answer comes: *For 2,300 evening-mornings, then the sanctuary will be put right* (14). Don't become so mesmerized with the 2,300 figure that you miss an important point. 'How long?' is the cry of desperation one hears from Yahweh's servants in the Psalter.[10] Only here in Daniel the cry comes from an angel. It is almost as if heaven's legions enter sympathetically into the anguish and duress of God's earthly people.

But what *are* we to make of the 2,300 evening-mornings? They are commonly taken in one of two ways. Since the regular offering was offered up twice each day, morning and evening, some take the figure as denoting 2,300 sacrifices on 1,150 days. Others hold that verse 14 is referring to 2,300 evening-morning units and so do not halve the number. The former number reduces to roughly three years and two months, the latter to six years and four months. Assuming the vision describes Antiochus IV's (more on him shortly) scourge of Israel, one finds difficulty fitting these possible time blocks into his time in any precise way. Antiochus set up an altar to Zeus in the temple in December 167 BC; the temple was cleansed and re-dedicated under Judas Maccabeus in December 164. If one focuses on the matter of temple worship the 1,150 view fits better (legitimate sacrifices might have been prohibited before the pagan altar was erected). However, if one focuses on the total persecution under Antiochus, say from the murder of Onias III, the legitimate high priest, in 171/170 BC, until the re-consecration of the temple in 164, then the 2,300 view works better.[11] Read Andrew Steinmann, and he'll convince you of the 1,150 view; read Stephen Miller, and he'll convince you of the 2,300 view. If I were held at gunpoint and told to make a decision, I would opt for the 2,300 position. But it's difficult, even without the gun. In any case, the 2,300 figure tells us this is a rather *long* period, yet the fact that it is calculated in days means it is a definitely *limited* one.

c. What sort of 'end'?

At verse 15 we leave the vision itself and move into its interpretation. Daniel was seeking to understand what he'd seen (15), and God

[10] E.g., Pss. 6:3; 74:10; 80:4; 94:3.

[11] Some would see the number 'as a figurative representation of a significant but limited period of suffering on the part of the people of God' (Duguid, p. 132; see also Harman, p. 197).

graciously provided an interpreter and interpretation of the vision
(16–18). The interpretation (19–26) helps immensely, although we
do have our questions about interpreting the interpretation! Before
we move on to the fulfilment and function of the vision, I want to
touch on one of these questions.

Daniel not only knew the perplexity of trying to understand (15)
but also endured the terror of meeting the heavenly interpreter
(17–18). We calmly stand at our desks or sit in our chairs and read
the text but Daniel is devastated over receiving the revelation (27).
Who can tell what this cost Daniel? However, the first point the
interpreter presses on Daniel is that the vision is *for the time of
the end* (17). What is the *end*? We should not easily assume this refers
to matters in connection with the second coming of Christ. The *end*
in this context seems related to the *how long?* question in verse 13,
the end of the oppression spoken of in verses 13–14. The phrases
in verse 19 appear to carry similar freight. The word *indignation* (in
the latter end of the indignation, 19a) is *zā'am*, a noun used twenty-
two times in the Old Testament, always but once of Yahweh's anger.[12]
Some see Israel as the object of this *indignation*, but it makes more
sense in the context to take it as Yahweh's indignation against Persia
and Greece and the latter's later Syrian satellite ruled by a slick and
godless piece of scum called Antiochus. At the latter time of the
indignation he would meet his end and be disposed of *by no human
hand* (25).

d. A brief bio and more

If this vision reached its fulfilment in the career of Antiochus IV
(Epiphanes), what did the fulfilment look like? We should provide
some historical filler.

After the death of Alexander the Great, Judah came under Egyptian
(Ptolemaic) control for roughly a century (ca. 300–200 BC). That
changed in 198 when Antiochus III (the Great) shattered the
Egyptians at Baniyas and Palestine passed into Seleucid (Syrian)
hands. Antiochus III for all his success was humiliated by the
Romans in 190 at Magnesia and met his end shortly afterwards in
187. By 175 Antiochus IV had wormed his way into power.[13]

---

[12] John R. Kohlenberger III and James A. Swanson, *The Hebrew-English
Concordance to the Old Testament* (Grand Rapids: Zondervan, 1998), p. 496. The
one exception is Hos. 7:16.

[13] For this background, see the lucid discussions in John Bright, *A History of Israel*
(Philadelphia: Westminster, ³1981), pp. 412–423; Emil Schürer, *The History of the
Jewish People in the Age of Jesus Christ (175 B.C.-A.D. 135)*, rev. and ed. G. Vermes
and F. Millar, 3 vols. (Edinburgh: T&T Clark, 1973), 1:138–163.

Psycho-history, of course, can be a perilous enterprise, but Antiochus was, apparently, a bit quirky, able to slide easily on the scale from warmly gregarious to terribly tyrannical. On his coins he placed the self-descriptive logo 'Epiphanes' (which was an abbreviation for 'god manifest/revealed' – the god in question being Olympian Zeus); some, however, opined that 'Epimanes' ('Madman') would have been more accurate. Antiochus IV seems to have been an able soldier and administrator, but he was always strapped for cash, primarily because he was always fighting wars and owing tribute to Rome, both very expensive propositions. Like a suave politician, Antiochus never met a substantial contributor he didn't like. His need to be a perennial fund-raiser partly explains his behaviour toward Jerusalem in 169 BC.

Antiochus had invaded Egypt at that time and on his way home he came to Jerusalem, where his lackey Menelaus (the highest bidder for the high priesthood) handed over a horde of temple treasures (including sacred furniture) to him (1 Macc. 1:20–23), so that he carted off, so it was said, 1,800 talents (2 Macc. 5:15–16, 21). This was only the half of it. For while Antiochus had still been in Egypt, Jason, a previously ousted high priest and Menelaus' rival, suddenly attacked Jerusalem but with only temporary success. Antiochus, however, saw this as a revolt – hence on his 169 visit he looted the temple but also carried out a horrific blood bath.[14]

Worse was on its way. The next year Antiochus invaded Egypt again. His success was frustrated by the appearance of the Roman general Popillius Laenas, who told Antiochus he could finish his Egyptian conquest if he also wanted to fight Rome. Otherwise, he should go home. And he must make up his mind on the spot. It may be that Rome's bullying stirred up Antiochus' rage against Jerusalem (cf. Dan. 11:30). However, what Antiochus did matters more than why he did it. In 167 BC he sent his chief tax collector, Apollonius, to Jerusalem, and pillage, massacre and ruin were the orders of the day (see 1 Macc. 1:29–40). Now Antiochus insisted on a forced paganization programme,[15] meant to corrupt and decimate every aspect of Israel's faith and practice. This scheme called for

the abolition of the Temple cult and of the observance of the Law, and the substitution of pagan cults. The observance of all Jewish

---

[14] According to 2 Macc. 5:14, a total of 80,000 were destroyed in three days, half in fighting, the other half sold into slavery. The figures are likely exaggerations but yet exaggerations that underscore the terrible extremity.

[15] There had already been a 'hellenization' process going on in Jerusalem, a gradual and increasing importing of pagan culture and practice. A number in Israel, eager to 'chummy' with the ruling power, welcomed such developments; it relieved them of the burden of standing firm for their ancestral faith.

ordinances, in particular those relating to the Sabbath and circumcision, was prohibited on pain of death. In every town in Judaea sacrifice was to be offered to the heathen gods. Overseers were sent everywhere to see that the royal command was carried out. Where the people did not comply willingly, they were obliged to do so by force. Once a month a check was made, and whoever was found with a scroll of the Torah or had had a child circumcised, was put to death. On 15 Kislev of . . . December 167 B.C., a heathen altar was built in Jerusalem on the great altar of burnt-offering, and on 25 Kislev the first heathen sacrifice was offered on it.[16]

That sacrifice was offered to Olympian Zeus, to whom the Jerusalem temple had been dedicated. A little taste of Antichrist ahead of time.[17]

e. Why all the fuss?

But is it really necessary to spill all this ink and pay all this attention to someone who is really a minor character on the roster of history? The answer is that he was not so minor. That is the point Robert Dick Wilson pressed years ago.[18] Wilson said that God's people had never before faced what they met under Antiochus – a systematic programme designed to eradicate completely every trace of Israel's faith, worship and life. Hence the extreme emergency justified the detailed prediction. The day would come when Israel would need this revelation. That is the assumption of verse 26: Daniel is to *close up* the vision, to keep and preserve it, for it will have relevance for *many days* down the timeline.[19] Is it not the kindness of the Lord to prepare his people for the extreme trouble they will have to endure?

The principle is easy to grasp. Not long ago I was walking down the hallway in our home that leads to our bedroom. On my way I passed the doorway to the guest bedroom. Unbeknownst to me, my wife had hidden inside that door and with her 'Boo!' scared the wits out of me as I went by. (Is she trying to collect life insurance proceeds?) But what if I happen to see her duck into that room unknown to *her*? Then I walk down the hall with two options. I can walk by the door, as if unsuspecting, and remain unmoved when she

---

[16] Schürer, 1:155. See 1 Macc. 1:41–64; 2 Macc. 6:1–11.

[17] The verb *šāḥat* (ruin, destroy) occurs three times in vv. 24–25, depicting this king's activity. NKJV renders: 'he shall destroy fearfully' (24b); 'he shall destroy the mighty and also the holy people' (24d); 'he shall destroy many in their prosperity' (25c). Destruction is the hallmark of his rule.

[18] See Introduction and the section, 'When was it published?', pp. 15–22.

[19] Those who date Daniel in the second century and in the Antiochus-crises (167–165 BC) have to view v. 26 as a bit of a cover-up, a second-century writer making it appear that his current production is an earlier prophetic revelation.

'boos' (which deprives her of pleasure) or I can suddenly jump in front of that door and scare her (which gives me pleasure). But the fact that I know what awaits me makes all the difference. So the *little horn* revelation should settle and steel Israel when the *many days* arrive.[20]

Jesus extends the very same kindness to his servants. Check his words in John 16:1–4a. Jesus has just been speaking of the hatred the world has both for him and for his disciples. 'These things [in 15:18–27] I have spoken to you in order that you not fall away.' He gives samples of the hatred they will face: they will be 'de-synagogued' and religious bigots will be sure they are expressing devotion to God by executing them. And so Jesus explains: 'But these things I have spoken to you in order that when their hour comes, you might remember them, that I [emphatic] told you [about them].' Jesus hides nothing in fine print; he buries nothing in obscure footnotes. In faithful candour he forewarns us and so fore-arms us. Not to do so would be cruelty rather than love. In late April 1942, sixteen US B-25 bombers, under the command of Lieutenant Colonel James Doolittle, carried out a raid on Tokyo. It inflicted little substantial property damage. But the people in Tokyo nearly panicked. They had been assured no US bomb would ever strike the home islands.[21]

The God of the Bible, however, does not operate like Japanese war propaganda. That's why Israel's knowing about a two-bit king is so all-fired important. We might say John 16:1 sums up the purpose of Daniel 8.

[20] Calvin (2:95–96) nicely catches this 'forewarning' function of Daniel's vision; e.g., 'For if nothing had been predicted, the pious would have glided gently downwards to despair in consequence of their heavy afflictions'; and: 'If this had not been predicted, they would have thought themselves deceived by the splendid promises concerning their return. But when they perceived everything occurring according as they had been opportunely forewarned, this became no slight solace in the midst of their woes.'

[21] William B. Breuer, *Secret Weapons of World War II* (Edison: Castle Books, 2005), p. 113.

Daniel 9:1–19
9. A tutorial in prayer

Leon Morris told how at one stretch of his life Howard Hughes would eat two scoops of banana nut ice cream at every meal. Then, one day, out of the blue, he switched to French vanilla. The effect in the latter part of Daniel is a bit like that, if not as extreme. The reader has become accustomed to visions in chapter 7 and chapter 8 (and will face one in ch. 9 as well – see v. 23), but the routine abruptly changes in 9:1–4: instead of another vision we have run into a Bible study and prayer session. And the prayer is fairly extensive; Daniel takes the time to spread it on the record in verses 4–19. He must have a reason for doing so (more on this later). The fact that he 'writes it out' invites us to ponder it and use it as an instruction piece for our own practice of prayer.

1. The immediate stimulus to prayer (1–3)

The date Daniel gives is very significant – *the first year of Darius, son of Ahasuerus*, for it means that there has been regime change and that Babylon has fallen.[1] This historical circumstance meshed with the prophetic assurances of Jeremiah. Daniel has been reading in the scrolls of Jeremiah's prophecy (in what would be Jer. 25:11–12 and 29:10–11 in our text) and notes that *seventy years* is the period allotted for both Babylon's domination and Jerusalem's desolations.[2]

[1] On the identity of this Darius, see note 30, ch. 5. 'Ahasuerus' need not refer to the later Xerxes I (485–465 BC) but may be a royal title or dynastic name (cf. D. J. Wiseman in *Notes on Some Problems in the Book of Daniel* [London: Tyndale, 1965], p. 15).
[2] There is no unanimity on calculating the seventy years. In the book of Daniel itself it makes most sense to me to begin the period with the big Babylonian 'moment' in 1:1–2, Nebuchadnezzar's ascendancy and his carting off the first wave of exiles (Daniel & Co.) in 605 BC; Darius' first year (9:1) would be 538. This covers sixty-seven or so years, which seems pretty close.

Daniel is not mystified or baffled by Jeremiah's prophecies;[3] he is stirred by them, for if Babylon's hegemony is at an end, Jerusalem's restoration is about to begin. Yahweh's word was: 'When the seventy years granted to Babylon are over, I shall intervene on your behalf and fulfil my favourable promise to you by bringing you back to this place';[4] and Daniel's response was: *So I set my face toward the Lord God to seek (him) by prayer and pleas for grace, with fasting and sackcloth and ashes* (3), as he begged for Jerusalem's restoration (16–19). It's quite simple: the Lord's promises drive his servant's prayer. It's as if God's promises have Velcro on them and our prayers are meant to 'get stuck' there.

In practice this promise-to-prayer pattern means Christians should let the Bible become their prayer book. What if I am reading, for example, in Micah 4, of that marvellous description of Yahweh's kingdom in which converted nations are salivating over the word of God, and then I come to verse 4:

And they shall sit
– each man under his vine
and under his fig tree –
with no one terrifying them,
for the mouth of Yahweh of hosts has spoken.

The verse depicts the individual and secure enjoyment of the peace of Yahweh's kingdom. And it should goad me to prayer. Should I not think of Jesus' flock in Orissa state and elsewhere in India where they are burned out of house and home, or of Christian girls in Egypt and Pakistan who are abducted, raped, and forced into Islamic marriages, of believers beaten and bombed in Nigeria, of Christ's disciples shut up in prisons from Eritrea to China? And should I not pray for the fulfilment of Yahweh's promise in Micah 4:4 for the sake of his devastated people? Yet it is Yahweh's promise itself that triggers the prayer. Or when I happen on to Romans 11:23–24, ought it not incite me to pray that God would graft Israel into his people again, bringing them from unbelief to faith? Does that item often appear on my intercessory radar screen? And yet it may not be a promise as such that stirs prayer; it may be an assurance or a description. When one reads that assurance about Yahweh in Isaiah 33:6 ('and he will be the stability of your times') or that description of the exodus God in Isaiah 63:9 ('in all their affliction he was afflicted'), don't wavering and suffering believers come to mind? And don't you

---

[3] As Harman (p. 212) rightly points out.
[4] Jer. 29:10, NJB.

115

delight to ask that this God will show himself to them in his character
that is so suited to their need? It is the Daniel way. Let Scripture
drive your prayer.

2. The thoughtful adoration of prayer (4)

After setting the stage in verses 1–3, Daniel actually begins his prayer
in verse 4:

> *And I prayed to Yahweh my God, and I made confession and said,*
> *'Ah, O Lord, the great and fearful God, keeping covenant and*
> *faithful love for those who love him and are keepers of his*
> *commandments . . . '*

This is the address of the prayer and consists of a little piece of
adoration. Even when the main burden of prayer is confession of sin
and petition, this adoration is not missing. Sometimes Bible pray-ers
are under such pressure that they rush immediately to their burden
(cf. Ps. 3:1–2). But often there is an explicit address, whether brief
('Our Father in heaven')[5] or rather extended (e.g., Dan. 2:20–22). But
such an 'address' is perfectly right. We should stop to consider who
it is to whom we are speaking.

Traces of Daniel's phraseology both precede (Exod. 20:6; Deut.
7:9, 21) and follow (Neh. 1:5; 9:32) Daniel. Deuteronomy 7 contains
both components of Daniel's ascription: Yahweh is 'in your midst,
a great and fearful God' and he is the one who 'keeps covenant and
faithful love to those who love him and keep his commandments'.[6]
This God then is both fearful and faithful (keeps covenant, etc.); he
is both great and good, both one who makes us tremble and one who
keeps us secure. Daniel teaches us how to adore and to rejoice over
God, to do so briefly but genuinely – and this is something we can
do in our prayers in spite of circumstances or feelings, simply because
God is who or what he is and that does not change despite the mess
I may be in.

When Lyndon Johnson was US vice-president during the Kennedy
administration, Russell Baker was working for the *New York Times*
covering Capitol Hill. Early in 1961 Baker was coming out of the
Senate when he ran into the Vice-President. Johnson grabbed him.
'*You*,' he cried, 'I've been looking for *you*.' He pulled Baker into his
office and began a long harangue on how crucial he was to the
Kennedy administration and what an insider he was. While Johnson

[5] Matt. 6:9.
[6] Deut. 7:21, 9.

bludgeoned on, he scribbled something on a slip of paper and rang the buzzer. His secretary came in and exited with the paper. She returned a few minutes later and handed the paper to LBJ. Still talking, Johnson looked at the paper, crumbled it up, threw it away and finished his speech. Later Baker tracked down what it was Johnson had written on the paper: 'Who is this I'm talking to?'[7] That should not be the case with our prayers. Do you know to whom you are speaking? And are there times when you are tempted to set the list of petitions aside and simply go on with the adoration?

3. The sad content of prayer (5–14)

The prayer is sad because it is a prayer of confession and Daniel is awash in Israel's sin. I think a quick walk-through of this section of the prayer will be the best way to get a handle on Daniel's chief concerns.

Daniel begins by speaking of *gross guilt* (5–6), guilt apparent in Israel's doings (*we have sinned* [also in 8, 11, 15] *and done wrong and acted wickedly*, 5a), defiance (*and rebelled*, 5b), defection (*turning away from your commandments and rules*, 5c), and deafness (*and we have not listened* [also in 10, 11, 14] *to your servants, the prophets . . .* , 6). Daniel then mourns the *obvious consequences* of such compounded guilt (7–8), especially the *clear shame* of these homeless waifs whom Yahweh has banished from covenant turf. And so their only hope is *abundant mercy* (9–10). In verse 7 Daniel had said, *To you, O Lord, belongs righteousness*, but now in verse 9 he says, *To the Lord our God belong compassions and forgivenesses*. The literal plurals sound a tad cumbersome but they refer to multiple, repeated acts of compassion and forgiveness. In short, he is 'rich in mercy'[8] and must be so if guilty people are to have any hope, *for we have rebelled against him* (9).[9]

Daniel, however, will not allow mental loitering on God's warm mercy but pushes us on to remember his *faithful anger* (11–13a). Israel, he confesses, *has stepped over your law* (11a), *so the curse and the oath written in the law of Moses . . . have been poured out upon us* (11b); God *put into effect his words, which he had spoken against us and against our rulers* (12) – *all this disaster has come upon us* (13a). The curse and the oath most likely refer to the 'covenant curses' of

---

[7] Paul F. Boller, Jr, *Presidential Anecdotes* (New York: Penguin Books, 1982), p. 317.
[8] Eph. 2:4.
[9] Some take the 'for' of verse 9b as 'though', which is permissible (e.g., NIV, NKJV); but 'for' is perhaps preferable, as long as it is not understood in a causal but in an explanatory way, i.e., showing 'not why God is merciful, but why there is need for His manifesting mercy' (Leupold, p. 386).

THE MESSAGE OF DANIEL

Leviticus 26:14–39 and Deuteronomy 28:15–68, where Yahweh spelled out in explicit, gory, scary and unnerving detail the multiple disasters he would inflict upon a people who turn away from him. Daniel's point is that Yahweh has been faithful in his anger; he *has* inflicted upon unfaithful Israel precisely what he said he would. We can forget this. We sing, 'Great Is Thy Faithfulness!' and forget there can be a dark side to that faithfulness (cf. Josh. 23:15–16). All of which brings us to the *great omission* (13b–14): *All this disaster has come upon us – and we have not entreated the favour of Yahweh our God, by turning from our iniquity and paying attention to your truth* (13b). Daniel seems to be saying that though Israel has gone through the ravages of God's curse, the people remain unchanged, unbroken, unrepentant. *Yahweh has superintended the disaster and brought it upon us . . . , but we have not listened to his voice* (14). On that futile note the 'confession' section of Daniel's prayer comes to an end.

That is a quick survey of Daniel's confession. I want to append two notes to it, one about inclusion and one about omission. By 'inclusion' I refer to the way Daniel grieves and mourns over Israel's guilt. Note that he does not foist blame on 'those people'. The pronouns are predominantly first person plural – we, our, us. Daniel includes himself in Israel's guilt.

By 'omission' I refer to what I called the 'great omission' in verse 13b. I want to touch on that in more detail. Here we meet the nagging matter that so distresses Daniel: Israel has a history of rebellion and idolatry and has suffered God's judgment for it *but it has not driven them to godly grief and genuine repentance.* What concerns him, it seems, is not so much the return to the land as the *people* who must return. What good will it do to have a people back in the land with still no sense of their sin and no exercise in repentance? Who have never been crushed in spirit over their idolatry? It's not Israel alone – humanity in general is averse to admitting sin and guilt.

Geoff Thomas tells of making a hospital visit to a lady who had broken her arm. After talking with her he went round to other people in the ward. One elderly lady there kept repeating 'I want to die'. So Pastor Thomas gave her the beginning of the good news wrapped in bad news. He said to her, 'Well, if you die, you know, you are going to meet God, and so you must start praying now if you are going to meet God. This is what you must pray: "God, be merciful to me, a sinner."' 'I'm not a sinner,' she shot back, and added, 'And if you knew me you'd know I wasn't.'[10] Someone like that can't even begin to scratch at the screen door of the kingdom of God.

But if you let Daniel teach you, you will know better. In fact, one

---

[10] Thomas, p. 93.

of the primary marks of a Christian is that he or she continually mourns over his or her sins. Herman Veldkamp puts it well:

> What distinguishes us from the world is not that we are less wicked but that by the grace of God we have learned to see our wickedness for what it is and that we confess our sins. The church is the only body on earth that confesses sin. Where the confession of sin dies out, the church is no longer church.[11]

You may think Veldkamp hyperbolic, but he is right. The Rotary Club does not engage in confession of sin; the city council doesn't do it; the United Nations doesn't confess its sins, nor do senates and parliaments. Only the church (when it's really 'church').

The prophet Ezekiel hammers home the same doctrine. In Ezekiel 36:22–32, where he gives a sketch of Yahweh's restored people, the prophet speaks of Yahweh cleansing them (36:25), giving them a new heart and a new spirit, giving them a heart of flesh in place of a heart of stone (36:26), of placing his Spirit within them (36:27). The assurances continue, and then we come on to verse 31: 'And you shall remember your evil ways and your doings which were not good, and you shall loathe yourselves because of your iniquities and because of your abominations.' You can go back over the passage and follow the flow of the grammar; Ezekiel's point is clear: loathing ourselves over our sins is a mark or evidence of having a new heart and a new spirit.[12] A new spirit will produce a *new sadness* that mourns and agonizes over sin, bringing about what the Puritans would call perpetual broken-heartedness.

Daniel's concern (at 13b–14) seems to be that there is precious little of such sadness and mourning among Israel in his own time. They have gone through *all this disaster* (13a) and are without home, without temple, without freedom, and – sadly – without repentance. Perhaps that's why Daniel wrote up his prayer – perhaps a model prayer could help.

4. The primary concern of prayer (15–19)

The *And now . . . '* (15a; also 17a) signals that Daniel is about to make his request. The bulk of his prayer is so consumed with lamenting

---

[11] Veldkamp, p. 202. Sadly, the church in our time may be on its way to being 'no longer church'. In many of our assemblies prayer itself has little place in worship (I do not refer to lengthy prayer but simply to earnest, thoughtful prayer), much less prayers of confession.

[12] Ezekiel's language may sound a bit shocking to generations who've been suckled on the flat fare of the self-esteem cult.

sin (4–14) that only now does Daniel express his petition. His *primary request* comes in verse 16: *Let your anger and your fury turn away from your city Jerusalem, your holy hill.* This is also an implicit plea for restoration. But notice the basis for his petition, the *primary argument* he presses. We catch hints of it when Daniel alludes to how the Lord made for himself a 'name' by his Exodus-deliverance (15b) and when he speaks of Israel now being *a cause for derision* (16b) to all around. Yet note especially how Daniel batters heaven with appeals to God's honour as he mentions:

> *your city Jerusalem, your holy hill* (16a);
> *your people* have become a cause for derision (16b);
> make *your face* shine upon *your devastated sanctuary*
>   for the Lord's sake (17b);
> the city which is called by *your name* (18a);
> do not delay, for *your own sake*, my God,
>   for *your name* is called over *your city*
>   and over *your people* (19b).

The emboldened phrases here do not indicate grammatical emphasis but constitute the 'leverage' Daniel seeks to bring to bear. Even beyond Yahweh's *many compassions* (18b), Daniel appeals to Yahweh's *reputation*.

Of course, the Lord 'ruined' his own reputation when he 'gave' Judah's king and temple vessels into Nebuchadnezzar's control (1:1–2). It was part of his judgment on Judah, but, as so often, the media didn't get it right. The popular interpretation was that Yahweh was simply another little-league deity unable to keep his provincial people from being steamrolled by mighty Babylon and her victorious gods, Marduk and Nebo – Babylon's helps in ages past, their hopes for years to come. Yahweh seemed to be just another poor choice in the world's cafeteria of divine also-rans. Daniel pleads with Yahweh to reverse all this and to restore his own reputation and 'name'. Genuine believers always have this concern close to their hearts.

It was 1945 and a Congress of Cults was convened in the Rumanian Parliament building. Four thousand clergy of all stripes were present. Loud applause greeted the announcement that Comrade Stalin was Patron of the Congress. Various politicians made lavish assurances of support. Then bishops and others expressed their delight over a 'red' stream now flowing into the river of the Church. Calvinist, Lutheran, the Chief Rabbi – all rose in turn to speak, to express their willingness to cooperate with the Communist regime. In that assembly sat a prominent Lutheran pastor and his wife. After speech after speech of clerical grovelling and boot-licking, Sabrina Wurmbrand could stand it no longer; she turned to her husband Richard and exclaimed, 'Go and wash this shame from the face of Christ!'[13] He did and went to prison for it.

Daniel teaches us then that Yahweh's reputation should be the driving concern of our prayers. Our petitions should be sprinkled with the incense of pleading his honour. What honour it will bring you, Lord, if that son of mine is converted; what praise will come to Christ if this marriage is renewed; what credit to Jesus' name if that saint can walk through this hard trouble growing stronger and sweeter in faith.

There is such a pleading note at the end of Daniel's prayer. It reaches an intense pitch. He seems reduced to short, staccato-like begging-notes: *O Lord, hear; O Lord, forgive; O Lord, pay attention and act – do not delay* (19a). And why? *For your own sake* (19b).

Who would have thought that it would be a government bureaucrat in the vast maze of the Persian empire who would teach us to pray?

[13] Richard Wurmbrand, *Christ in the Communist Prisons* (New York: Coward-McCann, 1968), pp. 20–21.

Daniel 9:20–23
10. Not so fast!

In the 1950s–60s, what some would call the heyday of American baseball, Willie Mays was the iconic centerfielder of the New York (later, San Francisco) Giants. He was fast, powerful, and electrifying. But he was a bit slow at first in picking up on major league ways. Once in his rookie year, Mays and Earl Rapp, a teammate who was not known for his speed, were walking across the ball field toward the clubhouse. Rapp suddenly bargained: 'Race you the rest of the way for five dollars.' Off they went. Mays won easily. Rapp said, 'Okay, let's have the five.' Mays was flabbergasted; he'd beaten Rapp, so Rapp owed him. 'Wasn't anything said about beating anybody,' Rapp noted – 'I just said I'd race you.'[1] The same problem carries over into our Bible reading; we tend to 'jump the gun' and make rash assumptions. In Daniel 9, for example, we can be so eager to get to the *seventy weeks* (24) that we ignore this very instructive interlude between Daniel's prayer and Gabriel's revelation; we are prone to dismiss verses 20–23 in a sentence or two so we can bury ourselves in the seventy weeks. That is a mistake; slow down and think it through.

For the rest of Daniel 9 I'll be working from my own translation. Here is our 'interlude' passage:

> *Now while I was speaking and praying and confessing my sin and the sin of my people Israel – and presenting my plea for grace before Yahweh my God for the holy hill of my God* (20),
> *and while I was speaking in prayer, the man Gabriel, whom I had seen in the vision at the first (I was very weary) – he was reaching me at the time of the evening sacrifice* (21).

[1] James S. Hirsch, *Willie Mays: The Life, the Legend* (New York: Scribner, 2010), p. 112.

And he gave me understanding and spoke with me, and said, 'Daniel, now I have come out to give you insight and understanding (22). At the beginning of your pleas for grace a word went forth, and I have come to tell you, for you are deeply loved; so ponder the word and discern the vision (23).

One way to profit from this text is to begin with observations about Daniel himself. So notice . . .

1. The proper focus of his concern (20)

Daniel is, to be sure, primarily introducing us to the revelation in verses 24–27, showing how it was that he came to receive that puzzling word. As he does so, however, he recapitulates in verse 20 what he had been doing in his previous prayer: he had been making personal and corporate confession of guilt (20a; see 4–11) and pleading for restoration of ordered Jerusalem worship (20b; see 16–17). Many of us likely sense a 'Daniel gap' here, for we wouldn't spend much time *speaking and praying and confessing my sin and the sin of my people Israel* as he did. We tend to view confessing guilt as at best a passing preliminary in our prayers rather than a primary burden of them. Calvin provides a correction for us. Reflecting on Daniel's 'guilt focus,' he says: 'This, then, is *our righteousness* [emphasis mine], to confess ourselves guilty in order that God may gratuitously absolve us.' He then draws attention to Jesus' prescribed prayer, 'Forgive us our debts'[2] and draws the application:

> For whom did Christ wish to use this petition? Surely all his disciples. If any one thinks that he has no need of this form of prayer, and confession of sin, let him depart from the school of Christ, and enter into a herd of swine.[3]

In short, we are to never cut loose from this 'mourning' over sin as if it belongs to some elementary stage of Christian experience we leave behind. It is a proper preoccupation of our prayers.

The other burden in Daniel's prayer was what we could call the low condition of the church: *presenting my plea for grace before Yahweh my God for the holy hill of my God* (20b). The city was desolate, the temple in ruins, and Daniel pleads for their restoration and the flourishing of faithful worship again. However true it is that we have a better altar now (cf. Heb. 13:10), even Golgotha, we

[2] Matt. 6:12.
[3] Calvin, 2:190.

should yet have the same anxiety over the welfare of the 'visible church'. Across the world Christ's church has either to endure pressure from without or escape rot from within. Tyrants and terrorists batter the church, apathy and apostasy eat at her. Are we not then called to plead for 'the holy hill' of our God? Had Daniel heard Timothy Dwight's hymn – 'For her my tears shall fall, for her my prayers ascend' – he would say, 'Yes, that's it; that's how you must pray.'

2. The revealing traces of his mind-set (21)

Daniel reports the arrival of Gabriel whom he had seen in a previous vision – perhaps the one of 8:15–17, though some suggest it may be that of 7:16 (though Gabriel is not explicitly named there). 'I was very weary' translates a phrase I take as a parenthetical aside, referring to the exhaustion of Daniel; some, assuming a different root, think it refers to the flight of Gabriel.[4] But what is so fascinating is the way Daniel mentions Gabriel's arrival: *he was reaching me at the time of the evening sacrifice*.

The evening sacrifice was the daily burnt-offering offered around 3 pm.[5] But why would Daniel tell time this way? It had been well-nigh seventy years since Daniel, as a very young teenager, had been in Jerusalem and perhaps at the time for an evening sacrifice; and it had been almost fifty years since the last evening sacrifice had been offered (the temple had been burned in 587 BC[6]). Yet Daniel still tells time liturgically! After decades of time and in a foreign land he still functions on 'Jerusalem time'. There are simply some things that years in Babylon cannot erase. Clearly, Daniel had been in, but not of, Babylon. Daniel's clock is tied to Yahweh's ordinances, non-existent as they are at that moment.

I recall helping my mother with the dishes one evening when I was about fifteen. No dishwasher then; she was washing, I was drying. As she gazed out the kitchen window with her hands in the suds, she suddenly exclaimed, 'I miss my father!' I didn't follow that up. I was fifteen. I had no psychological finesse for 'probing' that remark; if I had, it would have been wrong-headed to do so. Yet it was very revealing. I remembered that my mother had always spoken highly of her father. Her only disappointment in him was that he sometimes smoked a pipe! I knew Grandpa Wilson had lived with my mother and father in his last years – my older brothers used to speak of him. But grandpa had been dead by the time I was born. And now I am

---

[4] See Steinmann, p. 444, for discussion.
[5] Cf. Exod. 29:38–42.
[6] Cf. 2 Kgs 25:8–9.

standing by the kitchen sink with a woman in her late fifties and out of the blue she says, 'I miss my father!' That was no throwaway line. Rather it was a concise compendium packed with respect and affection spilling out of a thoughtful and overflowing heart. *At the time of the evening sacrifice* is like that. It reveals far more than Daniel's ability to tell time; that time-indicator is packed with years of yearning and longing and affection for Yahweh's ordinances, a passion for the 'means of grace' of true Jerusalem worship. Sometimes what may seem incidental reveals a soul thirsting after God.

3. The moving description of his standing (23a)

Gabriel assures Daniel that *at the beginning of your pleas for grace a word went forth, and I have come to tell you, for you are deeply loved.* The word translated *deeply loved* is *ḥămûdôt* (occurring also in 10:11, 19); it occurs nine times in the Old Testament and means something like 'preciousness'.[7] The root is *ḥāmad*, which appears as 'covet' in the commandment (Exod. 20:17). So our noun refers to what is desired, craved, highly esteemed (cf. NIV), precious or loved. Here it indicates how Yahweh regards Daniel. How welcome this word must have been. To be assured he was *deeply loved* would give him confidence that his prayer would be favourably received. And how instructive it is for ourselves as readers of the text, for we can easily become wrapped up in curiosity over the *seventy weeks* (24) that we neglect to notice God's holy anxiety that is so concerned to assure Daniel himself.

Though the word here specifically addresses Daniel, this assurance may 'slosh over' to comfort other servants. In 1751 Philip Doddridge was near the end of his life and ministry. Only forty-nine years old he was dying of consumption, and his doctor suggested the only hope for some limited recovery lay in a voyage to the warmer climate of Lisbon. Selina, Countess of Huntingdon, arranged for Doddridge and his wife to travel by way of Bath so that she might see and care for them before departure for Lisbon. The morning Doddridge was to leave Selina came unexpectedly into his room and found him weeping over the Scriptures open in front of him. The words that moved him to tears were from Daniel: 'O Daniel, a man greatly beloved' (the AV rendering). Selina could only say, 'You are in tears, Sir.' He assured her, 'I am weeping, but they are tears of comfort and joy.'[8] Why so? Was it not because he sensed that the assurance given Daniel belonged to him as well in that solemn hour, and if he also

---

[7] Cf. DCH, 3:249.
[8] Faith Cook, *Selina, Countess of Huntingdon* (Edinburgh: Banner of Truth, 2001), pp. 139–140.

was the object of heaven's holy coveting then all was well? 'For you are deeply loved.'

4. The continuing responsibility of his privilege (22, 23b)

Gabriel both provides Daniel with a gift and calls him to a task. Daniel himself says that Gabriel *gave me understanding* (22a); then Gabriel's own words support that: *I have come out to give you insight and understanding* (22b). That is the divine gift, but this is to be followed by human effort: *so ponder the word and discern the vision* (23b). The two elements go together; the divine gift is not to be neglected but exercised so that it might become fruitful. The gift of understanding presumably relates, at least in part, to the *seventy weeks* revelation in verses 24–27, but it is that very word and vision that Daniel is to ponder and figure out. This is always the Bible's balance: a divine gift is not meant to stifle human effort but to stimulate human initiative (23b). The gifts of God are not excuses for sloth but demands for sweat.[9]

In the task of expounding Scripture we can easily pander to an extreme. We can be very secular (even if 'evangelical') in that we dive into our grammars and commentaries and various Bible helps as though the whole venture depends on our savvy. Like the prodigal we 'come to ourselves' in the midst of it all and realize we've given no real thought to seeking light from the Lord. Even if not intentional, we find a certain essential arrogance in our procedure; we find we are committing hermeneutical idolatry. 'Lead me in your truth and teach me'[10] has not crossed either our minds or our lips. Or we commit the opposite error and make such a to-do of leaning on the Spirit yet never trace the logic or argument of a passage, pay no attention to vocabulary or grammar, expect no surprising theological claims (and so we don't find them), and refuse to use commentaries (because they only contain the opinions of men and women) – and so we come out with some anaemic topical thoughts that drive neither to repentance or joy. In this case we are sabotaging God's intention, for his whole purpose in giving divine discernment is to activate human diligence. Giving *insight and understanding* (22b) is his privilege; *ponder the word and discern the vision* (23b) – that is our responsibility.

---

[9] See Fyall, p. 142, for a nice summary of this point.
[10] Ps. 25:5.

Daniel 9:24–27
11. The long haul of the people of God

Let me first set down a working translation of the text, as a conveni-ent point of reference for the following exposition.

24 *Seventy weeks are determined*
   concerning your people and your holy city,
   to bring an end to rebellion,
   to seal up sins,
   to atone for iniquity,
   to bring in everlasting righteousness,
   to seal up vision and prophet,
   and to anoint a most holy place [*or:* one].

25 *Now you must know and have insight:*
   from the going forth of a word
      to restore and rebuild Jerusalem
   to an anointed one, a leader, seven weeks;
   and for [during?] *sixty-two weeks*
   it will be built again with squares and moat
      – but in distressing times.

26 *And after the sixty-two weeks*
   an anointed one will be cut off and have nothing,
   and the people of the leader who is coming
      will destroy the city and the sanctuary;
   and its end will be overwhelming
      – and to the end war is decreed with desolations.

27 *And he shall make a firm covenant with many*
   for one week;

in the middle of the week
he will make sacrifice and offering stop,
and on the wing of abominations
(will come) one causing desolation,
even until the predetermined destruction
is poured out on the desolator.

In a 'Peanuts' cartoon Linus is interpreting a nursery rhyme. He tells Charlie Brown, 'The way I see it, "the cow jumped over the moon" indicates a rise in farm prices.' Linus asks if Charlie agrees. Charlie confesses, 'I can't say; I don't pretend to be a student of prophetic literature.' We may be ready to disqualify ourselves in a similar way as we face Daniel's *seventy weeks* revelation. I well recall the first time I had to lecture on this passage in a liberal arts college. I worked through the Hebrew text and spent hours reading secondary sources – and almost came to a Charlie Brown position. But at least I had a title for my lecture: 'Seventy weeks and twenty problems.'

If you pry open that can of problems, you ask, what are these *sevens* or weeks? Just *weeks* or weeks of years? Are they to be taken literally (of 490 years) or in some symbolic way? How are we to understand the fulfilment of the purpose clauses (e.g., *to bring an end to rebellion,* etc.) in verse 24? Are they fulfilled in a decisive way in Christ's first advent? Or do they point to an ultimate fulfilment in the wake of his second advent? Is the *most holy* at the end of verse 24 a place or possibly a person? What *word* (*to restore and rebuild Jerusalem*) is meant in verse 25a? Is it some prophetic word (e.g., of Jeremiah)? Is it Cyrus' decree of 538 BC (Ezra 1:1–4)? Or that of Artaxerxes I in 458 BC (Ezra 7) or that of the same king in 445 BC (Neh. 2:1–8)? Is the *anointed one* of verse 25a referring to the Messiah or to some other leader? Are the *sixty-two weeks* (25b) a distinct segment of time? Or are they to be combined with the preceding *seven weeks,* so that the anointed one of verse 25a actually comes after sixty-nine weeks? When verse 26a speaks of **after** *the sixty-two weeks,* does it mean the rest of the verse describes what happens in the seventieth week (cf. 27) or does it imply a hiatus between the sixty-two segment and the 'last' week? Who is the *anointed one* who is cut off in verse 26? Is he identical to *the anointed one* of verse 25? Who is *the leader who is coming* in verse 26b? Does *its end* in verse 26c refer to the end of the city and sanctuary or should it be 'his end', referring to the leader who is coming? Who is the *he* who makes *a firm covenant* in verse 27a? The anointed one/Messiah or the leader who is coming? What sort of covenant is it? Beneficial or detrimental? Is it positive or negative when *sacrifice and offering stop* in verse 27b? One could add to this collage of queries. What does all this mean? It means that if you are driving home late at night and tune in to the 'Prophecy Hour' on your radio and hear the preacher refer to 'what is perfectly clear in Daniel's seventy-weeks prophecy', you know he hasn't read the text carefully.

All this does not mean we are left in a morass of mush. I think we can focus on the broad terms of the text and end with more than bland platitudes; below I try to wrap up the primary teaching points of the text in the headings. For the most part, I think these teaching points remain solid even if I disappoint or appal the reader by decisions I make about textual details.

On the whole we should expect verses 24–27 to prove a positive piece of revelation for Daniel and his people. That is what we expect at least in the wake of Daniel's prayer (9:1–19) and heaven's favourable response to it (9:20–23). Indeed Gabriel packs encouragement into the very first line: *Seventy weeks are determined concerning your people and your holy city* (24a). What welcome innuendo! *Concerning your people* – what does that say except that Yahweh has not cast them aside but is still dealing with them and holding on to them? Yet even though the seventy years of the exile (9:2) are coming to a close, Yahweh's people face 'seventy sevens'. Clearly, then, the end of the exile will not usher in any full or final restoration. In their overall context, verses 24–27 seem to say to Israel: The kingdom of God will *not* immediately appear and you must prepare for 'a long obedience in the same direction'.[1]

1. The right perspective: the scope of the hope (24)

Verse 24 tells us what God's programme for God's people involves in the *seventy weeks*, itemizing it in six purpose clauses. The first three are 'negative', having to do with sin,[2] the second three are 'positive', dealing more with fulfilment. The majority of these purposes will only be accomplished at the final establishing of the

---

[1] The title of Eugene Peterson's book on the psalms of ascent (Downers Grove: IVP, 1980), for which he thanks Nietzsche.

[2] We meet a gamut of sin-words here: 'rebellion', *peša'*, is a willful, deliberate act of disloyalty and disobedience, covenant treachery in fact (cf. NIDOTTE, 3:707); 'sins', *ḥaṭṭā'ôt*, an overall term for offences tinged with the idea of failure, of falling short of a standard or goal (TWOT, 1:277–278; NIDOTTE, 2:87–88); and 'iniquity', *'āwōn*, may refer to an act, the guilt of the act, or the punishment for the guilt (cf. BDB, 730–731), its root idea implying 'twistedness' or 'perversion' that comes from a nature of the same stripe (cf. Alec Motyer, *Look to the Rock* [Leicester: IVP, 1996], pp. 131, 198). The pile-up of sin-terms in Dan. 9:24 is probably not meant to focus on their individual nuances but to suggest that God intends to deal finally and fully with sin in *all* its guises.

kingdom of God. *To bring an end to rebellion*[3] is an ultimate and not an interim piece of work. *To seal up sins* may fall into the same category. Job 14:17 provides a useful parallel, where Job says to God, '*My transgression [pešaʻ] would be sealed up in a bag*' (ESV). Here Job imagines a time beyond his death when God would 'remember' him and 'long for' him, and at that time his rebellion would be sealed and 'bagged up' and so could do no damage.[4]

From our New Testament reading we gladly confess that *to atone for iniquity* is a 'final' matter (Heb. 10:11–13) that clearly occurs before the final time (e.g., Mark 10:45; Titus 2:14; 1 Pet. 1:17–19). However, *to bring in everlasting righteousness* points to the coming of an era and the imposition of an order in which righteousness, justice and godliness prevail, a time in which the righteousness will be as *everlasting* and ongoing as the kingdom and dominion in which it flourishes (7:14, 27; cf. Isa. 9:7; 11:4–5; Jer. 23:5). Understanding *to seal up vision and prophet* is a bit tricky. Some see 'to seal' as implying a *disposing* function. When a piece of prophecy is sealed it is, as perhaps in 12:4, 9, placed out of reach or off limits, so that no use may be made of it; it is sealed off. On this view *to seal vision and prophet* means that once the seventy weeks are ended no further prophecy or divine revelation will be needed.[5] Or one may place emphasis on the *authenticating* function of a seal (see 6:17), in which case 'the idea would be that God will someday set his seal of authentication upon every truly God-given revelation . . . by bringing about its complete fulfillment' (cf. Rev. 10:7).[6] In any case, both the *righteousness* clause and the *seal* clause presuppose the full establishment of God's visible regime.

The sixth purpose clause is, literally, *to anoint a most holy*. Holy place or holy person? Some would link the language to the *anointed one* (or Messiah) of verse 25, hence a 'most holy one'.[7] More likely, it refers to a place, since this superlative phrase (holy of holies, most holy) regularly refers to objects or items used in connection with the tabernacle or temple.[8] The Exodus materials themselves speak of

---

[3] The intended verb is *kālâ* (finish, bring to an end, consume), not *kālāʾ* (to restrain, hold back); see for explanation Steinmann, p. 445. Jesus the servant would be 'pierced through on account of our rebellions' (Isa. 53:5), but his death did not 'bring an end' to rebellion.

[4] For the proper and 'positive' interpretation of Job 14:16–17, see D. J. Clines, *Job 1–20*, Word Biblical Commentary (Dallas: Word, 1989), pp. 333–334. All three of the 'sin words' of Dan. 9:24 occur in Job 14:16–17.

[5] So Steinmann, p. 466; Harman, pp. 235–36.

[6] Miller, p. 261; TDOT, 5:269.

[7] See Steinmann, pp. 466–467.

[8] E.g., Exod. 29:37 (altar of burnt-offering); 30:29 (various tabernacle furniture); Lev. 2:3, 10; 7:1, 6 (offerings, sacrifices).

anointing the various items in the tabernacle when Moses was to inaugurate the wilderness worship. Moses was to use a specially formulated anointing oil to consecrate the various furnishings of the tabernacle as well as the priests who served there (Exod. 30:22–33; 40:9–15). Perhaps *anointing a most holy* is a way of saying, 'inaugurating Yahweh-ordained worship'. This becomes fascinating when in verse 26 we read that the people of the leader who is coming *will destroy the city and the sanctuary* (lit., 'holy place').[9] I propose that 'sanctuary/holy place' (*haqqōdeš*) in verse 26 is shorthand for the previous *most holy place* (*qōdeš qŏdāšîm*) in verse 24. Then verse 24 can be read as a pre-emptive 'answer' to the devastation of verse 26. Near the end of the seventy 'weeks' hostile forces will do their best to eradicate the true worship of God (26), but that will not be the final word, for God will see that his worship revives and thrives (*to anoint a most holy*). If I am correct, the sense of the text would be akin to the delightful dogmatism of Jesus in Matthew 16:18, 'I will build my church, and the gates of Hades will not prevail against it.'[10]

The upshot of this overview is that at least the first, fourth and fifth purposes stated in verse 24 will only occur when Christ's kingdom is fully and openly established. That is the scope of the hope, and it packs immense practical importance. It tells God's people not to fall for the 'immediacy heresy'. The seventy years of exile are drawing to a close but God's purposes for his people involve *seventy sevens* before they reach completion. The restoration to the land will not bring in the restoration of all things. Don't be suckered, verse 24 implies, into holding a false hope.

Constitutionally the Lord's people have trouble with the 'long haul' position. We eagerly grab at the sudden solution or the quick finish. One wonders if Lord Percy was doing that in August 1776 when, after the American troops had abandoned Brooklyn and drifted away in a thick fog, he wrote: 'Everything seems to be over with them. This business is pretty near over.'[11] Well, maybe not. In any case, we are not thrilled by the call to ongoing obedience and long-term endurance. We want a god with microwavable ways[12] and imminent solutions. In the West it is the way we live. I buy petrol by credit card. I prefer to pay cash, but to do that I would have to take the cash into the station, leave it with the clerk, go back and

---

[9] This would ill-fit a second-century 'fulfilment' under Antiochus IV, for his henchmen desecrated but did not destroy the temple (cf. 1 Macc. 1:29–40).

[10] Cf. the *Belgic Confession* (Article 27), which says that Christ's church 'is preserved by God against the fury of the whole world, although for a while it may look very small and as extinct in the eyes of man'.

[11] David McCullough, *1776* (New York: Simon and Schuster, 2005), p. 192.

[12] Cf. Duguid, p. 167.

pump petrol, then go back into the station to get my change or to pay more. It takes too long. So I pay at the pump with a card. It is sometimes the same story at the grocery. I may go out via the self check-out. To wait in line in a normal check-out lane takes too long! And we can carry the same mindset into our faith and discipleship. We want relief from trials now. We expect Christian maturity now. We demand answers to prayer now. And God says to us, as he seems to be saying to Daniel and his people here: Now this is what I am going to do, but not right away; hunker down and settle into a long faithfulness toward your final hope.

2. The unseen preservation: the tone of the times (25–26)

Here I hope we can move from the confusing to the clear, so we'll begin with *what can be confusing.*

First, what is one to make of these *weeks* (or, 'sevens')? Are they weeks of years, as many argue, so that a total of 490 years is intended?[13] Or are they meant in some figurative way? M. G. Kline links our passage with the 'seven weeks [lit., 'sabbaths'] of years' in Leviticus 25:8–17, where the forty-nine years are followed by the fiftieth year or Jubilee, the year of 'redemption, release, and restoration'. He sees Daniel's seventy sevens of years as emblematic of ten jubilee eras and so serving as an 'intensification of the jubilee concept' pointing to the ultimate jubilee.[14] This view of Daniel's *seventy sevens* as leading up to the super-jubilee may prove helpful; it could function with either a literal or figurative view of the *weeks*. For the moment, however, let us leave the week-problem unresolved.

Not only is there dispute about what the weeks/sevens are but also when they begin. Verse 25a is clear about the starting-point: *from the going forth of a word to restore and rebuild Jerusalem.* But Bible students are not clear about which *word* the text intends. It is usual to associate the *word* with a royal decree, so that one chooses among the decree of Cyrus in 538 BC for the exiles to return and rebuild the temple (2 Chr. 36:22–23; Ezra 1:1–4);[15] the decree of

---

[13] See Miller, pp. 257–258, who argues for weeks of years; see Steinmann, pp. 452–453, 459–462, who holds that the 'weeks' are meant metaphorically and that Dan. 9 gives no indication that the weeks are meant as groups of seven years.

[14] M. G. Kline, 'The Covenant of the Seventieth Week', in John H. Skilton (ed.), *The Law and the Prophets* (n. p.: Presbyterian and Reformed, 1974), pp. 458–462.

[15] Some object that Cyrus' decree focuses on rebuilding the temple not the city, while v. 25 specifies rebuilding Jerusalem. But the either-or is false. One can hardly conceive of a royal decree to rebuild the temple at the same time withholding permission to rebuild homes and infrastructure. Moreover, the Cyrus-plan announced in Isaiah already includes both the rebuilding of city/cities and temple (Isa. 44:26, 28; 45:13). Cf. Young, pp. 202–203.

Artaxerxes I in 458 BC making provision for Ezra to refurbish temple worship and enforce Yahweh's torah (Ezra 7:1–26);[16] or the decree of the same king granted in 445 BC on behalf of Nehemiah's design to rebuild Jerusalem (Neh. 2:1–8).[17]

There is another possibility: the *going forth of a word* may refer to a *prophetic word* rather than a royal decree. Gabriel uses this idiom in verse 23 when he tells Daniel that 'a word went forth'. He refers to the revelation communicated in verses 24–27. But where would one find this prophetic word to restore and rebuild Jerusalem? McComiskey reminds us that Daniel had been meditating on Jeremiah's prophecies (v. 2; indeed, 2 Chr. 36:22 and Ezra 1:1 specifically state that Cyrus' 538 decree permitting the exiles to return was to fulfil 'the word of Yahweh by the mouth of *Jeremiah*'). Daniel seemed to be considering especially Jeremiah 25 and 29, and the latter chapter does deal with Judah's restoration. McComiskey even draws attention to the similar phraseology between Jeremiah 29:10 and Daniel 9:25 (*word to restore*); in Jeremiah it refers to restoring the people to Jerusalem, which assumes the city is also restored, especially in view of promises like Jeremiah 30:18.[18] If the promise of Jeremiah 29 is the *word that went forth* in Daniel 9:25, it would date from sometime after 597 BC (see Jer. 29:1–2), perhaps around 594 BC (Harman).

Let us again walk away from this problem momentarily and look at a third confusing matter: how to construe and translate the 'week

[16] If (1) one takes the 'weeks' as seven-year periods and (2) combines the seven and sixty-two weeks into an overall sixty-nine weeks segment (NIV, NKJV), then the 483 years (7 x 69) from 458 BC bring one to about AD 26, arguably the beginning of Jesus' public ministry (see discussions in Miller and Archer). Yet one wonders if anyone would naturally identify the 'word' of Dan. 9:25 with the decree of Ezra 7 except that it permits a plausible way to mesh the mathematical calculations.

[17] The strength of this option is its stress on rebuilding the city itself (see v. 25). This view operates on the same assumptions as that in note 16; the calculations, 483 years from 445 BC, however, bring one down to about AD 39, beyond the ministry and crucifixion of Jesus – a poor fit. So advocates appeal to a 'prophetic year' as opposed to a solar year to 'back up' the calculation to AD 32 or 33. It seems to require too much interpretive gerrymandering. But other views run into math problems as well. The 'historical' interpretation that sees the seventy weeks climaxing in the scourge of Antiochus Epiphanes in 167 BC, tends to begin the seventy weeks at 587/586 BC; even sixty-nine weeks or 483 years bring them to the no-man's land of ca. 104 BC, some sixty-five years and decades after Antiochus (cf. Montgomery, pp. 390–393). If the prophecy was produced by a second-century writer near the eve of Antiochus' scourge, one would think such a late writer with surely some sense of chronology would have gotten the calculations right and not messed them up so badly.

[18] See T. E. McComiskey, 'The Seventy "Weeks" of Daniel against the Background of Ancient Near Eastern Literature', *Westminster Theological Journal* 47 (1985), pp. 25–28; also cf. Robert B. Chisholm, Jr, *Handbook on the Prophets* (Grand Rapids: Baker, 2002), pp. 314–315.

clauses' of verse 25. Are the seven weeks and the sixty-two weeks to be combined into one overall period (NIV, NKJV, NASB, NJB) or separated into two distinct periods (NRSV, ESV, NJPS)? How one answers this can affect interpretation. For example, if one connects them (into one united segment of sixty-nine weeks) the *anointed one* of verse 25 and of verse 26 can be the same person; verses 25 and 26 may then refer to the coming and the cutting off of the Messiah respectively.

However, I think the balance of probability favours separating the seven and sixty-two into two distinct periods. First, the traditional Hebrew text has an accent on *seven weeks* which indicates it is not to be closely combined with the *sixty-two weeks*. Of course such accents are not part of the original text and stem from Jewish scholars (Masoretes) working on the text from AD 500–1000. It is not difficult to cough up some examples of when they have been wrong, but they should be given credit for being more familiar with Hebrew than most of us. Since they did their work well into the Christian era someone may claim that they deliberately construed the text this way in order to 'throw off' a messianic interpretation, since they packed an anti-Christian bias. But this will not hold, for the dominant view in the early church (before the Masoretes) seems to have kept the two segments distinct.[19] Moreover, 'seven and sixty-two' is a strange way of saying 'sixty-nine', if that's all one meant to say. Why bother mentioning 'sixty-two' unless it marked off a distinct segment? Hence the text should be taken as translated at the beginning of this chapter – with a semi-colon after *seven weeks*.

Time to bite the bullet. I have decided, against my natural prefer-ence, that I cannot take the 'weeks' as weeks of years. I suppose that means that I do not take the 'weeks' literally; instead, I take them schematically and would characterize them this way:

7 weeks = relatively restricted time

62 weeks = relatively extended time

1 week = clearly climactic time

At the risk of displeasing most everyone, how then would I under-stand verses 25–26 on the whole? I take the *word to restore* as the prophetic word of Jeremiah in ca. 594 BC (Jer. 29:10–11) and the *anointed one* in 25a as King Cyrus (ca. 559–530 BC), who permitted the exiles to return home. Yahweh had already referred to Cyrus as 'his anointed' ('his messiah' – with a lower-case 'm') in Isaiah 45:1,

[19] See McComiskey, pp. 19–25, for detailed argumentation on this whole matter; also Chisholm, p. 313.

so there is nothing incongruous about Cyrus being an *anointed one* here.[20] Then there is an extended time characterized by both rebuilding and distress, after which (26a) an anointed one will be cut off. This seems to refer to the death of *the* Messiah in the wake of which the city and sanctuary will be destroyed.[21] Daniel had prayed these would be restored (9:16–18) and they would be (25) – then reduced to ruins once more.

We have tried to wend our way through this interpretive minefield, isolating some of the most important and confusing issues in it. Now it is time to press on to *what may be helpful.* One is prone to become so transfixed on all the debatable issues that one misses the clear pattern in it all. So it is crucial to see the character of these segments in verses 25–26. First, the seven weeks (25a) are *a time when hope returns.* This segment begins with the going forth of a word *to restore and rebuild Jerusalem.* Whether the *anointed one* is Cyrus or someone else, the word of restoration (whether a prophetic word or a royal edict) had to strike an encouraging note for Daniel and his people. Then the sixty-two weeks is *a time when life goes on* (25b). It is a time when the 'word' of restoration (25a) is accomplished – the city built again, completely done up as we might say, but *in distressing times.* But distressing times are not the same as wreck and ruin. So life progresses in an apparently extended period that seems to reflect the proximate answer to Daniel's prayer (9:16–19). This then brings us to *a time when clouds gather* (26). This occurs *after the sixty-two weeks.*[22] Apparently it encompasses the death and

[20] Some translations (e.g., NKJV, NIV) take *mašîaḥ* here in the 'technical' sense of 'Messiah' (referring to Christ). However, if one takes the seven weeks and sixty-two weeks as two distinct periods, the 'anointed one' at the end of the seven weeks cannot be *the* anointed one par excellence. There are plenty of uses of the noun/adjective (39 times in the OT) in a non-technical sense. Cf. J. A. Motyer, 'Messiah', *New Bible Dictionary*, 3rd ed., p. 753. My view of v. 25a assumes that Yahweh had begun to answer Daniel's prayer long before Daniel prayed. I see no major problem with this; if the seventy weeks present Yahweh's whole programme for restoration, why quibble if part of that plan was already afoot? V. 25 does not have to be future to Daniel; there is no 'will be' in the text – it simply says that from the word to an anointed one 'seven weeks'.

[21] H. C. Leupold takes the 'messianic' view here but uses the clause, 'And there shall be nothing belonging to Him', to explain what being 'cut off' involved, viz., 'losing all influence and prestige that ever He had before man. The season of the successful building of the city and the sanctuary is at an end. As far as the world is concerned, Messiah shall be a dead issue. His cause will seem to have failed' (Leupold, p. 427). Leupold does not see the Messiah's 'cutting off' as a specific reference to his death so much as the general eclipse of his cause in the world.

[22] What happens in v. 26 is not explicitly said to occur in the 'one week' (see v. 27) remaining. One could infer that if these occur *after* the sixty-two weeks then they must occur *in* the seventieth week or the one week remaining. But the text falls short of actually saying so. Yet neither can one be sure from the text itself that there is any 'gap' between the end of the sixty-two segment and the seventieth.

desolation of the Messiah (*an anointed one will be cut off*) and the destruction of the city and sanctuary that had been restored. Some take this as referring to the Romans' destruction of Jerusalem in AD 70.[23] All this leads, it seems, to ongoing tumultuous times (*to the end war is decreed with desolations*).

Years ago on a cold and cloudy day I was changing the oil in my car. I had it elevated on portable ramps, had drained the old oil out, replaced the drain plug, then focused on the always tedious job of removing the old oil filter and installing a new one. All that done, I rolled it off the ramps and started it up. Never heard it run so noisily. Then, with a glance taking in the cans of new oil sitting in state on my driveway, I realized I hadn't dumped the new oil into the engine. I had been so intent on all the collateral details that I had neglected the main matter. Which is why you must pay attention to *what you may miss* in verses 25–26.

And what is that? It is the assurance given God's people for that more extensive sixty-two weeks period: *it will be built again . . . but in distressing times*. The picture is of a city intact, people presumably residing there. There the covenant people have a home, and, even though the times are difficult, they are *there*. You can do worse than that. And in all our hermeneutical hubbub over weeks and numbers and allusions we can easily miss this testimony. What is this but the unseen preservation of God?

It reminds one of the scene in Bunyan's *Pilgrim's Progress*, in the Interpreter's house, where Christian is shown a fire burning, supposedly in a grate. One was in front of the fire heaving water on to it and yet, for all that, the fire 'burned higher and hotter'. The Interpreter indicated that the fire represented the work of grace in the believer's heart and the 'baptizer' in this case was the devil, doing all he could to extinguish it. Then the Interpreter took Christian behind the wall – there was a man with a vessel of oil, which he was continually throwing into the fire. 'This is Christ,' says Interpreter, 'who continually with the oil of His grace maintains the work already begun in the heart.' And he is behind the wall, doing his work secretly and hiddenly.[24]

That example focuses on the individual believer, but what is true for one of the Lord's sheep is true for them as a body, as in Daniel 9. You can be so preoccupied in interpretive conundrums that you miss this testimony about Yahweh's 'low-key' preservation. For doesn't this clause of verse 25 sum up the status of the Lord's people most of the time? *Built again . . . but in distressing times*. Both in the

---

[23] See Young, p. 207; Steinmann, p. 473; Archer, p. 116.
[24] John Bunyan, *The Pilgrim's Progress* (1678), ch. 2.

flow and sometimes in the fury of history God keeps his people intact.

3. The final crisis: the elimination of the enemy (27)

The end of verse 26 seems to move us on to final matters – *and to the end war is decreed with desolations*.[25] As Baldwin says, 'the mention of war *to the end* implies continuing conflict between a powerful enemy and God's cause till the end of the seventy weeks.'[26] No peace process there. And verse 27 brings us to that seventieth week.

The first question to ask of verse 27 is: Who is doing what here? Some think that the anointed one/messiah of verse 26 is the subject of the first two verbs. The messiah then will *make a firm covenant with many* for one week and in the middle of that week will *make sacrifice and offering stop*. The use of *the many* (lit.) would support this 'positive' view, for this terminology is used of God's own people elsewhere (Isa. 53:11–12; 54:1; Dan. 12:10). Those who take this messianic view see the stopping of sacrifice and offering as a plus, the result of Christ's once-for-all sacrifice as Hebrews 10:12–14 indicates. I think this view is erroneous. First, the subject of the verb (*make a firm covenant*) is not expressed; it is simply *he*. So it is more natural to identify that 'he' with the more recently mentioned *he* of verse 26b, the *leader who is coming*, rather than with the more remote *anointed one* of 26a. Second, the verb form (*higbîr*) is a power-word and suggests a coercive imposing of a covenant.[27] Finally, elsewhere in the book of Daniel when legitimate worship is stopped or taken away it is a hostile act by an ungodly ruler (8:11–12; 11:31). One expects the same to be the case here.

What then is the picture of verse 27? Apparently the final (remember we are in the last 'week') enemy of God and his people seeks to impose idolatrous worship (*abominations*) until he meets the end God has decreed for him.[28] A final ruler then exalts himself,

---

[25] In the last clause of v. 26 ('its end will be overwhelming') the 'its' refers to the city and sanctuary taken together. It could also be translated 'his end', referring to the leader who is coming.

[26] Baldwin, p. 171.

[27] Cf. Baldwin's oft-cited remark: 'it has the implication of forcing an agreement by means of superior strength' (p. 171). The same 'stem' of the verb is used in Ps. 12:4 (Heb., v. 5) where swaggering oppressors are quoted as saying, 'with our tongues we will power our way'.

[28] 'Abomination/s' is *šiqqûṣ* (s.), a noun that 'focuses exclusively on certain aspects of idolatrous worship, whether the idol itself or part of an idolatrous ritual' (Michael A. Grisanti, NIDOTTE, 4:244). On the grammar and translation of v. 27b, see Steinmann, pp. 449–450, and Collins, p. 347.

imposes his authority, forbids true worship, instigates idolatrous worship – and runs into the meat-grinder of God's decree.[29] Predetermined. On target. Certain.

I am not sure even believers have a lively appreciation for that 'predetermined destruction'.[30] In an editorial piece Mona Charen told how the Aegis class cruiser Lake Erie was operating in heavy seas west of Hawaii on the night of 20 February 2008. It was charged with shooting down a disabled satellite tumbling toward earth's atmosphere. The satellite carried a toxic fuel that could pose health risks should it hit a populated area. The deadline for action was 1 March; on that date the bus-sized satellite would bounce against the outer reaches of the atmosphere and begin a more erratic orbit. Actually the firing window was only about 30 seconds long. At 10.30 pm Eastern time, the USS Lake Erie fired an SM-3 missile 150 miles into space and scored a direct hit on a target moving at 17,000 miles an hour. One tends to be impressed. The timing was precise, the shot accurate, the destruction complete. All had to be carefully calculated ahead of time. And the calculations have been made; the time has already been set for the last tyrant who would assault God's kingdom and crush God's people to be terminated. Somehow that injects a ground-floor assurance into the souls of God's servants and makes it possible for them to walk on with a certain godly fearlessness.

So what is the message of Daniel 9:24–27 to Daniel and to us? Something like this: You are called to a long obedience; your people will be sustained even in distressing times; and the great hater of God's people sits in the Lord's cross-hairs with the date of his demise clearly marked on God's calendar. You may have wished for more than that, but that's mostly what Daniel 9:24–27 is about. And that's not bad.

[29] Very like 'the man of lawlessness' Paul depicts in 2 Thess. 2:1–12.
[30] The same Hebrew phrase occurs in Isa. 10:23 and 28:22.

Daniel 10:1 – 11:2a
12. Intimidating introduction

We sometimes visited a church served by a fine teaching pastor. Each Lord's Day the sermon outline was printed in the worship folder. The outlines were reasonably detailed. Sometimes a quick glance at the day's outline revealed that the mere introduction to the sermon would not be, well, mere. One could tell it might be eighteen minutes before the first 'point' was reached. Daniel 10 is something like that. It brings us into the last major section of the book of Daniel. Chapters 10 – 12 are all one vision – with a long introduction. One could scope it all out this way:

Heading (10:1)
Preparation for the revelation (10:2 – 11:2a)
Communication of the revelation (11:2b – 12:4)
Footnotes to the revelation (12:5–13)

So it takes all of chapter 10 simply to get to the vision itself. And the chapter *is* a formidable introduction – it nearly sucked the life out of Daniel himself. But the question we must ask is: what does a long introduction like this mean to teach us? It may have been terrifying for Daniel and yet it should prove instructive for us. I think the teaching of the text can be gathered up in several propositions.

1. Faithfulness may be more difficult than we suppose (10:1)

This verse is the heading for all of chapters 10 – 12. The vision came in the *third year* of Cyrus. This probably means the third year after Cyrus' conquest of Babylon and so ca. 536 BC. Daniel says that *the word* [i.e., the revelation he was given] *was true and it was a great conflict* (ESV). Some think the *conflict* consisted of Daniel's difficulty in understanding the revelation. More likely, the *conflict* alludes to the content of the vision. *Conflict* renders *ṣābā'*, which means 'army' and 'warfare,' and includes extended meanings like 'hard service'. Leupold seems to pick up on this last option and translates, 'it involved great suffering'.[1] This is likely on target. To be sure, the vision will major on 'warfare' (e.g., 11:21–28) but such warfare will also include severe suffering for the people of God (e.g., 11:29–35; see also 12:1).

It is a bit haunting that this reminder should come at the very first, in the heading to the whole vision. We who live under governments that, for all their godlessness, at least do not inflict overt persecution can forget that we are in an abnormal situation. Our brothers and sisters who are daily savaged and ravaged for Christ's sake – whether in North Korea or Myanmar or Pakistan or Iraq or elsewhere, where they are hated and hunted – are wading through what is far more normal for Christ's servants. We need instant recall that both faith in Christ and suffering for Christ are equally gifts of grace, as Philippians 1:29 teaches us: 'Because to you it has been graciously given on behalf of Christ, not only to believe in him but also to suffer for his sake.'

Spurgeon told of a Mr Mack, a Baptist minister in Northampton-shire. He had been a soldier but, upon obtaining release from military service, became a minister. On one occasion when he went to preach in Glasgow, he went to visit his aged mother. Though he had not seen her in years he knew her the moment he laid eyes on her, but the elderly woman did not recognize him. Once in his childhood his mother had accidentally wounded his wrist with a knife. To comfort him at that time his mother had exclaimed, 'Never mind, my bonnie bairn, your mither will ken [know] you by that when ye are a man.' So when Mack's mother would not believe that a fine-looking minister could be her very son, he turned up his sleeve and cried, 'Mither, mither, dinna ye ken *that*?' In a moment they were in each other's arms. Spurgeon was pointing out that affliction is the identification mark of God's people. It is simply what is characteristic of them. And Daniel's heading underscores that. He is saying that the future history of the people of God will 'involve great suffering'. It is simply 'par'. But we are not told this to break us down but to brace us up, not to make us morose but only to make us prepared.

2. Prayer is more crucial than we suppose (10:2–3, 12–14)

Perhaps we can't know. Certainly the text does not tell us in so many words. But we are curious creatures: Why is Daniel *mourning for*

---

[1] Leupold, p. 443. This was also Keil's view. Cf. Ringgren, TDOT, 12:214, who thinks that here it means approximately 'great tribulation'.

three weeks (2)? Why the semi-fasting regimen on a subsistence-level diet? Why the ban on using aftershave lotion (3)? Clearly, as verse 12 makes clear, this period was a time of extended and focused prayer. But what was behind the prayer? Why was Daniel driven to such intense petitioning? We may suggest two reasons.

First, he was seeking further understanding of the future awaiting his people. Whatever we make of 8:27, it clearly indicates that Daniel had less than full comprehension of what the vision in chapter 8 depicted. In addition, he may have still been trying to put the revelation of 9:24–27 together. Apparently some such concern motivated him, for in verse 12 the heavenly messenger speaks to Daniel of the first day *that you set your heart to understand.* Then subsequently he indicates that he himself came to *make you understand what is to happen to your people in the latter days* (14, ESV).

Second, Daniel may have been disturbed by reports filtering back from Judah of the ongoing, unrelenting opposition the returned exiles were meeting.[2] If the exiles had returned to Judah in 537 BC, sufficient time had likely passed by the *third year of Cyrus* (1; ca. 536/535 BC), the date of the present vision, for the schemes and malice depicted in Ezra 4:1–5 to hit the fan.[3] If Daniel was still serving in some governmental capacity (cf. 1:21) he would have access to reports on provincial affairs. Hearing of Judah's distress drove Daniel into his prayer closet.

Of what use was his prayer? Baldwin is spot on when she says, '*I have come because of your words* [v. 12b] implies that this visitation would not have occurred apart from Daniel's specific prayer'.[4] Then the speaker's continued explanation in verse 13 (more on this verse later) implies that Daniel's prayer sustained a behind-the-scenes triumph over the malicious designs of the invisible powers in charge of Persia. Veldkamp sums it up like this:

> As we shall see, Daniel's prayers succeeded in drawing angels from heaven to earth. These angels formed an invincible heavenly guard around the people of the Lord, with the result that the plans of the enemy failed. In the mighty battle then being fought between the Kingdom of God and the kingdom of this world,

---

[2] See Ezra 4:4–5; the three participles in the Hebrew text underscore the continuing nature of the hostility; there was no let-up in the enemies' attempt to dishearten and intimidate – nor in their pay-offs to Persian bureaucrats to influence policy against the returned residents of Judah.

[3] This would not be the case if Steinmann's view that the exiles' return did not occur until 533 proves correct; cf. Steinmann, pp. 29–30, 36–39.

[4] Baldwin, p. 181.

Daniel succeeded in mobilizing the angels as a spiritual air force against the satanic powers in the air.[5]

But why does God do it this way? Why does he bring his help through the cumbersome and agonizing process of Daniel's prayers? Why doesn't he directly apply heaven's muscles to Israel's troubles? The answer to that last question is that sometimes he does. Check out Numbers 22. There Balak, Moab's king, paid off the super-diviner, Balaam, to place a hyper-hex upon Israel; Balak would then be able to defeat them in battle. There is no indication that Israel at the time was even aware of her danger. There were no prayer groups meeting over the matter. Yahweh simply went to work on his own, using donkey, vision and threat to stifle any curse Balaam would have loved to declare. So often, however, God seems to take the long way round, the time-consuming way. One gets a glimpse of it already in Genesis 2:18–25. If it was 'not good' for the man to be alone, Yahweh God could have plunked that first loved female down in front of Adam with a clipped, 'Here – you need this'. But he didn't. Instead he put the man through an extended process of assessing the nature of other creatures through which it became abundantly evident that in all this delightful clutter of creatures there was no helper 'corresponding to him'. It was then Yahweh God set about to 'build' the woman. Yahweh seemed in no panic to 'fix' it. The Creator rather takes a leisurely approach and allows his servant to catch up to omniscience by discerning and sensing his own need. Then surely the man will all the more prize the fulfilment of that need (cf. 'At last!' in Gen. 2:23). But it's all so inefficient, isn't it?

God seems to choose this inefficient way in Daniel 10: he moves his servant to pray for his people, then in response to the sweat and struggle of prayer he begins to bring help to his people. *I have come because of your words.* Daniel prayed, and angels went to war.

3. Truth is more devastating than we suppose (10:4–19)

Now we must go back and survey the bulk of the chapter and especially consider this figure Daniel saw in his vision by the Tigris River (4–7). Who or what was he? Some think he is Gabriel, who was the angelic interpreter previously (cf. 8:16; 9:21). If so, it would have been easy to include his name here, but anonymity rules. Others think this is a theophany or Christophany (a pre-incarnate manifest-ation of Christ), and the latter is especially appealing in light of parallels between Daniel's vision and John's vision of the risen Jesus

[5] Veldkamp, p. 207.

in Revelation 1:13–16. The *linen* (5) that may point to a priestly function (cf. Lev. 16:23, 32), the rich gold sash, the face *like the appearance of lightning*, the eyes *like torches of fire*, arms and legs *like the sight of polished bronze* (6) – all tend to push one in this direction. But I cannot quite go there. I assume that the figure of verses 5–6 is also the speaker in verse 13, where he acknowledges that he received assistance in his conflict from Michael. There is something jarring about the supposition of omnipotence receiving help. Hence I hold that verses 5–6 depict an unnamed angelic figure, who packs the splendour, power and dread of the God he serves.[6]

Daniel is devastated. *I was drained of strength, my vigour was destroyed, and I could not summon up strength* (8b, NJPS). How could it be otherwise? We must remember why in this particular context Daniel's angelic visitor appears in this terrifying form. It is because he is an invincible *warrior*, well able to face such minions as the prince of the kingdom of Persia (13a). He may be one of God's bonnie henchmen but the sight of him will scare the liver out of you. And Daniel faced this. Ponder it: here is a man probably in his mideighties, having come through three weeks on fasting-level rations, and he is physically and psychologically flattened. There is nothing casual about a heavenly visitor.

Some in our contemporary Christian 'culture', however, seem to assume that a manifestation even of the Lord himself is no reason for trauma. A man once waited to speak with John MacArthur after a meeting somewhere. He told him how he often saw the Lord, had visions of him, and that Jesus talked with him often. As an example, the man said: 'He'll come and speak to me while I am shaving.' John MacArthur's response was: 'I have just one question. Do you stop shaving?'[7] As if to say: 'Does this tend to interrupt your routine at all?' Or there is the televangelist who claims Jesus appeared to him, stood no more than three feet from him, carried on a conversation on various topics, and then dictated a four-point formula of faith for the use of hearers/viewers.[8] I don't suppose one can decisively invalidate such claims; but we can suspect them. The near flippancy is so unlike what we meet in the Bible. In the Bible one doesn't chat with Shaddai. Even when one of the Lord's angelic servants brings the revelation, that experience is not 'just the neatest thing' but devastating anguish.

Back to Daniel 10. Most of the chapter describes the agonizing process of getting Daniel able to stand on his feet again. (The Bible

---

[6] For this view, see Leupold, p. 448, and especially Duguid, pp. 180–181, who also points out parallels with the cherubim beneath the divine throne in Ezek. 1.

[7] As told by Thomas, pp. 123–124.

[8] See Hank Hanegraaff, *Christianity in Crisis* (Eugene: Harvest House, 1993), pp. 74–75.

seems to assume that one cannot receive God's revelation when 'zapped out' – one, in this case Daniel, must be aware, standing, have his wits about him and be 'on top of things'.) But why does this arduous process of strengthening Daniel have to be described in such unhurried detail? Why 'waste' a whole chapter on this? Why not simply say something like 'Daniel had a fearful, gut-wrenching struggle when he had this vision' and get on with it? Because summaries don't impress, but itemizing tends to do so.[9]

Let us move from principle to particulars and trace Daniel's struggle in the text. We use the ESV in this listing.

> *no strength was left in me. My radiant appearance was*
> *fearfully changed . . . I retained no strength* (8);
> *and as I heard . . . I fell on my face in deep sleep* (9);
> *a hand touched me and set me trembling on my hands*
> *and knees* (10)
> *when he had spoken . . . I stood up trembling* (11);
> *When he had spoken . . . I turned my face toward the*
> *ground and was mute* (15);
> *by reason of the vision pains have come upon me,*
> *and I retain no strength* (16);
> *now no strength remains in me, and no breath is left*
> *in me* (17);
> *one . . . touched me and strengthened me* (18);
> *as he spoke . . . I was strengthened and said,*
> *'Let my lord speak, for you have strengthened me'* (19).

One might wonder if this helpless, sleeping, shaking, speechless, breathless man will ever be in shape to receive the angel's revelation. Verses 18–19 finally assure us that Daniel had been sufficiently *strengthened* to face more of the revelation ordeal.

The chapter's description in such painful detail emphasizes that receiving the truth takes a frightful toll on a man. Perhaps it's something like happened to John Bradley (and many others). He was one of those men in the famous picture of raising the American flag on the island of Iwo Jima in World War II. He was a medical corpsman and saw more than his share of the gore and horror of war. He almost never spoke about it at all. He only used seven or eight disinterested minutes speaking of it on his first date with his wife-to-be Elizabeth. But, Elizabeth later told their son, after they were married in 1946 John wept at night, in his sleep, for four

---

[9] For more discussion and biblical examples, see my *The Word Became Fresh* (Ross-shire: Christian Focus, 2006), pp. 18–19.

years.[10] The agony had left its mark – precisely what we see with Daniel in this text.

Where should this leave us? In gratitude. True, we seldom if ever think of it – of the horror and pain the Lord's servants endured in order to be the vehicles through whom his word is passed on to us in the Scriptures. We sit comfortably at our desks or tables with a companionable mug of coffee, read the prophets, and scarcely think of how Daniel was physically and emotionally wiped out or Ezekiel plunged into a mental morass of anguish and anger (Ezek. 3:14–15) – in short, of how much the word of God *cost* them. If we did, we would more highly prize and tenderly reverence what we have received at their hands.

4. History is more complicated than we suppose (10:13, 20–21)

Daniel's heavenly informant explains his delay in reaching Daniel in verse 13: *Now the prince of the kingdom of Persia was standing against me for twenty-one days – and, behold, Michael, one of the premier princes, came to help me, for I had been left there facing the kings of Persia.*[11] The prince of the kingdom of Persia must be an angelic power like Daniel's informant and Michael, and yet an evil angelic power since he opposes them. This prince then seems to be a demonic power that has Persia as his niche of responsibility and potential control, a powerful evil spirit assigned to work through Persia to bring harm to God's people. We seem to be dealing with a member of that collection Paul enumerates as 'all rule and authority and power and lordship and every name that is named'[12] over which the risen, exalted Jesus now reigns – and their doom had been promised long ago (Isa. 24:21).

The angel, however, indicates that he faces further conflict once he leaves Daniel (20–21). He must return *to fight with the prince of Persia*, and, when he finishes with that piece of combat, the *prince of Greece is coming*. War goes on. The only assistance Daniel's mentor receives comes from Michael, Israel's warrior-advocate (21b).

What are we to make of this? One must not sensationalize the text nor yet mute its testimony. The teaching seems to be that unseen evil

[10] James Bradley with Ron Powers, *Flags of Our Fathers* (New York: Bantam, 2000), p. 259.

[11] The verb *nātar* is capable of various nuances, but I think the customary 'be left' is proper here. The clause actually begins, 'And I had been left . . .', but I take it (à la Steinmann) as explanatory of the previous statement, i.e., why it was necessary for Michael to come and help. To make this connection clear I have used 'for' in place of 'and'. Expositors differ on how to take 'the kings of Persia': some take them as hostile evil powers, others as human historical kings.

[12] Eph. 1:21.

powers influence and control the kingdoms and governments of this world in order to inflict harm and havoc on the people of God.[13] There is what we see on the surface, but then there is this whole unseen arena; an invisible war is going on behind the 'seens'. It reminds me of the time George Wishart (d. 1546) received a note from a close friend, who had suddenly taken ill and longed to see Wishart before he died. Wishart started out with a few friends but had scarcely gone a quarter mile before he expressed a divine premonition of danger. He asked some of his friends to ride a little ahead to a certain hill and investigate. They did – and found sixty horsemen concealed and waiting to lay hands on Wishart.[14] There was what seemed obvious, a friend's illness and request (though the note had been a forgery), but beneath the surface, unseen, malicious treachery.

Walter Luthi had the right reaction: 'Dark powers encompass the king's palace in Persia. What a dreadful thought . . . the government offices of a nation occupied by the forces of anti-God!'[15] We don't usually think this way. We have no trouble believing that incompetence and bungling are endemic to governments and political machinery, but we don't as easily think of suave and sinister spirits of evil lurking in the corridors of our congresses or shaping the policies of our parliaments. Veldkamp speaks of any number of satanic assistants who are 'far more cunning than even the most clever human diplomats' and each is assigned to be an evil influence on the people of a country 'through lies, propaganda, and other means, with the overall goal of stirring up hatred of the church of the Lord'.[16] We would despair if we did not know of Daniel's visitor and Michael (cf. Rev. 12:7–9) and the legions Jesus spoke of (Matt. 26:53).

History, then, is not only long – stretching over time, but deep – beneath its surface unseen denizens carry on a hidden war, seeking to decimate the people of God. Given that, it is amazing, is it not, that – Psalm 124-like – the Lord's flock still endures in this flesh-eating, saint-hating world?

---

[13] On this matter and current debate about it, see David E. Stevens, 'Daniel 10 and the Notion of Territorial Spirits', *Bibliotheca Sacra* 157 (2000), pp. 410–431.

[14] Thomas McCrie, *The Story of the Scottish Church* (Glasgow: Free Presbyterian, n.d., [1874]), p. 19.

[15] Luthi, p. 142.

[16] Veldkamp, p. 215.

Daniel 11:2b–45
13. The case of Mr Hyde and Mr Hyde

It was too late. One Sunday evening in May I began to preach from Daniel 11. I did so even though I had read a commentator's stricture: 'This chapter might be treated in Bible classes. We do not see how it could be used for a sermon or for sermons' (Leupold). I read aloud the first segment of text (2b–4a):

> *Look – yet three more kings are going to arise in Persia, and the fourth will gain great riches more than all, and when he is strong due to his riches he will stir up everyone, even the kingdom of Greece. And a great king shall arise, and he shall rule a vast domain and shall do as he pleases; and when he has arisen, his kingdom will be broken and parcelled out to the four winds of heaven.*

The congregation's worst fears were likely confirmed. But then I brandished a three-page handout, which explained in reasonably lucid form the personalities, events, and references depicted in Daniel 11; they had received a copy of this as they came into the service. This document, however, may have stirred more despair than hope. It still makes one's head ache to try to follow the rushing tide of kings, battles, conspiracies and looting. And right here Fyall, who had also noted Leupold's comment, comes to our rescue, for he simply points out that chapter 10 is 'the most impressive intro-duction to any of the sections of the book'.[1] And that means that what such a weighty introduction introduces must be weighty material indeed – and therefore ought to be preached. I will therefore attempt to slice up this extensive chapter into manageable sections, hit the highlights, and sketch the details of historical fulfilments

---

[1] Fyall, p. 162.

without (hopefully) suffocating in them – in what I call this strange case of Mr Hyde and Mr Hyde.

1. The futile furore of history (2b-20)

This section of Daniel's vision spends one verse on Persia (2), two on Greece (3–4), and an extended segment on the kings of the south and the kings of the north (5–20); this last chunk covers 323–175 BC and a good part of it focuses on Antiochus III ('the Great,' 11–19).

We can trace the fulfilment of Daniel's vision in capsule form. The 'fourth' king (2) in Persia after Cyrus was Xerxes (the Ahasuerus of the book of Esther), who proved numerical advantage was not decisive in war. The Greek navy so mauled the Persian fleet in the battle of Salamis (480 BC) that Xerxes went limping back to Persia. Then Daniel's interpreter depicts in verses 3–4 *a mighty king* who is almost certainly Alexander the Great (334–323 BC), who will pass from the scene but not pass on his regime to his own descendants but to *others* (4), like Ptolemy Soter, the *king of the south*, and Seleucus I, the *king of the north* (5). It hardly seems right for Alexander the Great to get whisked off the page in just twenty-seven Hebrew words and all the attention be focused on these two dynasties of 'also-rans' (the Ptolemies of Egypt, the Seleucids in Syria). But Alexander doesn't matter that much. Not here. The reason for the zoom lens on the kings of the south and north is because the people of God (a substantial number of them) will be back in the land of Israel, living on that sliver of land at the east end of the Mediterranean, that crossroads where Africa, Asia and Europe come together, where they will be scrunched between and subject to the whims of these two opposing dynasties. Besides the fortunes of God's people Alexander's empire doesn't much matter.[2]

Verses 5–12 survey a period of mostly Ptolemaic (Egyptian) dominance. Readers must remind themselves, however, that though the text seems to go into intricate details, it gives only a selective survey not an exhaustive report. *After some years* in verse 6a alerts us to this. At this point Ptolemy II (Philadelphus) reigns in Egypt and fancies an attempt at romantic diplomacy. About 250 BC he gives

---

[2] For this emphasis, see Ferguson, p. 223. This 'imbalance' is typical in the Bible. Luke, for example, is careful to highlight both Caesar Augustus and Quirinius (Luke 2:1–2) but the real 'history' of note is what will happen when this Nazareth carpenter and his intended (v. 4) reach Bethlehem. In Luke 3:1–2 the evangelist almost seems guilty of overkill; he runs through Tiberius Caesar, Pontius Pilate, Herod, Philip, Lysanias, Annas and Caiaphas, and then comes to what matters: 'the word of God came to John the son of Zechariah in the wilderness.' It's as if Luke says: 'The big news is that the word of God came to the people of God – all the name-dropping was just background.'

his daughter Berenice in marriage to Antiochus II (Theos), with the proviso that Berenice's son would be heir to Antiochus' Seleucid throne. There was a slight 'hitch': Antiochus II was already married. But not to worry, Antiochus put Laodice away and went on with the plan. However, two years later Berenice's father, Ptolemy II, died; so Antiochus divorced Berenice and took Laodice back. Laodice, once scorned, was not mollified. She apparently poisoned Antiochus and saw to it that Berenice and her child were liquidated. Hence Laodice's son, Seleucus II (Callinicus) could reign.

All this blood-letting, however, was not smart. Berenice's brother was Ptolemy III (*One from her family line*, 7 [NIV]), who attacked the north, captured and executed Laodice, and enjoyed a resounding victory over Seleucid-land (7–8). About 242 BC Seleucus II made an unsuccessful foray against Egypt (9).

Seleucus II's sons will keep assaulting the king of the south (10). One of those sons, Antiochus III ('the Great'; 223–187 BC), will bring Israel/Palestine under Seleucid control. But not soon. The king of the south was now Ptolemy IV (Philopater; 221–204 BC), one of the sorrier excuses for a ruler that any kingdom ever had.[3] Amazingly, this pervert and playboy posted a decisive victory over Antiochus III. Verse 11b seems to describe this: *And he* [the king of the north] *shall raise a great multitude, but it shall be given into his* [the king of the south] *hand* (ESV). This occurred in 217 BC at Raphia, on the frontier between Palestine and Egypt. One senses from reading Polybius that a pre-occupied Philopater had able and alert underlings like Sosibius who saved his military and political bacon.[4] In any case, Antiochus III was humiliated: he lost 17,000 troops, the Egyptians only 2,200.

But something like thirteen years later Antiochus makes a comeback. In verses 13–17 the prophecy seems to sketch the success of Antiochus III. The time was propitious: Ptolemy IV had died and Ptolemy V (Epiphanes; 204–181 BC) was a mere four years old. Antiochus mustered a massive army, attacked Egyptian holdings in Phoenicia and Palestine (13), eventually driving General Scopas and the Egyptian forces into Sidon, where, under siege, the latter surrendered in 198 BC (15?). The land of Israel now passed into Seleucid control (16).

Nevertheless, even winners have frustrations. Antiochus met one in his daughter Cleopatra. He had betrothed her to Ptolemy V in order to infuse Seleucid influence into Egypt via matrimony. But the scheme

---

[3] Cf. Archer (p. 135): 'Ptolemy IV was a cruel debauchee who began his reign by murdering his own mother, Berenice of Cyrene, and then his wife, his sister, and his brother. He then gave himself over to a degenerate dissipation with male and female sex partners and finally succumbed to disease in 203.'

[4] Polybius, *Histories*, 5:62–64, 66–67.

'bombed' – Cleopatra was far more enamoured with her young husband and became decidedly pro-Egyptian (cf. 17). And then Antiochus attempted the conquest of some Mediterranean islands and coastlands and enjoyed some success. However, the Romans warned him to stay out of Greece. He nevertheless invaded Greece (192 BC), and the Romans, perhaps wondering what part of 'No' Antiochus did not understand, defeated him at Thermopylae, then pursued him into Asia and defeated him at Magnesia (190 BC; cf. 18). There Antiochus had the Romans outnumbered more than two-to-one (70,000 to 30,000) – and still lost. The Romans laid such a heavy indemnity on Antiochus that he was in dire need of funds. Hence the temptation to rob temples. While he was looting a temple in Elymas in 187 BC, an incensed mob of local Zeus zealots did away with him (cf. 19).

Antiochus the Great may bite the dust but Rome still wants its annual tribute. So Seleucus IV (187–175 BC) borrows a page from his father's playbook and sends a revenue agent, his prime minister Heliodorus, to seize funds from the temple treasury in Jerusalem (20a). According to 2 Maccabees 3, Heliodorus' sacrilege was stymied by a vision of terrifying and attacking angels. Some time later the same Heliodorus poisoned Seleucus IV and so he was *broken, neither in anger nor in battle* (20b).[5]

I have dubbed this segment the 'futile furore' of history, and the 'furore' fairly leaps at us off the page. From Xerxes to Seleucus IV we have an overflowing dossier of lies and schemes and conspiracies, of victories and disasters and tragedies, of the never-ending, hurly-burly confusion of wars and political turmoil. But the text doesn't merely want us to hear the racket but to see the *futility* of it. Repeatedly, the text calls attention to a 'frustration'-element that stymies the plans or actions of the 'history-makers'. We will be best impressed with this if we wade through the whole pile of instances.[6]

Verse 4:   *his kingdom shall be broken and divided*
           No sooner does Alexander amass his empire than it
           will be splintered.

Verse 6b: *but she will not hold on to the strength of (her) arm
           … but she will be given over*
           The alliance forged through Berenice's marriage to
           Antiochus II will not succeed.

---

[5] I have tried to keep this survey concise; for more detail in lucid form, see the commentaries of Steinmann and Miller, or Allan A. MacRae's discussion in *The Prophecies of Daniel* (Singapore: Christian Life Publishers, 1991), pp. 214–225.

[6] Sinclair Ferguson (p. 233) very helpfully notes that these futility-points can often be traced by looking for the conjunction 'but' in one's English translation.

Verse 9: *but he shall return to his land*
About 242/240 BC Seleucus II (king of the north) invaded Egypt but, being defeated, had to return to Syria.

Verse 11b: *but the multitude shall be given into his hand*
Raising a 'great multitude' seems to be the work of Antiochus III, the king of the north. Polybius says Antiochus' army at Raphia consisted of 62,000 infantry, 6,000 cavalry and 102 elephants – a formidable force, but 'given over' to Ptolemy IV.

Verse 12b: *but he will not remain strong*
After Ptolemy IV's (Philopater) smashing victory at Raphia, his power will evaporate; no surprise, considering his passionate commitment to dissipation.

Verse 14b: *Violent ones among your own people will assert themselves to fulfil a vision, but they will fail* (HCSB)
Expositors puzzle over this cryptic remark. Apparently, some Israelite thugs tie their fortunes either to Antiochus III or to the Egyptians and find that their hot-headed zeal comes to nothing.

Verse 17b: *And the daughter of women he will give to him to destroy it* [= the Egyptian kingdom?], *but it will not stand and will not prove to his advantage*
Antiochus III gave his daughter Cleopatra to Ptolemy V in order to undercut the latter, but she seemed genuinely to love her husband and all things Egyptian, and so Antiochus' scheme fell to pieces.

Verse 18b: *but a commander shall put an end to his arrogance*
Antiochus III enjoys successful conquest of Mediterranean islands and coastlands; but Roman consul Scipio inflicts a crushing defeat on him at Magnesia, with a crippling indemnity payable to Rome.

Verse 19b: *but he shall stumble and fall, and will not be found*
After his reverse at Magnesia and the humiliating treaty of Apamea, Antiochus III can only venture to the east; but this is short-lived – he is cut down while robbing a temple, seeking funds in order to pay off Rome.

Verse 20b: *but within a few days he will be broken, but not in anger or battle*
Seleucus IV (Philopater; 187–175 BC) succeeds his father Antiochus III but eventually he enters the royal 'landfill' when his head revenue collector poisons him.

Citing all these instances seems to place a reader under a literary sledge-hammer, but it is crucial to see how pervasive this futility-element is in the text. No one has summarized this matter better than Iain Duguid, who speaks of the 'profound perspective on history' in verses 2–20:

> On one level, it is the continual story of wars and rumors of wars, as one human ruler and empire after another seeks to gain power by cunning or force. Yet though the tide in the affairs of men comes in and goes out, in the end it accomplishes precisely nothing. The balance of power in earthly politics may shift but it never comes to a permanent rest. On the one hand, therefore, Daniel 11 shows us the fallen world pursuing the wind and finding it elusive. What do power and politics gain for all their toil?[7]

Or, as Habakkuk 2:13 asks, 'Why, is it not from Yahweh of hosts that peoples weary themselves only for fire and nations exhaust themselves for nothing?'

One dare not, however, leave the matter there. We must understand what *massive comfort this view of history provides for the people of God.* For how often God's people worldwide must feel they are caught in the gears of vicious regimes and that the corpulent heavyweights of this age simply mash them at will. But our text teaches that our Lord brings judgment not only at the climax of history but also *within history* as he injects futility into the designs of self-exalting, saint-ignoring rulers of this world, so that their schemes end in shambles. Not that he *always* does this; but the text, by its repeated examples, implies that this is his tendency, that he does it far more often than we may be aware. How could God's people bear to live if he simply allowed the self-styled deities of this age to fulfil all their plans?

2. The insane intensity of history (21–35)

Now we are dealing with a *despicable* person (21a). No one has conferred royal majesty on him but he slithers in while folks are *at*

---

[7] Duguid, p. 200.

ease (cf. NIV) and grabs the kingdom by flatteries and manoeuvrings. This is Antiochus IV (Epiphanes). Antiochus had been released from Rome in a 'hostage exchange' – Demetrius, the son of Seleucus IV (cf. 20) had gone to Rome, Antiochus was released and was in Athens when he heard his brother Seleucus had been murdered. With the help of the king of Pergamum Antiochus obtained an army and marched east. Antiochus took the Seleucid throne, seemingly as regent in place of his nephew Demetrius (now in Rome) and as co-regent with another nephew, Antiochus, who was an infant (and conveniently murdered five years later).[8] All of verses 21–35 focuses on Antiochus IV.

We may break down the passage into three 'chunks': first, a synopsis of his reign (22–24), which sketches his overall military success (22–23) and lavish rewards to those he favoured (24);[9] second, the objects of his hostility (25–31), the *king of the south* (25–27) but especially the covenant people (28–31);[10] and third, the cost of his savagery (32–35) – the great price the faithful in Israel will pay as they resist Antiochus' programme.

This savagery seems to have become especially brutal after Antiochus' second foray against Egypt (29; ca. 168 BC). Verse 30 *may* help explain it: *ships of Kittim shall come against him, and he shall be intimidated and return, and shall vent his rage against the holy covenant.* Antiochus would find that the Roman fleet (*ships of Kittim*) had come to greet him along with the Roman general, Popillius Laenas, who carried a senate decree requiring Antiochus to abandon his designs on Egypt or be regarded as Rome's enemy. Antiochus said something like, 'Well, of course, I must consult with my advisers.' But Laenas, having a vine stick in his hand, drew a circle in the sand around Antiochus' feet, and told him, 'You must decide before you step outside that.' Classic Roman arrogance perhaps, but Antiochus had no other rational option but to submit. Frustrated in Egypt, he erupted in maniacal fury against Israel.[11]

[8] See Steinmann, p. 525.

[9] The 'prince of the covenant' (v. 22) is often thought to be Onias III, high priest in Jerusalem, whom Antiochus deposed in favour of Jason and later Menelaus; the 'alliance' of v. 23 may have been with King Eumenes II of Pergamum who provided Antiochus with a working army (cf. Collins, p. 382).

[10] Vv. 25–26 depict Antiochus' victory over Ptolemy VI of Egypt. However, some Egyptians installed his younger brother as Ptolemy VII in Alexandria and Antiochus 'negotiated' with Ptolemy VI to restore him to Egypt's throne. The 'talks', however, would be riddled with duplicity and so we have that superb description of most all international diplomacy in v. 27: *they shall speak lies at the same table.*

[11] Lester Grabbe (*Judaism from Cyrus to Hadrian*, vol. 1, *The Persian and Greek Periods* [Minneapolis: Fortress, 1992], p. 248) rejects this implication because it provides 'no logical explanation' except the caprice of an unpredictable individual. But if the individual was unpredictable it may well be a reasonably logical explanation. Antiochus IV was likely an able administrator and general – and at the same time quirky and

153

I have dubbed this segment the 'insane intensity' of history. Just what is so 'intense' about it? Well, if we look back over the angel's disclosure in terms of its fulfillment, we notice that verses 2–20 cover matters from 530 to 175 BC, basically from Cyrus to Antiochus the Great – 355 years in nineteen verses; however verses 21–35 cover events with the span of 175 to 163 BC, the tenure of Antiochus Epiphanes – twelve years in fifteen verses.[12] That is what is so intense: the single reign of Antiochus Epiphanes gets essentially equal space with the 350-plus years before him. Why does he rate such space? Why is the angel so fixated on Antiochus Epiphanes?

Hopefully I have answered these questions in the introduction[13] and in the second half of the exposition of Daniel 8. Suffice it to say here that ca. 167 BC Antiochus instituted a religious rampage against the covenant people. He was set on emasculating the vitals of biblical faith and was determined to see every Jew apostatize. He stripped them of sacrament (the death penalty for circumcising male infants), sacrifice (unless they would offer pagan offerings to Zeus), Sabbath (observing it brought a death sentence), and Scripture (one's life was forfeit if caught with a torah scroll). In this reign of terror it seemed the only choice was to be a live pagan or a dead Israelite. Hence many in Israel 'caved'. But the severity of the trouble explains the amount of space given Antiochus. This was to be a terribly lethal time of tribulation for Israel; God's people therefore needed to know clearly about it in advance. Hence the fifteen verses of this prophecy dealing with the ruler who would be Antiochus Epiphanes.

In an autobiographical memoir, theologian Helmut Thielicke reflected on what kept him from falling for Nazism in the days of Hitler's rise to power in Germany. He wrote that he was one of the few people who had actually read Hitler's *Mein Kampf* and that the style and content of that book had to a certain degree 'immunized' him against Nazi ideology.[14] That is, I would hold, something of the function of the Antiochus Epiphanes prophecy here – not that it

bizarre. Cf. the convenient collection of testimonies from ancient writers in Walter K. Price, *In the Final Days* (Chicago: Moody, 1977), pp. 56–60. Will Durant calls Antiochus 'both the most interesting and the most erratic of his line, a rare mixture of intellect, insanity, and charm' (*The Life of Greece* [New York: Simon and Schuster, 1939], p. 573). In any case, the strange behaviour of rulers is not so mystifying if one remembers Barbara Tuchman's thesis in *The March of Folly* that stupidity is a correlate of power.

[12] Duguid, p. 201, makes the same point a bit differently: 'After fifteen verses [= vv. 6–20] that cover the reigns of seven Seleucid kings over a period of around 150 years, the next fifteen verses focus our attention on the reign of a single Seleucid king, Antiochus IV.'

[13] See 'When was it published?', pp. 15–22.

[14] Helmut Thielicke, *Notes from a Wayfarer* (New York: Paragon House, 1995), p. 86.

could 'immunize' God's people but that it would *fortify* them, would brace them to endure such a dark and evil time.

But the passage does more than warn of a coming storm. One hears a positive note of quiet encouragement in the repeated *refrain* of a *time* or *appointed time*. In verse 24b Antiochus will plot and scheme *but for a time*. A limit has been imposed on him. Verse 27 relates the skulduggery of Antiochus and Ptolemy VI at the conference table and declares it futile, *for there is yet an end at the appointed time*. This *end* may refer particularly to Antiochus' end and the time God has set for removing him from the playing field of history. Verse 29 indicates that Antiochus will make another foray against Egypt *at the appointed time*, that is, at the time God has set; it's as if Antiochus marches to God's calendar. Then verse 35 indicates some of God's *wise* ones will be refined by their sufferings *until the time of the end, for it is yet at the appointed time*. Contextually, I think the *end* in verse 35 means the end of Antiochus' scourge, and God has already appointed that termination date. These little notes, this repeated refrain, should prove heartening to suffering people who will weather years under a loose cannon like Antiochus, who inflicts madness and murder seemingly at will. Just as in Psalm 23 the way through the 'valley of deep darkness' is yet one of the paths of righteousness, so here, mysteriously, even chaotic time is *appointed* time. Antiochus will not be footloose and fancy-free as he may seem, for God determines even the terms of tyrannies and they are tethered to the dates on God's calendar. Antiochus will only operate within *appointed time*.

I recall several times in earlier years when our family had to relocate. The move might be of five hundred or even over a thousand miles. I would rent a truck, anguish over the best way to pack our household goods into it, and eventually we would be off, my wife and children following in the family auto. In those days at least, truck rental companies put a governor on their trucks, set for, say, sixty or sixty-two miles an hour. This proved frustrating. I might begin to pass another vehicle (usually another truck), would tramp the accelerator to the floor, pick up speed, and then – just as one needed that extra burst to pass successfully – would feel the engine go 'flat' as the governor refused to allow any further speed. One could end up going sixty miles an hour beside another vehicle for some distance, never being able to pass that vehicle because the governor on 'my' truck controlled my maximum speed. That's the point being made in this 'Antiochus' section. Antiochus himself will not likely have a clue, but he will be functioning within the confines of God's *appointed time*. Even the insane intensity of history is under the control of a 'governor'.

3. The final scourge of history (36–45)

We must face a preliminary scourge ourselves before looking at the 'final scourge' in this section, because a number of scholars do not think the scourge in these verses is so 'final' but simply more on Antiochus Epiphanes. A brief discussion is essential, if not painless.

a. Big debate

Verse 36 raises the disputed question: Who is *the king* who *shall do as he pleases*? The more natural answer seems to be Antiochus Epiphanes – he was the focus of verses 21–35 and it seems obvious to assume that verse 36 is introducing more of the same about the same ruler. Verse 35b, however, with its *until the time of the end* formula seems to close off the Antiochus segment (21–35),[15] drawing a line as it were across the page. If this is so, then *the king* of 36a could well refer to someone else.[16] But someone could claim that the writer is just opening up another presentation of Antiochus in verses 36–45 and recapitulating his rule. Hence the content and detail of these verses is crucial.

The passage describes this king's religious pretensions (36–37), military dominance (40–44) and final end (45). None of these fits what we know of Antiochus Epiphanes. For all his dallying with inscribing 'god manifest' on his coins,

> Antiochus did not exalt himself above every god (vv. 36–37), reject 'the gods of his fathers,' or worship 'a god unknown to his fathers' (v. 38); on the contrary, he worshiped the Greek pantheon, even building an altar and offering sacrifices to Zeus in the Jerusalem temple precincts.[17]

Nor did Antiochus ever have mastery of, for example, Egypt and her satellites (40, 42–43) – and he did not meet his end in Israel but in Persia (45).

Normally one would infer that if the description of verses 36–45 does not fit Antiochus Epiphanes it must not be about him, that *the king* (36a) must be someone else. Yet a block of scholarly opinion still insists these verses describe Antiochus. John Collins, for example, admits that the data of verses 36–38 go far beyond what

---

[15] The 'end' in this context refers to the end of Antiochus' persecutions; see Miller, p. 303.

[16] Note the similar abrupt 'jump' from (probably) Xerxes of Persia to Alexander of Greece in vv. 2–3.

[17] Miller, p. 305; see also Archer, pp. 143–145; and even Collins, p. 387.

Antiochus did but suggests that the writer is 'probably' engaging in deliberate distortion and exaggeration in order to underscore Antiochus' extreme godlessness. That could be possible; but one can't help but wonder if Collins is explaining or evading evidence.[18]

The slant taken on verses 40–45 is a bit different. Those biblical critics who hold Daniel was written about 165 BC in the wake of Antiochus' persecutions see no particular mystery about these verses. In their view all of chapter 11 (up through 35 or 39) was prophecy-after-the-fact. That is, the events had already taken place but they were written up in the guise of 'prophecy', cast in the form of prediction, which explains why most of chapter 11 is as accurate as it is. But in verses 40–45 the writer had come up to his own time and so, to wrap up the Antiochus saga, engaged in a segment of 'genuine' predictive prophecy. He predicted Antiochus would carry out extensive military conquests and meet his end in the land of Israel. He plainly botched it. I suppose the moral is that doing predictive prophecy is harder than it may appear. At any rate, these critics would say there is no real problem between what we know of Antiochus' last years and what we read in verses 40–45. The writer tried his hand at real prediction and simply did a 'butcher' job.

However, this position runs into serious difficulties. For example, if the prophecy of 11:40–45 was so erroneous, how does one explain the people of Israel accepting the book as authoritative Scripture, especially when they would know the true facts about Antiochus' final years?[19] Were they simply too naïve or 'pre-critical' to know better? Are we to imagine they were so adept in theological double-speak that they could conclude that this prophetic mess the writer had made was nevertheless in some way the word of God to them? Then there is an 'internal' problem. In verse 30 our writer had indicated that *ships of Kittim* would oppose Antiochus, a likely reference to the way the Romans would write 'verboten' across Antiochus' map of Egypt. Stay out or fight Rome. Would that writer, then, if composing his own prediction about Antiochus, have sent him on another invasion of Egypt (40, 42–43)?[20] Wouldn't he try to avoid such an improbable supposition?

Suffice to say I cannot buy into this common 'critical' view of this passage. If the content of the passage does not fit Antiochus

---

[18] See Collins, pp. 387–388. What evidence do we have that the biblical writer was distorting and exaggerating? Only that Collins says so. That is opinion but not evidence.

[19] See Robert Dick Wilson, *Studies in the Book of Daniel*, 2 vols. in 1 (Grand Rapids: Baker, 1972 [1917/1918]), 2:265–266.

[20] See A. R. Millard, 'Daniel', in *The New Layman's Bible Commentary* (Grand Rapids: Zondervan, 1979), p. 924.

Epiphanes it is because it is not about Antiochus but someone else. Hence I think *the king* of verse 36 is someone other than Antiochus Epiphanes.

It may be helpful to look at the overall structure of our passage. Sometimes 11:36–45 is thought to be a recapitulation of Antiochus' career; I hold that it forms a *parallel* to it. Notice the following broad breakdown:

11:21–35
Focus: *A despicable person* (21)
A   Rise and success (21–24)
B   Conflict and oppression (25–31)
C   Suffering and steadfastness (32–35)

11:36 – 12:3
Focus: *The king* (11:36)
A'   Rise and success (11:36–39)
B'   Conflict and oppression (11:40–45)
C'   Suffering and steadfastness (12:1–3)[21]

Though we are dealing with chapter 11, 12:1–3 (C') obviously belongs to it (*At that time* in 12:1a links to ch. 11), and brings us to the time of resurrection (2), which implies that *the king* of 11:36ff. is a figure of the 'last times', clearly post-Antiochus. But why the parallel pattern? Because the vision intends us to see Antiochus and 'the king' in tandem. I find it difficult to imagine why the writer would follow the same structural pattern if he were only describing Antiochus again. In Antiochus one sees a foreshadowing, a scale model, of the final opponent of God's people. This final scourge will be like Antiochus Epiphanes – only more and worse. Hence the title of this chapter. Only we are not dealing, as in Robert Louis Stevenson's tale, with a Dr Jekyll and Mr Hyde, with a reasonable, companionable fellow versus a reclusive, vicious, evil beast of a man. No, it's only the latter type, what we might call a case of Mr Hyde and Mr Hyde. Antiochus and the coming opponent are of the same ilk, only Antiochus is like Hyde and his antitype like a highly more hideous Hyde. One might say Antiochus is a lower-case 'hyde', and his ultimate successor is an upper-case 'Hyde'.

[21] I have found similar schemes in MacRae (p. 225) and Steinmann (p. 545). Note the shared themes of distributing favours in A and A' (11:24b, 39b), the oppression of Israel in B and B' (11:28, 30, and clearly implied in 41 and 45), and the division brought about within the professing people of God in C and C' (11:32 and 12:2).

b. Overall sketch

The brief bio of this oppressor alludes first of all to his *religion* (36–39a), which consists primarily in his self-deification:

> *he will exalt himself and magnify himself above every god and against the God of gods he will speak un-heard-of things (36); he will not pay attention to the gods of his fathers . . . and he will not pay attention to any god, for he will magnify himself above all (37).*

Shades of 2 Thessalonians 2:4. One assumes that his claim to deity also involves an insistence that men and women acknowledge him as such – otherwise, why make the claim? Verses 38–39a may seem to qualify his divine pretensions when, for example, we read that *he will give honour to the god of fortresses* (38a). Here Keil is helpful:

> The 'god of fortresses' is the personification of war, and the thought is this: he will regard no other god, but only war; the taking of fortresses he will make his god; and he will worship this god above all as the means of gaining the world-power. Of this god, war as the object of deification, it might be said that his fathers knew nothing, because no other king had made war his religion, his god to whom he offered up in sacrifices all, gold, silver, precious stones, jewels.[22]

If this is the case, then his devotion to the 'god of fortresses' does not counter his self-deification but is only a further expression of it. The text continues by noting his *seduction* (39b) by which he secures that adulation of lackeys and boot-lickers, his *dominance* (40–44) in international conquests, and his *termination* (45), welcome news for those crushed under his regime.

Readers must beware of a subtle form of unbelief that may infect them, especially as they read of the deity-claims of this 'final scourge'. At least we in the West may think we are too rational and cynical to ever be tempted to confess the divine status of such a pretender. We may imagine that no one would ever swallow such claims. On the contrary, otherwise reasonable people are only too eager to become god-makers. When in 1951 US President Harry Truman dismissed General Douglas MacArthur as commander of forces in Korea, the general came home to tumultuous accolades. Truman's action was in response to MacArthur's insubordination and criticism of US policy in the Far East. But Truman's name was mud; people despised

---

[22] Keil, p. 466.

him for the decision. MacArthur then addressed a joint session of Congress on 20 April – a packed house plus thirty million more by television. He kept his audience spellbound for a little more than a half-hour, making plain his own position on the Korean conflict. At the end of his speech he alluded to the adage, 'Old soldiers never die – they just fade away', and his last word was spoken in a whisper into a great hush: 'Goodbye.' Then it was pandemonium. People, it is said, were sobbing his praise, pressing in to touch his sleeve. One Missouri congressman shouted, 'We heard God speak here today, God in the flesh, the voice of God!'[23] What utter blasphemous nonsense – and yet how easily and eagerly we slide into the god-manufacturing business. 'Watch and pray that you may not enter into temptation.'[24]

c. Bottom line

Sometimes one can say much by saying nothing, or very little. Maria Louisa was the wife of Confederate general James Longstreet for more than forty years, endured the strain of being the spouse of a military man during the War between the States, and gave birth to their ten children (five survived to adult years). And yet Longstreet never mentioned her in his memoirs.[25] Perhaps a mere oversight. Or maybe it means Old Pete, as he was called, was an ingrate. At any rate, it seems like a put-down. And the last line of chapter 11 functions that way. Not that there is no mention of the king's end at all but that his obituary is so terse, so brief, so abrupt that it is dismissive.[26] *But he shall come to his end, with no one helping him* (45b). Fascinating treatment for a deity-clone who conquers nations and oppresses saints: he is wiped off the stage of history in a mere six Hebrew words.

The bottom line is instructive. It's as if the Lord says to us: You must be prepared; in the world you *have* tribulation (cf. John 16:33); but don't think *too* much of the 'tribulator', for though he may be dreadfully terrifying, he will be easily disposed off. That should put steel in our bones, in case we have to face the final scourge of history.

[23] Robert A. Caro, *Master of the Senate* (New York: Knopf, 2002), pp. 367–369.
[24] Mark 14:38.
[25] Cormac O'Brien, *Secret Lives of the Civil War* (Philadelphia: Quirk Books, 2007), p. 209.
[26] See Ferguson's helpful treatment (p. 238).

Daniel 12:1–13
14. Enduring to the end

In *The Guns of August* Barbara Tuchman writes that Russia's last czar, Nicholas II, gave people the impression of imperturbability. Yet, says Tuchman, it was nothing of the kind – it was apathy, indifference. When he received a telegram telling him that the Russian fleet had been annihilated at Tsushima, he read it, stuffed it in his pocket, and went on with his tennis game. A tragic response to tragedy. And a reader has to beware of a Nicholas-type response to Daniel's book, especially by the time he or she reaches Daniel 12. As noted before, the book of Daniel functions as a manual for the suffering church, as does its New Testament counterpart, the book of Revelation. Daniel 12 proves this again to be the case, for it tells us that the people of God will face their most frightful opposition in history bar none. Yet in Daniel we have heard repeatedly of the sufferings, perils and devastation the saints face or will face, and so we may become less and less moved by it, desensitized to it, a bit hardened. (Bible reading is a dangerous business.) We must not then turn a deaf ear when we hear even more of it in Daniel 12; we must not turn away in an equivalent of resuming a game of tennis.

I realize that Daniel 12 actually consists of two distinct pieces of material: verses 1–4 are the final piece of the revelation beginning in 11:2b and, more immediately, the last segment of 11:36–45 describing the 'final scourge' of history. Verses 5–13, on the other hand, constitute the concluding 'footnotes' to the revelation of 11:2b – 12:4. Nevertheless, all of chapter 12 presses one question upon us: Will the people of God endure when evil does its worst? Will they endure to the end, in the very last and most severe period of suffering? The answer is positive, because of what we have or will be given.

1. We will have security in the greatest trouble (1–4)

At that time (1a) most directly links up with 11:40, 'At the time of the end'. The reference is to the tenure of the 'king' with the self-deification itch (11:36–39) with his passion and programme of conquest (11:40–45), the one I have called the 'final scourge' of history.[1] Now, however, we hear of his 'internal policy' (Archer) toward the people of God. And it is not good:

> *And there shall be a time of distress;*
> *nothing like it has happened*
>   *from the time a nation came into being*
>   *up to that time;*
> *but at that time your people will be rescued* (1b).

The language of the text is not mere hyperbole – it is the language of extremity and uniqueness. Whether the *nation* refers to Israel or to the rise of any nation, the point is that never in history has there been a time of suffering so severe and intense (cf. Mark 13:19).

What strikes us, however, in verse 1 is its double affirmation of unparalleled distress *and* assured deliverance. One senses this security in the way Daniel's angelic interpreter describes the people of God. He says they are a *helped* people, for *at that time Michael, the great prince, will arise, the one who stands [guard] over the sons of your people.* We don't know all that is involved here, but from Daniel 10[2] we understand Michael to be the warrior-advocate of Israel who takes up the cudgels on their behalf. There are unseen legions (cf. Matt. 26:53; Heb. 1:14) standing behind the wobbly people of God in their darkest trouble. They are, moreover, a *known* people: *And at that time your people will be rescued – everyone found written in the book* (1d). The figure of the *book* is familiar from Exodus 32:32–33 and Psalm 69:28; it is the 'citizen list' of the kingdom of God or 'the roll of thine elect'.[3] *Written in the book* may be a literary figure but is no literary filler. Rather, in a time when God's people will be viewed as trash, scum and faceless protoplasm, they are assured that their names are known and precious to God (cf. Luke 10:20 in context).

When, however, Daniel hears that his people will be *rescued* or delivered (1d) we naturally wonder how that will take place. Part of an answer may come from verse 2: *And many of those sleeping in the*

---

[1] Paul calls him 'the man of lawlessness' (2 Thess. 2:3) and John alludes to him as 'the beast rising from the sea' (Rev. 13:1), which he would likely dub the (final) Antichrist.

[2] See ch. 12, 'History is more complicated than we suppose', p. 145.

[3] The latter from Henry Alford's hymn, 'Ten Thousand Times Ten Thousand'.

dusty ground will awake. That is, deliverance for some at least will come via resurrection. They are then a *vindicated* people, for though they may forfeit their lives in the time of suffering, their resurrection will prove to be their deliverance and more than that – an act of God's defiance to the ungodly 'terminators' of this age. Yet resurrection in itself is not deliverance, for, as Stuart Olyott points out, 'resurrection day will also be division day'.[4] *Some will rise to everlasting life and some to disgrace and everlasting abhorrence* (2b). With the encouragement also comes the warning that one may be a card-carrying Israelite and yet not be one of the 'rescued' people.

Verse 3 implies that this suffering people is also an *encouraged* people. It speaks of *the wise* who will *shine like the bright sky* and then describes the *wise* as *those who turn many to righteousness*, which I assume means that they influence others to go on walking in righteousness and assist them in remaining faithful in the pressure of the times. There is a similar scenario in 11:32–33, which depicts Antiochus' persecution. There 'the wise among the people will make many understand' (33) which keeps them from apostatizing as other Israelites will do (32a). Whether *the wise* are teachers (as a number of commentators think) is not certain, but they do seem to be those who have discernment about what God's people are facing, who remain faithful in the time of suffering, and who bolster others not to deny the faith in such a time. Such encouragement can make quite a difference for faltering saints. It was like that one day in 1540, when two Scots lads, Alexander Kennedy and Jerome Russell, were condemned to burn at the stake for their faith. As they plodded to the execution site, Russell noticed some signs of depression in his companion and so heartened him with: 'Brother, fear not; greater is He that is in us, than he that is in the world. The pain that we are to suffer is short, and shall be light, but our joy and consolation shall never have an end. Let us, therefore, strive to enter in to our Master and Saviour by the same strait way which he has trod before us. Death cannot destroy us, for it is already destroyed by Him for whose sake we suffer.'[5] And so they walked on, to the stake. But what a help it can be to have one of the *wise* come along beside and keep you on your feet.

Finally, verse 4 may indicate that God will see that he has a *prepared* people in these times. I say 'may' because expositors differ on how to construe this verse. Rather than take you through five pages of fascinating and engrossing discussion of disputed points I will simply explain what I think is the sense of the verse. Daniel is

[4] Olyott, p. 162.
[5] Thomas McCrie, *The Story of the Scottish Church* (Glasgow: Free Presbyterian, n.d. [1874]), pp. 13–14.

to *close off the words*, probably because the revelation is finished and there will be no more at this time. He is to *seal up the document until the time of the end*. The *document* could refer to the last revelation of chapter 10 to this point, or possibly to the whole book. One sealed a document not to hide it but in order to preserve and authenticate it. Note the process Jeremiah followed with the purchase deed for Hanamel's field in Jeremiah 32:9–15. Beside the 'sealed' deed there was also an open copy attached so that one could know the contents of the sealed material.[6] But what is the link with the enigma that follows? *Many will roam to and fro and knowledge will increase.* The first verb is *šwṭ* (to roam around or about), which occurs thirteen times in the OT. It refers to, among other things, Satan's extensive roaming through the earth (Job 1:7; 2:2) and to the comforting scrutiny of Yahweh's eyes 'ranging' throughout the same arena (2 Chr. 16:9; Zech. 4:10) and to Joab's detailed survey through Israel's territory (2 Sam. 24:2, 8). The verb connotes *thoroughness*.[7] If this roaming *to and fro* refers to thorough and intense activity directed to Daniel's document, the last clause (*knowledge will increase*) promises progress in the understanding of it.[8] As the Lord's people give diligent attention to this piece of Scripture, they will, especially nearer the end, have a clearer grasp of its meaning. (This seems to be the Lord's usual pattern in our use of Scripture: it is immersion that brings insight.) This feeds into their security, for if they are clearer about what may come their way, they are fore-armed to face it.

Yahweh is just so very 'God-like' in this passage. No sooner does he mention unheard-of distress than he peppers the text with tokens of our security. It helps immensely to know, among other things, that no church-crushing, saint-smashing regime can remove the names written in the indelible ink of God's book.

2. We will have certainty in the hardest misery (5–7)

In verses 5–6 we see another clip of a human vision (5) and hear an angelic question (6). Daniel saw two additional figures, apparently angelic ones, one on each side of the stream. The *man* originally described in 10:5–6 stands *above the waters of the stream*. It was

---

[6] Cf. the description in William L. Holladay, *Jeremiah 2*, Hermeneia (Minneapolis: Fortress, 1989), p. 215.

[7] Some (e.g., Young, Collins) take it as indicating *futility*, linking it to its use in Amos 8:12, where Israel will search everywhere ('they shall wander from sea to sea, and will *roam around* from north to east') for a word from Yahweh and 'will not find it'. But the 'futility' comes only from the last verb ('will not find'); the use of *šwṭ* earlier in the verse, as usual, connotes only the *thoroughness* of the search.

[8] See Calvin, Keil, Leupold and Miller for essentially the same view.

likely one of the additional angels who asked, *How long is it going to be until the end of the wonders?* (6b). The *wonders* may refer to the unparalleled *time of distress* in 12:1, or the term may take in the triumphs, sway and oppressions of the coming pseudo-god depicted in 11:36 – 12:3. The sense of the question is, 'How long will these "wonders" continue once they begin to occur?'[9] If it is one of the angels who asks this, then clearly it is a legitimate question and not at all a matter of idle curiosity.

In verse 7 Daniel's revelation-guide gives his answer: the matter is utterly certain (for contrary to usual practice in oath-taking, he raises not just one hand – see, e.g., Gen. 14:22, but *both* hands), and the time is both *definite* (*for a time, times, and a half*) and *devastating* (*and when they finish shattering the power of a holy people, all these things will be finished*). We have already met the 'three and a half times' in 7:25, where they refer to the period in which the saints are 'given' into the power of the 'different' king of the fourth and final earthly kingdom. The phrase seems to imply a restricted and limited time during which Yahweh's flock stands under the ravages of this final oppressor.[10] What is especially disturbing, however, is this *shattering of the power of the holy people* (ESV). Stuart Olyott has set forth a stark summary of the scenario:

> We will come to the point in history where it appears that darkness has really won the day. It will seem as if the Antichrist is going to continue for ever. It will seem as if the church has been entirely obliterated, for there will no longer be any sign of it.[11]

Can you think of anything so bleak? This is the hardest misery. This is, eventually, the future of the church. And it's not what we prefer to hear. In fact, you won't get invited back to speak at the prophecy conference if you preach like this! But the marvel of it all is that this shattered people has a God who 'shortens the days' (cf. Mark 13:20), a cross-centred God who knows the pains of his people (Exod. 3:7; Isa. 63:9) and sets a limit to their distress. Lest we be tempted to doubt, Daniel's visitor gives us a two-handed oath, so that misery is infected with certainty.

[9] Miller, p. 322.
[10] I cannot follow Calvin in holding that three and a half times denotes an indefinite period. The context seems to expect some kind of limitation. Whatever three and a half times denotes, it seems to import something definite, which is a strange way to indicate an indefinite period.
[11] Olyott, p. 165. Cf. Duguid: 'Certainly there is no expectation here of a gradual Christianization of the world. The prerequisite for the end is not the final fixing of our world's brokenness; rather, it is the final breaking of the holy people's strength' (p. 218).

3. We can have tenacity in the darkest days (8–12)

An attentive reader probably finds Daniel's confession in verse 8a somewhat comforting: *I heard, but I did not understand.* Even Daniel was perplexed, probably about the cryptic declaration in verse 7b. So he presses on for more light and asks, *What will be the outcome* [or: 'fall-out'] *of these things?* (8b). *These things* most likely refers to the statements in verse 7. 'His particular concern was doubtless directed toward the ultimate fortunes of the covenant people of God, especially in view of the intimidating language of v. 7. Would they survive after their power was "broken," or would they go under as a nation in their futile struggle for truth?'[12] Daniel's guide seems both to refuse an answer and to supply an answer. In verse 9 he signals that the current revelation is at an end, and yet in verses 10–12 he does provide him with some idea of the *outcome* for Daniel's devastated people.

What does he tell him? He says there will be *ongoing division* (10a), a clear distinction between the *many*, who are God's faithful ones, and the *wicked*. The *many* will be a suffering people (for they *purify themselves, make themselves white* and will *be refined*), likely to the point of martyrdom, while the wicked will – what else? – *act wickedly*. There will be the two humanities in all their stark difference, the seed of the woman and the seed of the serpent (Gen. 3:15) standing over against each other. But there will also be *increasing perception* (10b): *none of the wicked ones will understand, but the wise will come to understand* (this second verb can be translated this way). In 10a God's people are the *many*, in 10b they are *the wise*. The wicked remain in their accustomed darkness, but the Lord's wise ones will discern the issues of the time, will perceive what they are called to do and what it will cost them. Their 'understanding' may also include having more exact clarity about the meaning of the revelation given via Daniel's 'book' (see the treatment of verse 4b above).

Above all, however, the aftermath of the verse 7 situation will include *dogged endurance* (11–12):

> *And from the time that the regular offering has been taken away and the abomination making desolate is put in place – there will be 1,290 days. How blessed the one who waits and reaches the 1,335 days.*

Verse 11 is speaking of the repression of true worship (*the regular offering . . . taken away*) and the imposition of false worship (*an*

---

[12] Archer, p. 155.

appalling abomination [NJPS] put in place). We have already noted that Antiochus Epiphanes would do this sort of thing (8:11–13 and 11:31), yet there will be another near the end who will out-Antiochus Antiochus, one who will not only put a stop to legitimate worship (9:27b) but along with 'abominations' is himself one 'who makes desolate' or 'is causing horror' (9:27c); now in 12:11, under the aegis of this 'final scourge' of history, the *abomination making desolate* appears again. I think Jesus has 9:27 and 12:11 in view when he refers to the 'abomination of desolation' in Mark 13:14. Even though 'abomination' in that text is a neuter noun, the following participle is masculine – 'standing where *he* ought not' (emphasis mine). Jesus agrees with Daniel 9:27 that the 'abomination' is supremely a person and assumes that his appearance is future to Jesus' own earthly ministry.[13]

But what are we to make of these figures – 1,290 and 1,335? According to verse 11, the 1,290 days are a time in which true worship is repressed and believers would be under pressure to engage in perverted worship. Hence it is likely a time of intense suffering when faithfulness will come at immense cost. The most notable characteristic of the numeral 1,335 is that it is larger than 1,290. If then one makes it to the 1,335 days, he or she has outlasted the 1,290. Such persons have endured. They outlast the pressure, the persecution, the pain – they have gone through and beyond the trouble (cf. Mark 13:13; Heb. 10:36). The numerals may baffle us but the way they are used here simply implies that Yahweh has a people who will make it in spite of everything thrown at them.

This passage brings to mind an Associated Press news story. One weekend in St Louis, Missouri, a dog dubbed Quentin, a year old Basenji mix, was ushered into the city gas chamber to be euthanized

---

[13] For the record, one commonly meets the claim that at least a partial fulfilment of Jesus' words ('when you see the abomination of desolation . . . then let those in Judea flee . . . ', Mark 13:14 [parallel in Matt. 24:15–16]) came about in AD 70 when the Romans planted their standards with the image of the emperor on them on the temple site (cf. e.g., Alan Cole, 'Mark', in *New Bible Commentary*, 3rd ed., p. 970; and William Hendriksen, *New Testament Commentary: Exposition of the Gospel According to Matthew*, pp. 857–858). But Mark 13 (and Matt. 24) does not fit the Roman conquest. By the time the Romans had planted their standards in the temple, it was far too late for anyone to flee. The whole province as well as the city had already been sealed off and flight made impossible long before that moment. See Emil Schürer, *The History of the Jewish People in the Age of Jesus Christ (175 BC–AD 135)*, rev. and ed. G. Vermes and F. Millar, 3 vols. (Edinburgh: T&T Clark, 1973), 1:485–508; and Robert H. Gundry, *Mark* (Grand Rapids: Eerdmans, 1993), pp. 754–756. James Edwards (*The Gospel according to Mark* [Grand Rapids: Eerdmans, 2002], pp. 396–399) recognizes these difficulties but is not bound by them. One may find Roman armies in Luke 21, but the 'abomination of desolation' in Mark 13/Matthew 24 seems to be a strictly 'eschatological' entity.

with his fellow unwanted, unclaimed canine associates. Monday morning the death chamber's doors were thrown open, and among that ghastly scene of death there stood – with tail and tongue wagging – Quentin. The animal control supervisor said she never had seen such a survivor and didn't have the heart to slam the door shut. In her view the thirty-pound Quentin had earned the right to live.

These things are a parable, we might say. If you are Jesus' disciple, you are simply called to keep on going, to keep slogging on in your worship of Christ, to keep on refusing to bow to the latest idol. Who knows what hatred and damage may fall on you, what threats or enticements may be made to you? But God is going to have a thirteen-thirty-five people. After evil does its worst, the church of Jesus will be there, Quentin-like, standing on their feet.

4. We have direction for the present moment (13)

God never loses sight of his servants: *But you . . .* Here the heavenly instructor leaves a word for Daniel himself. He underscores two matters for Daniel. He tells him first, Your duty is clear: *But you, go on to the end* (13a); and second, your future is settled: *and you will rest and you will stand in your allotted place at the end of the days.* Interestingly, this command and assurance uses the word 'end' in two distinct ways; the first occurrence seems to refer to the end of Daniel's life, the second to the post-resurrection era.

Daniel was up in years – he was not going to see the little horn of chapter 8 nor the little horn of chapter 7. He was simply to go his way until the end. In other words, 'Get back to your desk and filing cabinet, Daniel, and finish your day's work; plod along in living quietly and working with your own hands and being faithful to King Cyrus, your Persian employer.' But, of course, there is more, as if to say: 'You'll die here – no, you will rest, and then, at the right time, you will be raised and stand in your allotted place.' *Allotted place* translates the word *gôrāl*, which is used over twenty-five times in Joshua 14 – 21; it refers both to the *lot* that is cast and to the al*lot*ment that the lot determines, so that it frequently designates the turf or the towns assigned to a tribe or group. Hence the Lord's assurance to Daniel is: You have an allotted place, an assigned space, designated for you in the resurrection age at the end of the days (cf. John 6:39).

So, what if you, like Daniel, are not one of the heroic faithful near the end? What if you never live to encounter the final edition of the Antichrist? What if you don't go through the 'shattering' of the power of the holy people? Are you then deficient? Is yours a second-class experience? Rather, do you not have all you need? Your duty is clear and your future is settled. Is that not enough? If your Lord says to you, 'And you will rest and will stand in your allotted place at the end of the days', isn't that about all you really need?

The Bible Speaks Today: Old Testament series

The Message of Genesis 1 – 11
The dawn of creation
David Atkinson

The Message of Genesis 12 – 50
From Abraham to Joseph
Joyce G. Baldwin

The Message of Exodus
The days of our pilgrimage
Alec Motyer

The Message of Leviticus
Free to be holy
Derek Tidball

The Message of Numbers
Journey to the promised land
Raymond Brown

The Message of Deuteronomy
Not by bread alone
Raymond Brown

The Message of Judges
Grace abounding
Michael Wilcock

The Message of Ruth
The wings of refuge
David Atkinson

The Message of Samuel
Personalities, potential, politics and power
Mary Evans

The Message of Kings
God is present
John W. Olley

The Message of Chronicles
One church, one faith, one Lord
Michael Wilcock

The Message of Ezra and Haggai
Building for God
Robert Fyall

The Message of Nehemiah
God's servant in a time of change
Raymond Brown

The Message of Esther
God present but unseen
David G. Firth

The Message of Job
Suffering and grace
David Atkinson

The Message of Psalms 1 – 72
Songs for the people of God
Michael Wilcock

The Message of Psalms 73 – 150
Songs for the people of God
Michael Wilcock

The Message of Proverbs
Wisdom for life
David Atkinson

The Message of Ecclesiastes
A time to mourn, and a time to dance
Derek Kidner

The Message of the Song of Songs
The lyrics of love
Tom Gledhill

The Message of Isaiah
On eagles' wings
Barry Webb

The Bible Speaks Today: New Testament series

The Message of the Sermon on the Mount (Matthew5– 7)
Christian counter-culture
John Stott

The Message of Matthew
The kingdom of heaven
Michael Green

The Message of Mark
The mystery of faith
Donald English

The Message of Luke
The Saviour of the world
Michael Wilcock

The Message of John
Here is your King!
Bruce Milne

The Message of Acts
To the ends of the earth
John Stott

The Message of Romans
God's good news for the world
John Stott

The Message of 1 Corinthians
Life in the local church
David Prior

The Message of 2 Corinthians
Power in weakness
Paul Barnett

The Message of Galatians
Only one way
John Stott

The Message of Ephesians
God's new society
John Stott

The Message of Philippians
Jesus our Joy
Alec Motyer

The Message of Colossians and Philemon
Fullness and freedom
Dick Lucas

The Message of Thessalonians
Preparing for the coming King
John Stott

The Message of 1 Timothy and Titus
The life of the local church
John Stott

The Message of 2 Timothy
Guard the gospel
John Stott

The Message of Hebrews
Christ above all
Raymond Brown

The Message of James
The tests of faith
Alec Motyer

The Message of 1 Peter
The way of the cross
Edmund Clowney

The Message of 2 Peter and Jude
The promise of his coming
Dick Lucas and Christopher Green

The Message of John's Letters
Living in the love of God
David Jackman

The Message of Revelation
I saw heaven opened
Michael Wilcock

The Bible Speaks Today: Bible Themes series

The Message of the Living God
His glory, his people, his world
Peter Lewis

The Message of the Resurrection
Christ is risen!
Paul Beasley-Murray

The Message of the Cross
*Wisdom unsearchable, love
indestructible*
Derek Tidball

The Message of Salvation
By God's grace, for God's glory
Philip Graham Ryken

The Message of Creation
*Encountering the Lord of the
universe*
David Wilkinson

**The Message of Heaven and
Hell**
Grace and destiny
Bruce Milne

The Message of Mission
*The glory of Christ in all time and
space*
Howard Peskett and Vinoth
Ramachandra

The Message of Prayer
Approaching the throne of grace
Tim Chester

The Message of the Trinity
Life in God
Brian Edgar

**The Message of Evil and
Suffering**
Light into darkness
Peter Hicks

The Message of the Holy Spirit
The Spirit of encounter
Keith Warrington

The Message of Holiness
Restoring God's masterpiece
Derek Tidball

The Message of Sonship
At home in God's household
Trevor Burke

The Message of the Word of God
The glory of God made known
Tim Meadowcroft

The Message of Women
Creation, grace and gender
Derek and Dianne Tidball